IMAGES
of America

African Americans of Orangeburg County

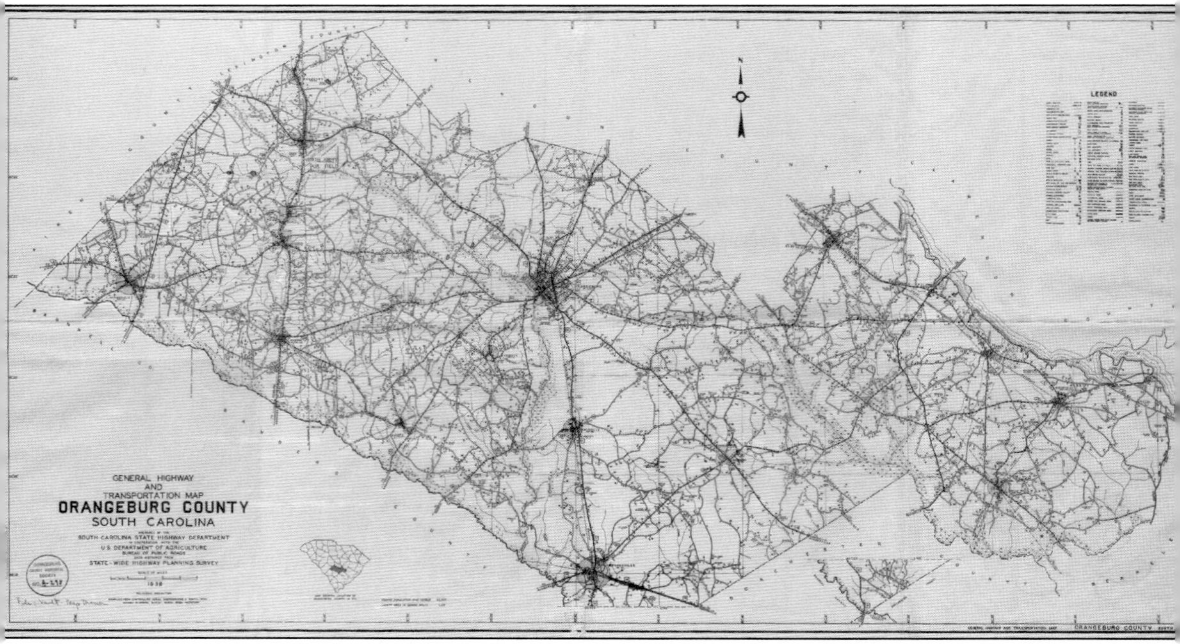

This is a 1938 map of Orangeburg County. There are 16 other towns located in the county of Orangeburg, which is the second-largest county in the state of South Carolina. (Courtesy of the Orangeburg County Historical Society.)

ON THE COVER: Lillie Gaffney (center row, third from left) and other Army wives wrap gifts for a Red Cross project at Dunton Memorial School in Orangeburg in the early 1950s. Gaffney is the wife of Maj. Raymond Gaffney Sr. (Courtesy of Lillie Gaffney.)

IMAGES
of America

African Americans of Orangeburg County

Lauritza Salley Hill

ARCADIA PUBLISHING

ISBN 978-0-7385-9880-2

Published by Arcadia Publishing
Charleston, South Carolina

Printed in the United States of America

Library of Congress Control Number: 2012950478

For all general information, please contact Arcadia Publishing:
Telephone 843-853-2070
Fax 843-853-0044
E-mail sales@arcadiapublishing.com
For customer service and orders:
Toll-Free 1-888-313-2665

Visit us on the Internet at www.arcadiapublishing.co.

In memory of my parents, Leona and Fred Douglas Salley,
and my grandmother, Clarrie R. Spell.

Contents

Acknowledgments

Writing this book has been a wonderful and enlightening experience, as I ventured back to the past and researched information about people and places in Orangeburg County. I met many wonderful and interesting people, some of whom actually lived through events that are illustrated in the book.

I wish to thank everyone who invited me into their homes and opened up their photograph albums and spent countless hours with me going through photographs to find just the right one. I wish to thank all of the pastors and members of various churches who contributed the history of their congregations. I wish to thank Maggie Bullwinkel for her help and patience. I wish to thank Lillie Gaffney, Ruth Harrison, and Beatrice Blount for always being there when I called at all times of the day and night for information. I wish to thank Betty Huff, of the chamber of commerce, and Danny Dantzler, of the City of Orangeburg, for their help. Eric Powell, Wayne Hughes, and the volunteers of the Orangeburg County Historical Society were most helpful in providing me with valuable photographs and information.

Many, many thanks to Richard Reid, John D. Spells, Ruth Hodges, Charles Payne, Jeanette Bailey, Cecil Williams, Michael Stafford, Beressee Summers, Fairey B. Zeigler, Carmen S. Thomasson, Barbara Williams Jenkins, Janice Carson, Minnie Johnson, Isabelle Maple, Mary Smalls, Barbara Townsend, Brenda Williams, Sarah DeWeever, Annette Disher, Doris J. Felder, Diane Floyd, and Marilyn Gibbs, who were invaluable in helping me with facts and offering advice from other sources.

I am truly appreciative of all the people who contributed images for this book. Their names are listed in the courtesy lines following each caption. Other sources for images include Orangeburg-Calhoun Technical College (OC Tec); Orangeburg County Historical Society (OCHS); Orangeburg National Fish Hatchery (ONFH); Orangeburg Consolidated District Five (OCDF); South Carolina Department of Archives and History (SCDAH); City of Orangeburg (CIOR); County of Orangeburg (COOR); Claflin University Archives (CU); South Caroliniana Library, University of South Carolina, Columbia (Caroliniana); South Carolina State University Library and Archives (SCSU); and the Regional Medical Center (RMC).

Introduction

This book is about the lives and contributions of African Americans in Orangeburg County, South Carolina, during the 20th century. The various towns and events described here are located within the county. The city of Orangeburg, the county seat, is a small town with a big history. The town was founded by an Indian trader named George Sterling in 1704, and was named by Lt. Thomas Broughton in honor of William IV, Prince of Orange, the husband of Princess Anne, daughter of George II of England. The center of the original village was located near what are now Broughton and Henley Streets, according to a marker there. The great people in the various communities have contributed to what Orangeburg County is today.

The county is located between the city of Columbia, South Carolina, which is the capital, and the city of Charleston. It is nicknamed the "Garden City" and is the largest community in the county. According to the 1860 census, the Orangeburgh District, as it was known before the Civil War, was populated by a majority of slaves and free blacks. This status began in 1820, when the white population was 6,760 and the black population was 8,893. From that point until today, blacks have been the majority in Orangeburg County. According to the *South Carolina Handbook* of 1908, Orangeburg (which included Calhoun County prior to 1907) had a black population of 41,442 and a white population of 18,220. Orangeburg is also one of the largest agriculture-producing counties in South Carolina. The major crops are cotton, soybeans, corn, turf grass, and watermelons.

There are about 16 other towns within Orangeburg County, and some of them hold events or festivals throughout the year, including: the Festival of Roses and the Edisto Memorial Gardens, which are major attractions for Orangeburg; the Raylrode Daze Festivul in Branchville; the Hummingbird Festival in Woodford; and the Governor's Frog Jump and large flea market in Springfield. The town of Cope's Depot is listed in the National Register of Historic Places. Every March, the town of Elloree, with a population of about 742, hosts approximately 7,000 horse lovers who come to town for the famous races, the Elloree Trials. The last major battle of the American Revolution was fought near the town of Eutawville.

The book features a few of the earlier Baptist, United Methodist, African Methodist Episcopal, and Presbyterian churches and some popular ministers in Orangeburg. Churches were often a haven in the worst of times and played a major role in the education and advancement of African Americans.

The town of Orangeburg is quite unique because of the four colleges located there, two of which, Claflin University and South Carolina State University, are historically black colleges. The other two are Orangeburg-Calhoun Technical College and Southern Methodist College. Claflin and South Carolina State have produced thousands of graduates, some of whom have become quite well known throughout the country, such as South Carolina Supreme Court justice Ernest A. Finney Jr., Rep. James Clyburn, and the late Judge Matthew Perry, to name a few. Orangeburg County is the birthplace of several celebrities, including actress and singer Eartha Kitt of North,

South Carolina; exercise rider Charlie Davis of Holly Hill, South Carolina; and trainer of Triple Crown winner Secretariat, Eddie Sweat of Vance, South Carolina.

In some captions for Claflin University and South Carolina State University, "college" and "university" will variously appear, because throughout their histories, the institutions' names were changed. African Americans will at times be referred to as colored, blacks, or Negroes, depending on the time period of the image under discussion. Most of the information for the captions was provided by the people or families from whom I received the images. The information for colleges and towns was provided by those entities' various historical publications. Early school information was provided by a publication by Ellen P. Chaplin, a former superintendent of Orangeburg County Schools, and from various school reunion committees. All other content was public information from various newspapers or census records.

African Americans have struggled through many hard times. The Orangeburg Movement, a testament to the struggles of the 1950s and 1960s, involved civil rights marches and sit-ins. South Carolina State University was the site of the Orangeburg Massacre of 1968, in which three students were killed on the front lawn of the campus. Through it all, the heroes who accomplished acts for the betterment of the community, regardless of the obstacles confronting them, must be recalled. A local historian, Richard Reid, wrote in the *Times and Democrat* that African Americans were very active in politics and owned prosperous businesses before Reconstruction. Benjamin F. Randolph became the first state senator for Orangeburg in 1868 and was a leader in helping to establish a public school system. Henry Dickson, Edward Cain, William McKinley, James P. Mays, and T.K. Sasportas became the first state representatives for Orangeburg County in 1868. Henry Dickson Sr. became the first African American elected to city council, in 1870. At that time, they were called aldermen. London Dickson and A.S. Hibbler became the first county council members in the 1870s. At that time, they were known as county commissioners. James P. Mays became the first coroner in the 1870s. The first black sheriff was Edward Cain from Fort Motte; his son James was an 1892 graduate of Claflin University. In medicine, Dr. Saul Mickey became Orangeburg's first known black doctor in 1890. Reid further stated that the true history of Orangeburg reveals that whites and blacks began to document their heritage upon their arrival in Orangeburg in 1704. For historical reasons, the black heritage had to be extracted so as to provide a better understanding of their role in our county.

While this book includes some images from before 1900, the majority depict 20th-century African American life. The important thing about this book is that it portrays not only the already well-known people in the community, it also portrays ordinary people who have contributed to the area in extraordinary ways. The author would like to note that the images included in the book are just a glimpse into the lives of some of the many African American pioneers who helped to make Orangeburg a better place to live. The author hopes that the book will pique the interest of readers, and prompt them to seek more information about the people of Orangeburg County's past and present.

One

The Religious Life

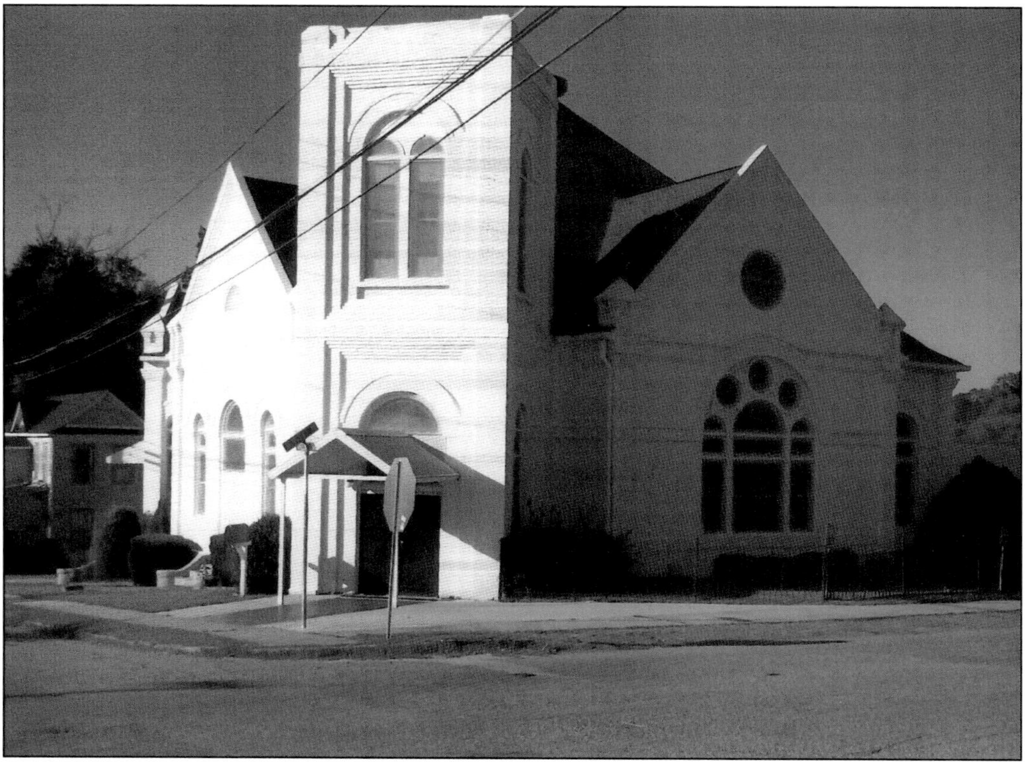

Mount Pisgah Baptist Church, located on the corner of Green and Henley Streets in Orangeburg, is believed to have begun during slavery, in 1853, as a bush harbor with a small group of Christians. In 1865, blacks belonging to First Baptist Church of Orangeburg withdrew and formed their own church. The new church was initially called Sunny Side Baptist Church until the name was changed to Mount Pisgah Baptist Church in 1870. In 1902, the first building burned down, and the present building was erected in 1903. A.W. Thorne was the builder. The first known pastor was Rev. Jacob Govan, and he was followed by Reverend J. Harvey. About five pastors followed Reverend Harvey until Rev. Charles Salley, who served from 1890 to 1900. Rev. Nelson C. Nix was the ninth pastor, serving for 45 years. Rev. John D. Rhodes served from 1945 to 1968. The church is listed in the National Register of Historic Places. (Courtesy of Lauritza Hill.)

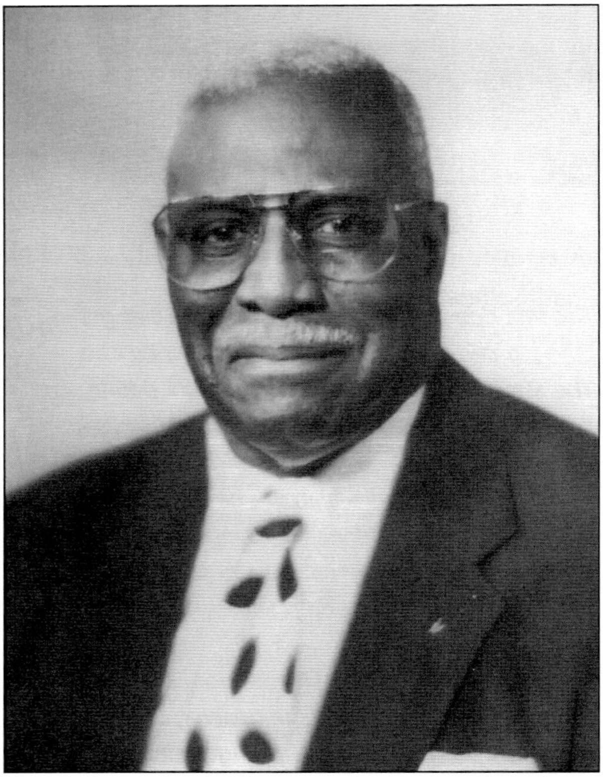

Francis Gordon Samuel Everett (1925–2005) was a minister, educator, councilman, and community leader. He and all of his brothers were ministers. He entered the ministry at age 24 and served 50 years as pastor of churches in South Carolina. He was pastor of Mount Pisgah Baptist Church starting in 1969 and served for 34 years. He was employed at Elloree Training School as a teacher and principal. Reverend Everett was a significant part of history for Orangeburg County as he, Fred Mack, and Chappelle Davis were the first African Americans to serve on the Orangeburg County Council. After the creation of single-member districts, Everett served from 1976 to 1984. (Courtesy of Mount Pisgah Baptist Church.)

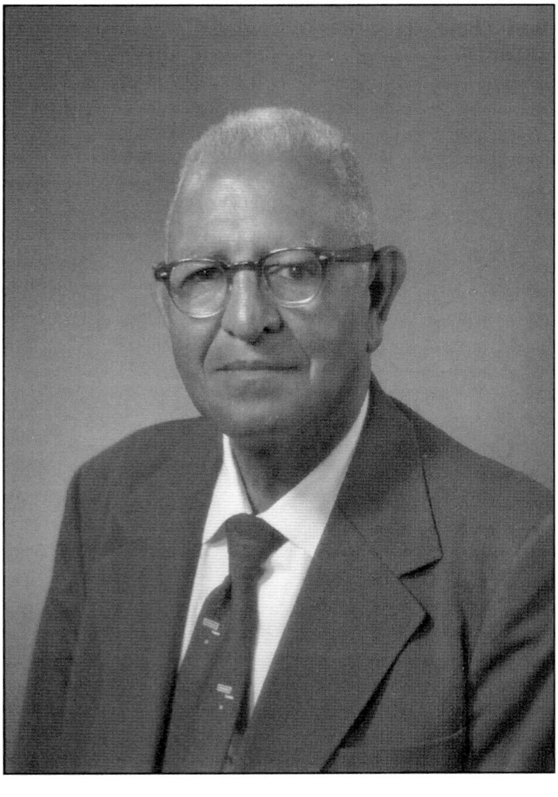

Eddie Gaffney Jr., of Orangeburg, served as chairman of the deacon board of Mount Pisgah Baptist Church for many years. He joined the church in the early 1920s and, as a deacon, he was a mentor to many young men who came to the church. The brother of Raymond Gaffney Sr., he served as deacon chairman under Rev. Nelson C. Nix and Rev. John D. Rhodes. (Courtesy of Lillie Gaffney.)

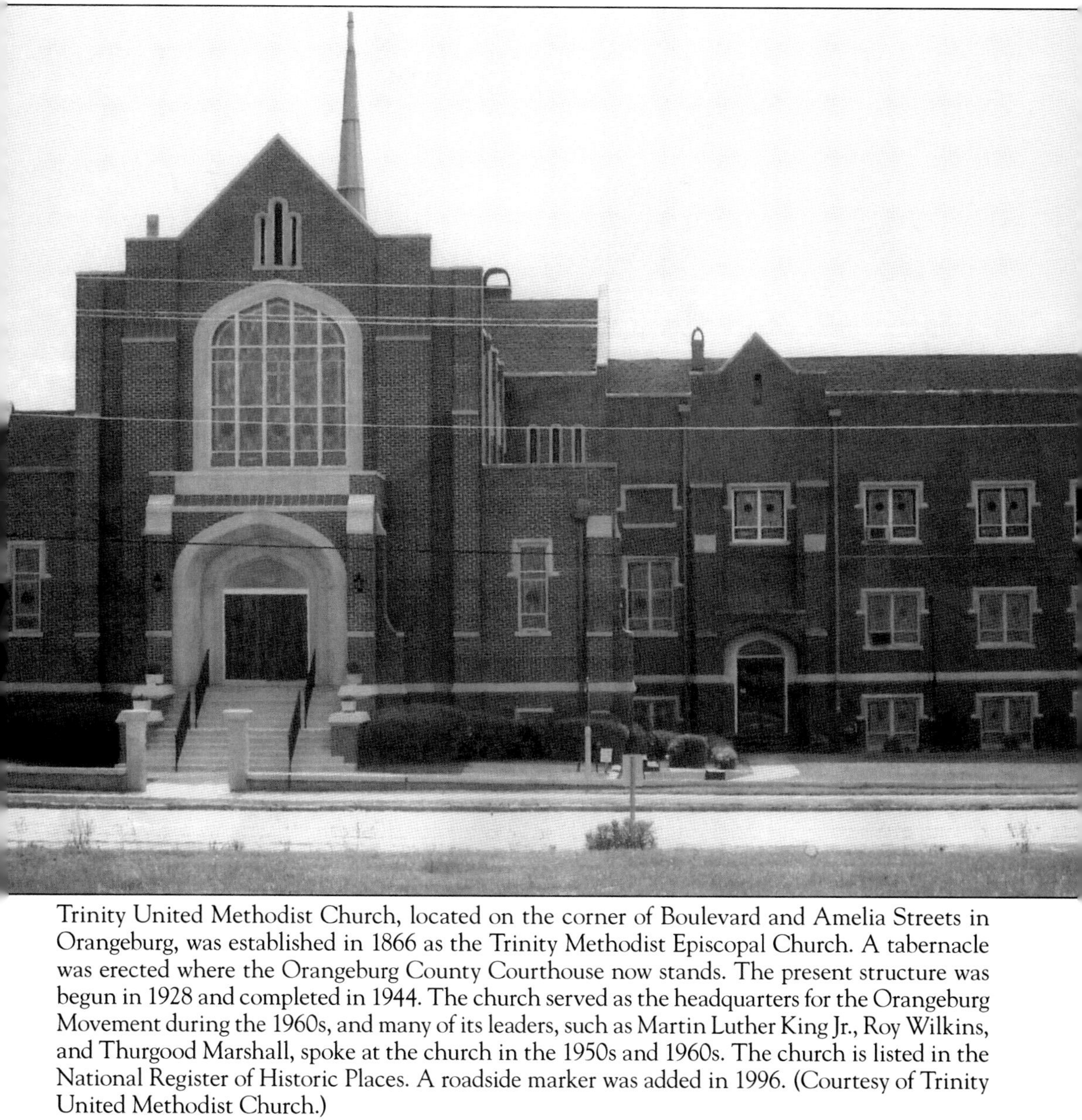

Trinity United Methodist Church, located on the corner of Boulevard and Amelia Streets in Orangeburg, was established in 1866 as the Trinity Methodist Episcopal Church. A tabernacle was erected where the Orangeburg County Courthouse now stands. The present structure was begun in 1928 and completed in 1944. The church served as the headquarters for the Orangeburg Movement during the 1960s, and many of its leaders, such as Martin Luther King Jr., Roy Wilkins, and Thurgood Marshall, spoke at the church in the 1950s and 1960s. The church is listed in the National Register of Historic Places. A roadside marker was added in 1996. (Courtesy of Trinity United Methodist Church.)

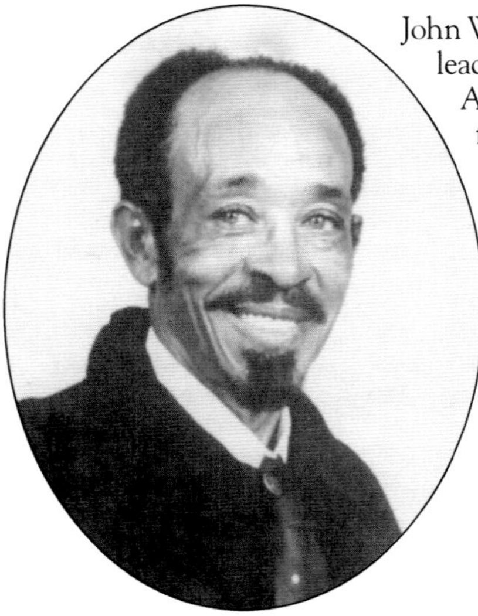

John W. Wright (1925–1995) was a popular minister, community leader, and president of the Holly Hill chapter of the National Association for the Advancement of Colored People (NAACP) for 20 years. He served in the US Army during World War II. He was a graduate of Voorhees College (Denmark, South Carolina) and Morris College (Sumter, South Carolina), where he received his BA and BD degrees. Wright was pastor of many churches, including Rock Hill Baptist Church (Sumter), Mount Zero Baptist Church (Paxville), and Olive Grove Baptist Church (Coward). (Courtesy of Gwendolyn Wright-Barksdale.)

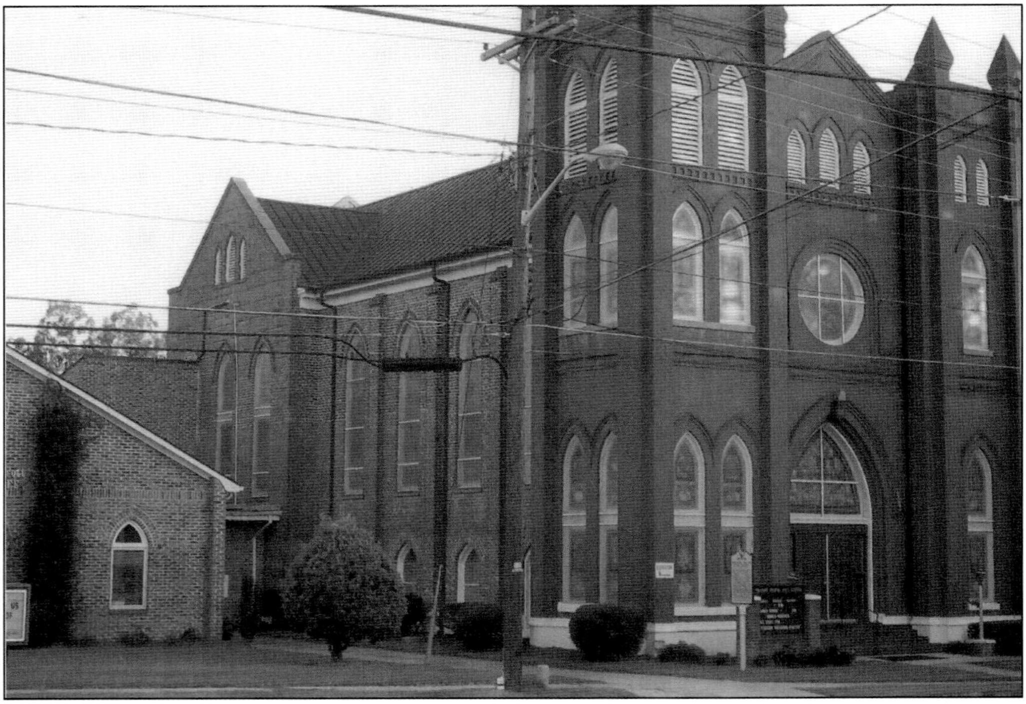

Organized in 1873, Williams Chapel African Methodist Episcopal Church is located on Glover Street. In 1877, trustees Emily A. Williams, Richard Howard, and Irwin Mintz purchased a small plat of land on then Market Street, on which a frame church was built. In 1919, a new church was constructed at the junction of Glover and Middleton Streets. Miller F. Whittaker (1892–1949), third president of State A&M College (now SC State University), one of the first black architects in South Carolina, designed this unique Gothic Revival structure. Whittaker was a member of the congregation and professor at State A&M College. Daniel A. Straker, prominent African-American lawyer and legal scholar during Reconstruction, prepared the church deed. Rev. Dave Christie served as the first pastor. In 1985, the church was listed in the National Register of Historic Places. Approved by the South Carolina Department of Archives & History, in 2006, the congregation erected a South Carolina historical marker. (Courtesy of Lauritza S. Hill.)

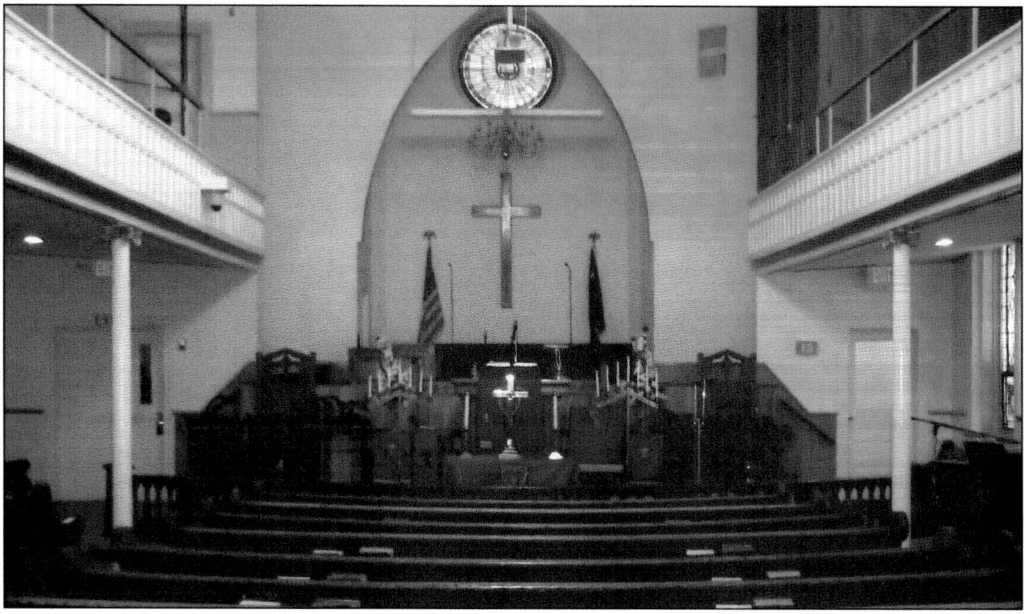

The sanctuary of Williams Chapel is quite interesting, with Gothic arched stained-glass windows. The front doors give access to a two-story narthex, and staircases on each side lead to the nave and balcony. The lower level was designed for large gatherings, a popular practice at the time the church was designed. Rose windows are displayed at the front and rear of the church. Dr. M. Maceo Nance (1926–2001) and Dr. Andrew Hugine, the fifth and ninth presidents, respectively, of South Carolina State University, were members of the church. Bishop Richard Allen Hildebrand (1916–2011), elected 88th bishop in the African Methodist Episcopal Church, the highest position in the church, was a member of Williams Chapel as a young man. In 1956, Agnes Brogdon Hildebrand (1881–1986) was selected National Mother of the Year by the *Afro-American* newspaper. (Courtesy of Lauritza S. Hill.)

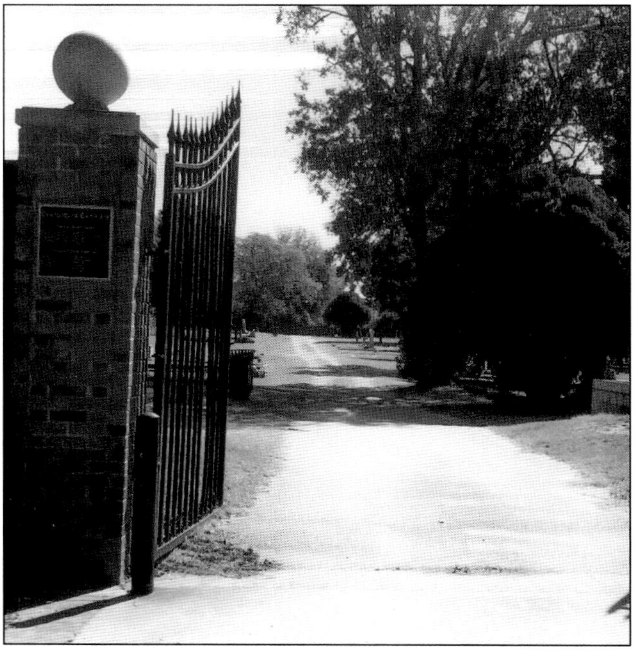

Orangeburg City Cemetery, at the intersection of Bull and Windsor Streets, is considered to be the oldest non–church affiliated private cemetery for African Americans in Orangeburg County. Chartered in 1889, citizens listed on the original charter were Rev. E.C. Brown, Maj. John H. Fordham, Rev. A.G. Townsend, Rev. Abram Middleton, B.J. Lloyd, W.L. Buckley, and R.W. Jewell. For many years, a group of private citizens contributed to its upkeep with help from community organizations. Management of the property was transferred to the city of Orangeburg in 1994. In 1996, the cemetery was listed in the National Register of Historic Places. (Courtesy of Lauritza Hill.)

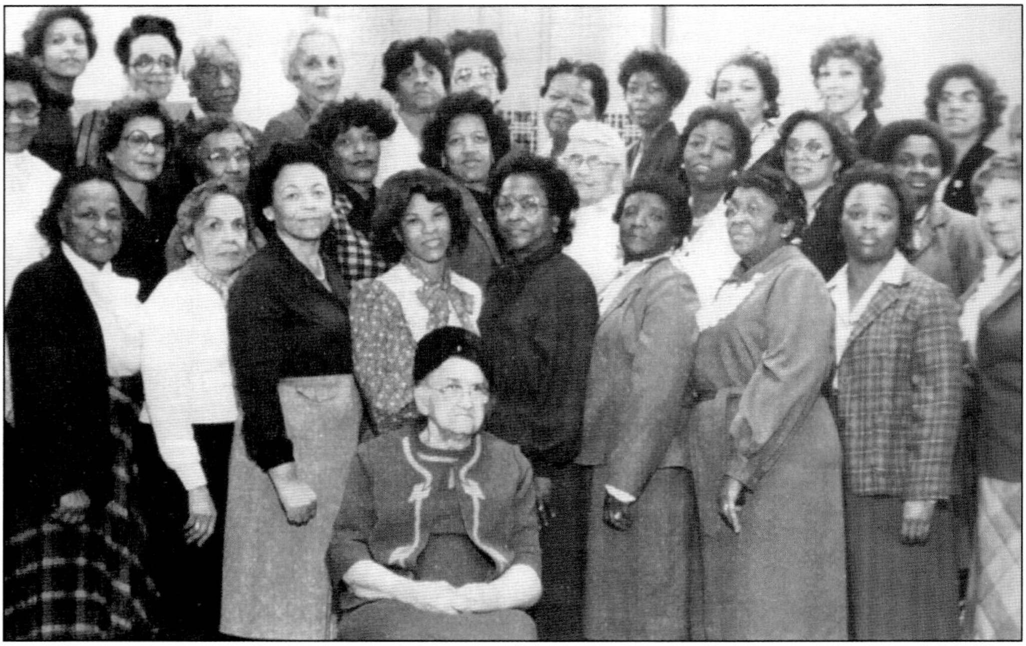

United Presbyterian Women of Saint Luke Presbyterian Church, USA, pose for a photograph at the church's 86th anniversary in 1983. A church history book, spanning the years 1897 to 1983, was completed to commemorate the event. Rev. Lawrence Bethel served as the pastor that year. The women of the church serve in various capacities at church events. The major event sponsored by the church is the Sepia Fashion Revue, held every October. The highly successful event presents Chicago models exhibiting the latest styles for men and women. (Courtesy of Saint Luke Presbyterian Church, USA.)

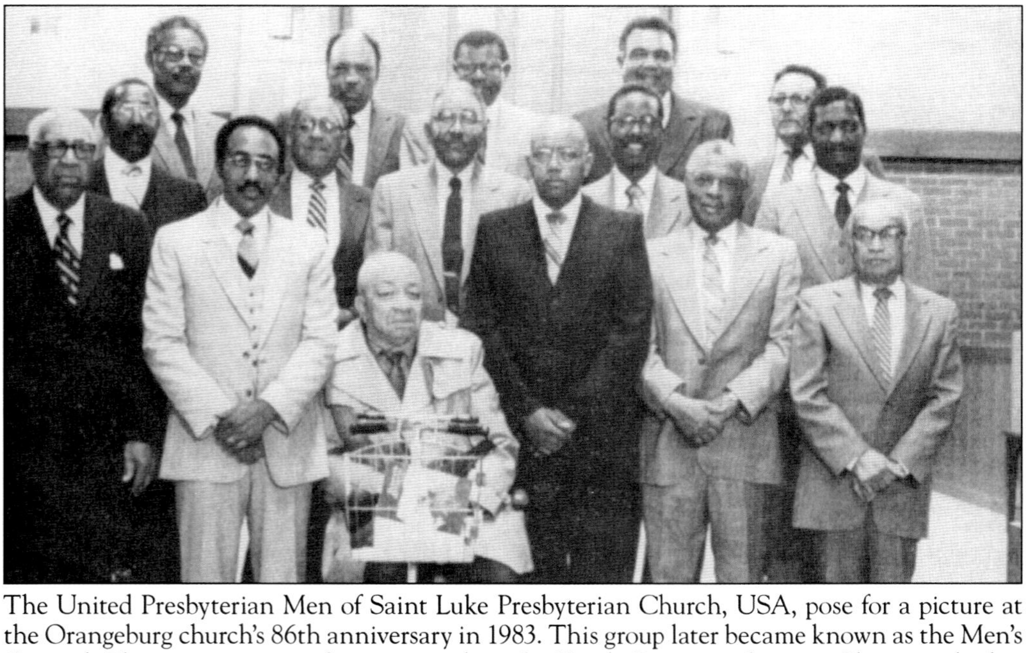

The United Presbyterian Men of Saint Luke Presbyterian Church, USA, pose for a picture at the Orangeburg church's 86th anniversary in 1983. This group later became known as the Men's Council. The group supports functions such as the Youth Camp, graduation, Christmas basket sales, and other fundraisers. (Courtesy of St. Luke Presbyterian Church, USA.)

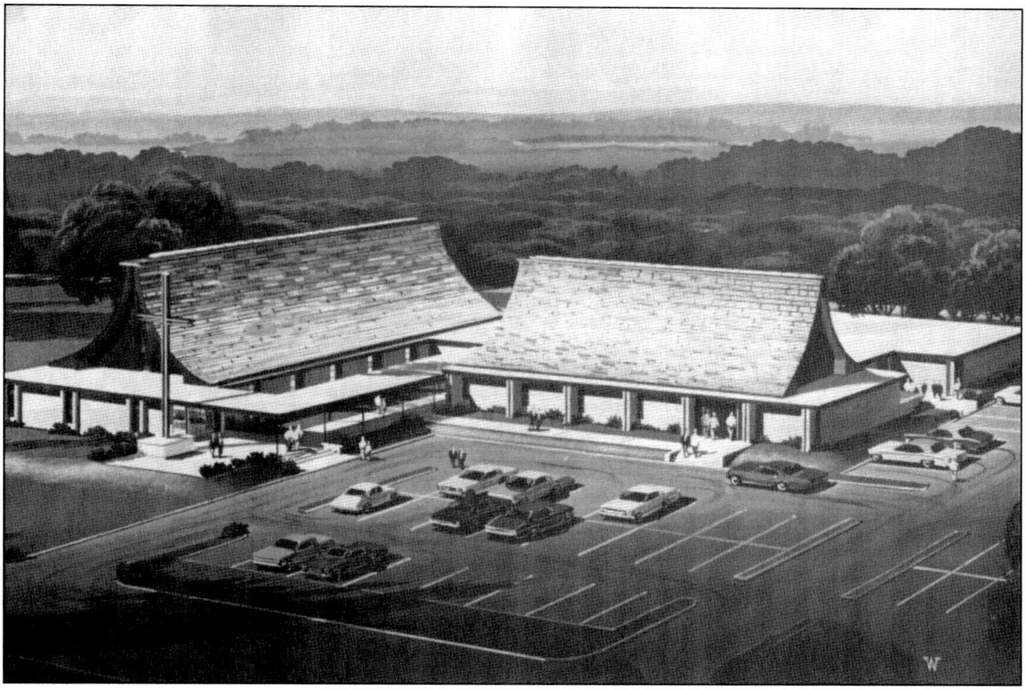

Saint Luke Presbyterian Church, USA, located on Mingo Street in Orangeburg, was founded in 1897 by Thomas E. Miller, the first president of South Carolina State Agricultural and Mechanical College. The name of the first church was Railroad Avenue Presbyterian Church, USA, and later was changed to Saint Luke United Presbyterian Church, USA. The church was once located on Treadwell Street and then Lowman Street. It was rebuilt in 1968 at its present location. The church records reveal that from 1906 to 1909, Rev. C.M. Uggams, grandfather of movie and television star Leslie Uggams, served as pastor. (Courtesy of Saint Luke Presbyterian Church, USA.)

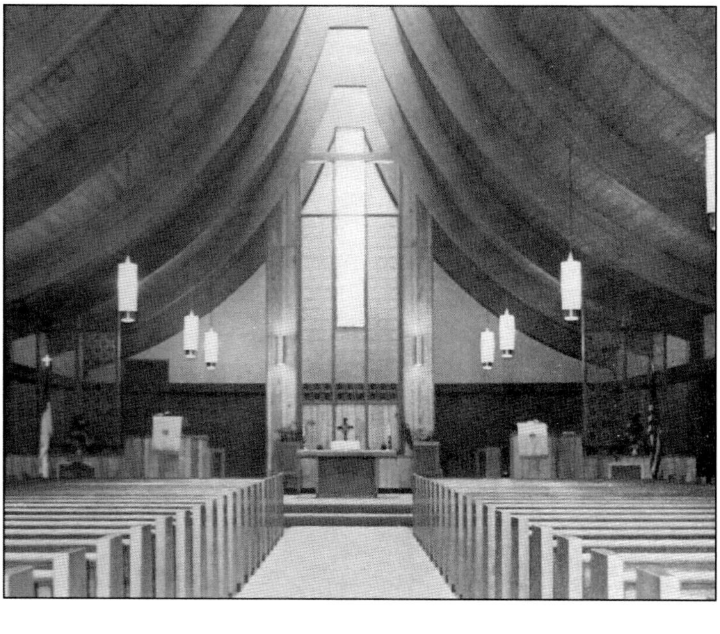

The inside of Saint Luke Presbyterian Church, USA, reveals an interesting design. The church was designed by William Clement and built by the H.A. DeCosta firm, both of Charleston. St. Luke played a vital role in the Orangeburg community in the early 1960s, hosting civil rights meetings. It was one of the first congregations to conduct early education programs from within the church. (Courtesy of Saint Luke Presbyterian Church, USA.)

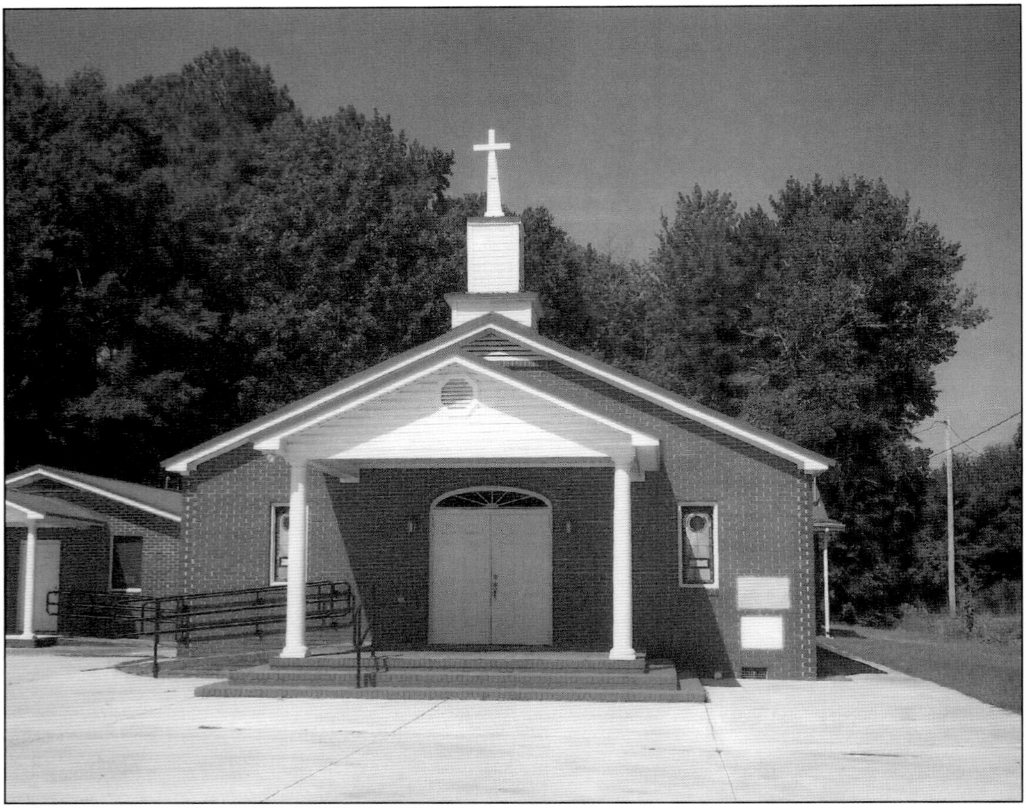

Saint Stephen Missionary Baptist Church, located on Freedom Road, Highway 21 in Branchville, was established in 1875 by Cecil Stephen under a bush harbor. Stephen became the first pastor. A wood frame was erected in 1900, and the church was rebuilt in 1972 while Rev. Arthur Young was the pastor. It went through other major improvements while under the leadership of Reverends W.J. Tyler, J.L. Tindal, and W.J. Ellis Sr. (Courtesy of Lauritza Hill.)

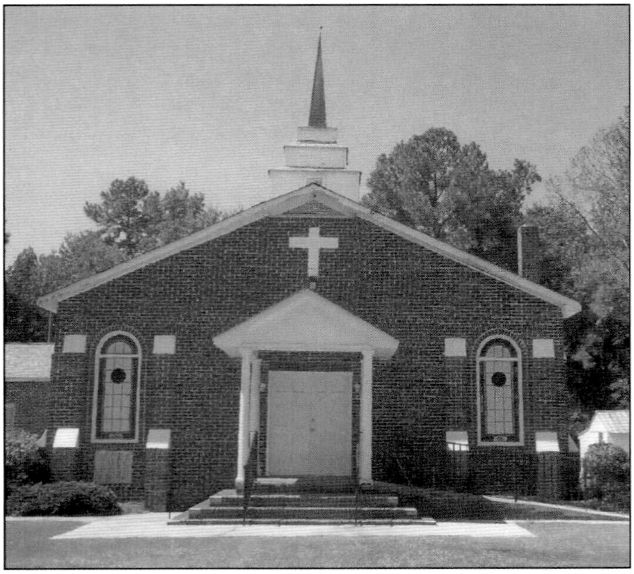

McBranch Missionary Baptist Church, located on Hoghaven Road in Branchville, was established in the late 19th century. The founders were the Reverend E.C. Coker, Deacon Henry Owens, Deacon Lewis Owens, Deacon Jeff Owens, Deacon Morgan Owens, and their families. A brick church was constructed under the leadership of Rev. Jervy S. Utsey, who served from 1948 to 1982. Some of the early ministers were Reverends Barnwell, Benny Freeman, W.K. Rickenbacker, S.D. Rickenbacker, J.D. Riley, Harry Jenkins, and John Preacher. (Courtesy of Lauritza Hill.)

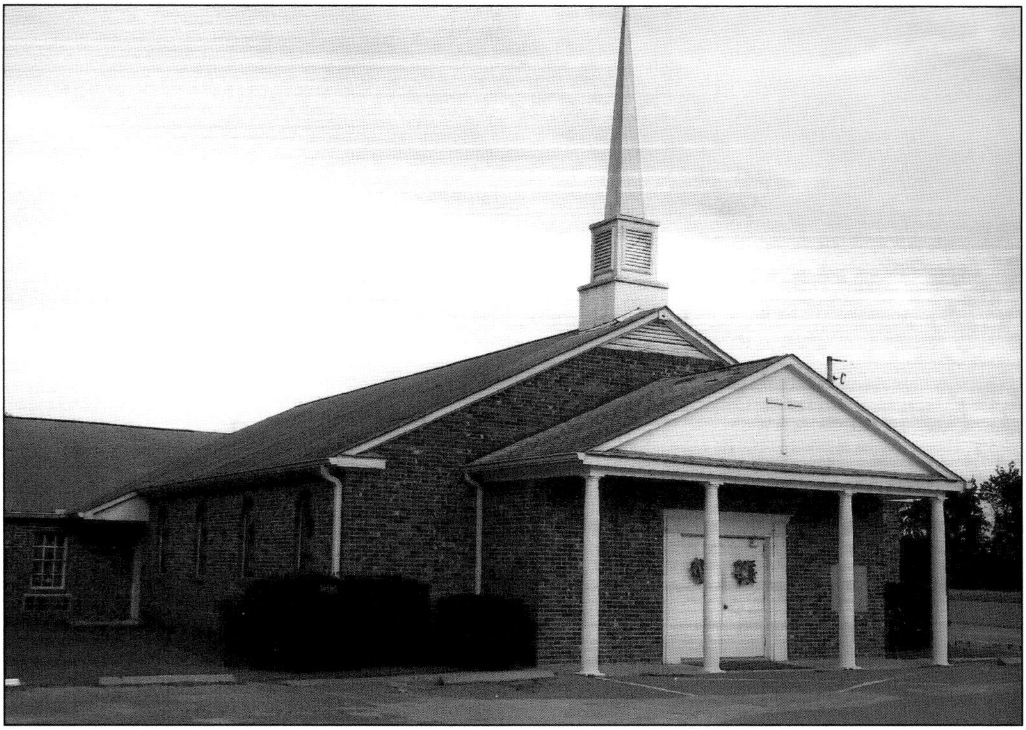

Canaan United Methodist Church is located on Slab Landing Road in Cope and is believed to have been built in the early 1900s. The first church building was constructed on a site on Highway 70 on land given by the Salley and Boyd families. It is thought to be one of the six churches that made up the Edisto Fork Circuit as far back as 1874. The second church was built in 1979 under the leadership of Rev. Warren Jenkins. The first service, the service of consecration, was held in 1980. (Courtesy of Lauritza Hill.)

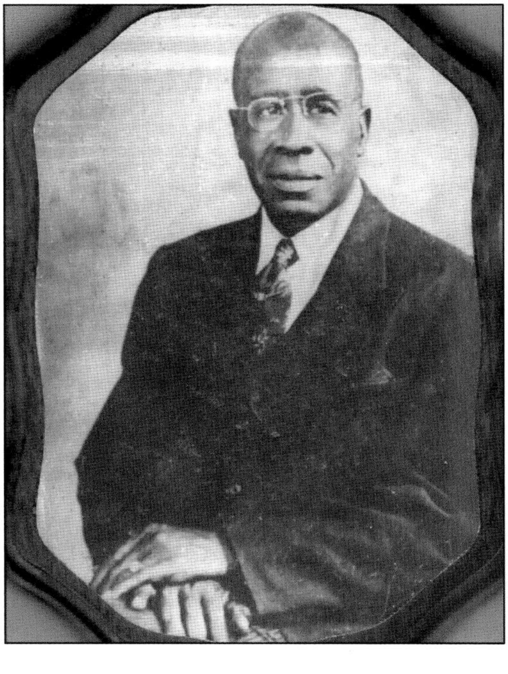

Thomas Franklin Owens (1886–1955) was a minister and educator. He was a 1912 graduate of what is now known as South Carolina State University. In 1925, under his leadership as pastor, Canaan Baptist Church in Branchville became a brick structure. Reverend Owens helped to organize the New Mount Zion Baptist Church in Orangeburg and served as a teacher and principal of the Lockett Normal School in Branchville for many years, as well as pastor of the First Baptist Church of Far Rockaway, New York, for 18 years. (Courtesy of Charles Owens.)

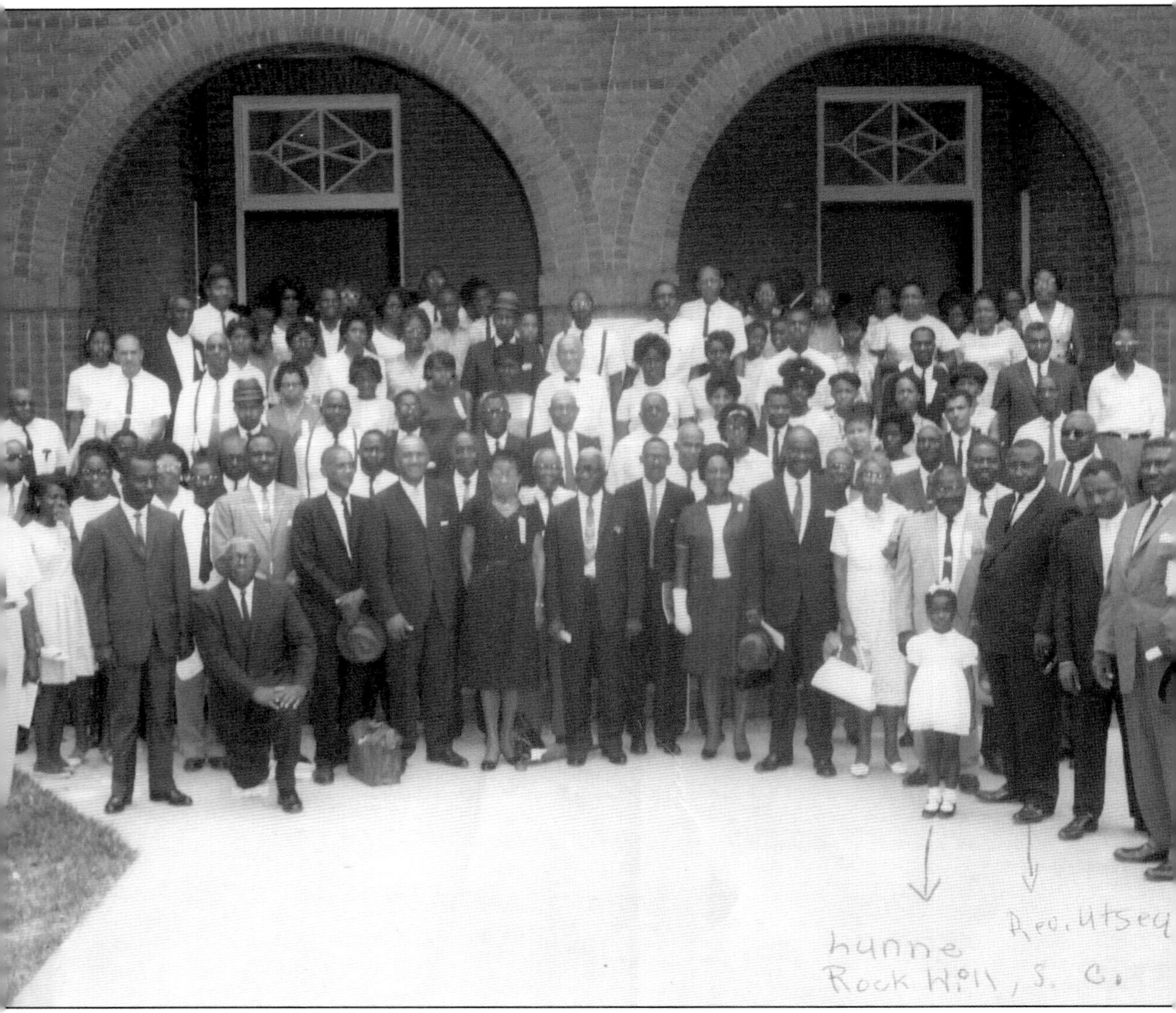

Members of the Sunday School Congress of the Lovely Hill Baptist Association pose for a photograph after a weeklong meeting at the National Sunday School Congress in Rock Hill, South Carolina, around 1967. Rev. Jervy S. Utsey (front row, third from right) was the president of the local Sunday school congress at that time and lived in Branchville. (Courtesy of Ruth Harrison.)

J. Herbert Nelson of Orangeburg was a minister, educator, veteran, community leader, and civil rights activist. He was an instructor at Morris College in Sumter before serving in the US Army from 1944 to 1946. He received an AB degree and a theological seminary degree from Johnson C. Smith University in 1949. He participated in many civil rights demonstrations and was the first vice president of the state NAACP in the 1960s. He was pastor of Saint Luke Presbyterian Church, USA, from 1963 to 1981 and was a prolific speaker. Reverend Nelson was the son of a Presbyterian minister, and three of his brothers were ministers. In this photograph, Eddie Jones Sr. (left), Eddie Jones Jr. (center), and Reverend Nelson stand on the grounds of the church after Sunday services in the early 1960s. St. Luke Presbyterian Church and the community suffered a great loss when Reverend Nelson died suddenly in 1981. (Courtesy of Jonalee Nelson.)

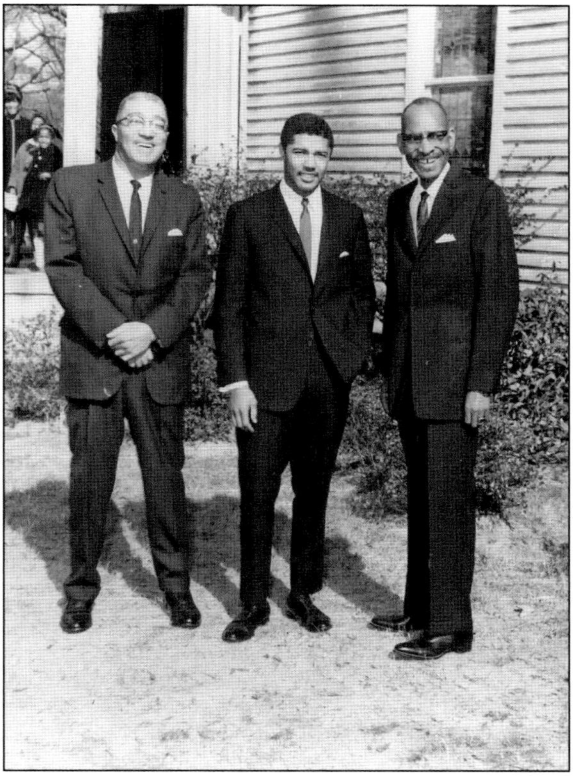

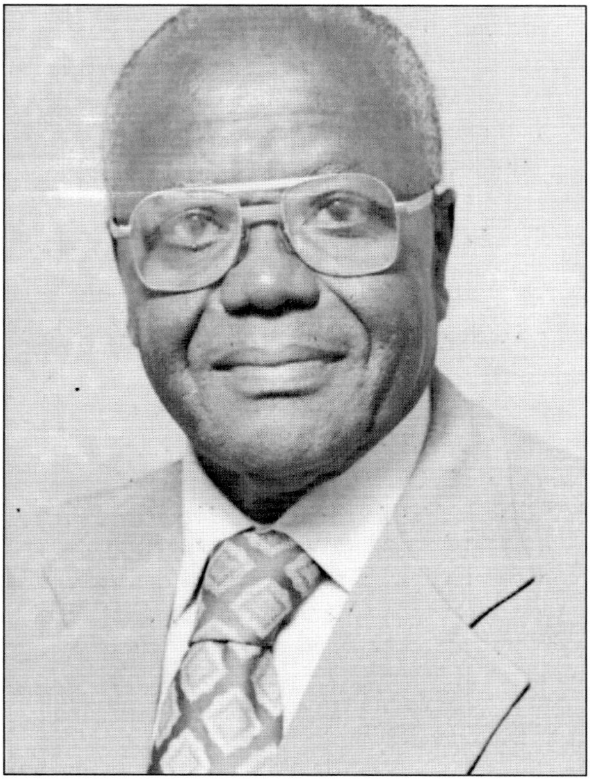

John W. Curry of Orangeburg was a minister, educator, author, and community leader. He was pastor of Trinity United Methodist Church from 1962 to 1974. Reverend Curry, the members of his church, and the members of many other churches were in the forefront of the civil rights movement during the 1960s. In 1980, he was the author of *Passionate Journey*, a book chronicling the events of the 1866 South Carolina Church Conference. (Courtesy of Claflin University Archives.)

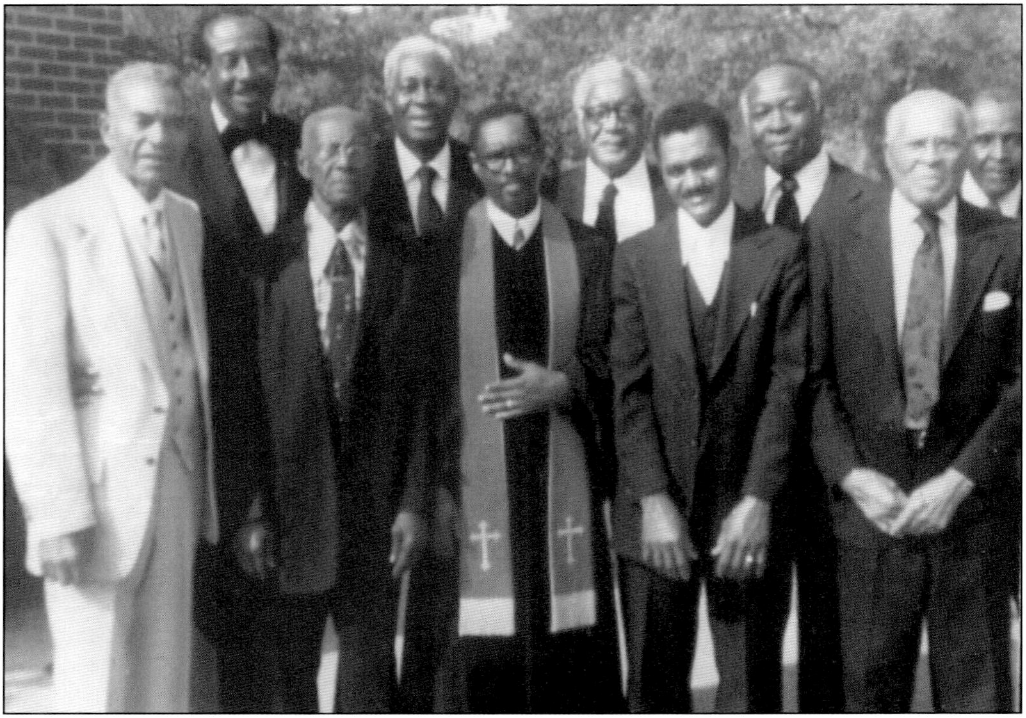

Harry Zimmerman poses with the pastor and fellow deacons of Mount Carmel Baptist Church in Cameron, South Carolina. Zimmerman was employed at Saint Paul Baptist Church on the plaza in Orangeburg for over 20 years. Shown here are, from left to right, (first row) Robert Thomas, Frank Johnson, James Council (pastor), Robert L. Green, and T.H. Scoville; (second row) Sumpter Green, Harry Zimmerman, Clarence Perry, Hercules Pinkney, and Walter "El" Green. (Courtesy of Dorothy Elmore.)

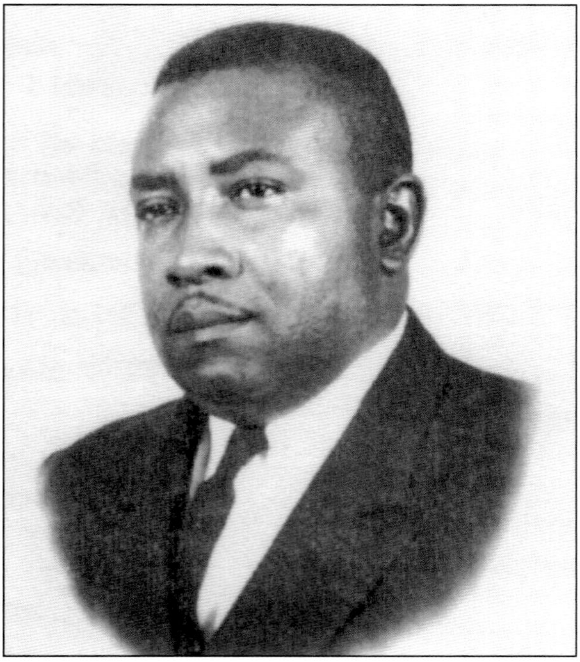

Jervy Samuel Utsey (1914–1991) of Orangeburg was a minister, educator, and community leader. He was a graduate of Morris College in Sumter and did further studies at South Carolina State College in Orangeburg. He taught school in Colleton County for many years and was assistant principal of Bethel Elementary School in Smoaks. He later became a trustee of Morris College. He served as pastor of several churches for over 50 years, including McBranch Missionary Baptist Church and Free Gift Missionary Baptist Church in Branchville, and Lovely Hill Missionary Baptist Church in Smoaks for 34 years. (Courtesy of Ruth Harrison.)

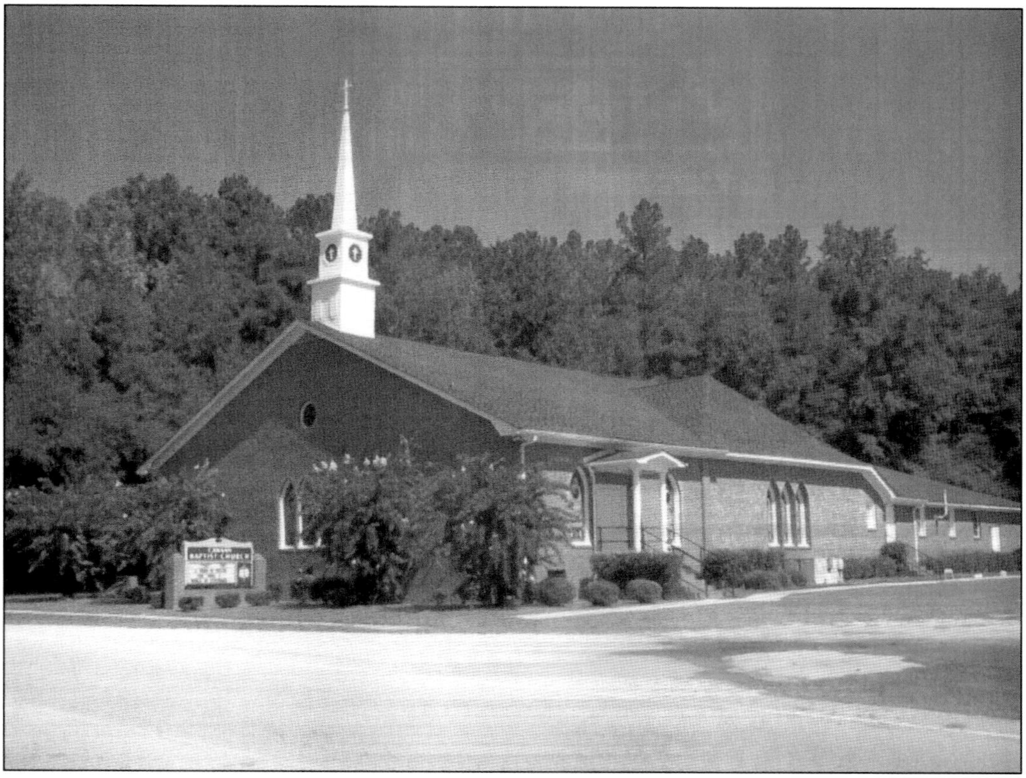

Canaan Missionary Baptist Church in Branchville started as a tent site in the late 1800s. A few years later, a board church was erected. The children of George and Luvenia Williams were instrumental in Canaan Baptist Church's initial construction. In 1925, under the leadership of Thomas Franklin Owens, a brick structure was built. (Courtesy of Lauritza Hill.)

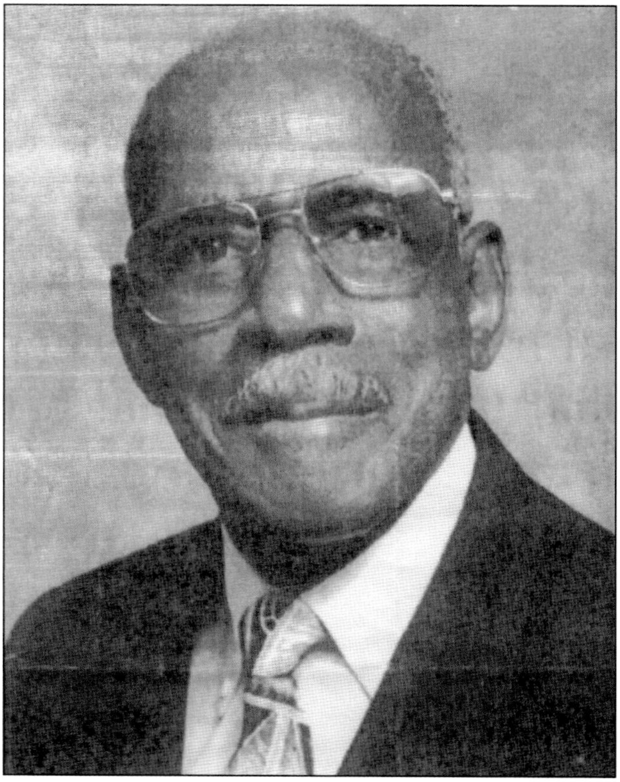

Alfred C. Wright (1927–2000) was a minister and community leader. He was the pastor of Lovely Hill Baptist Church in Holly Hill, South Carolina, for over 35 years. (Courtesy of Gwendolyn Wright-Barksdale.)

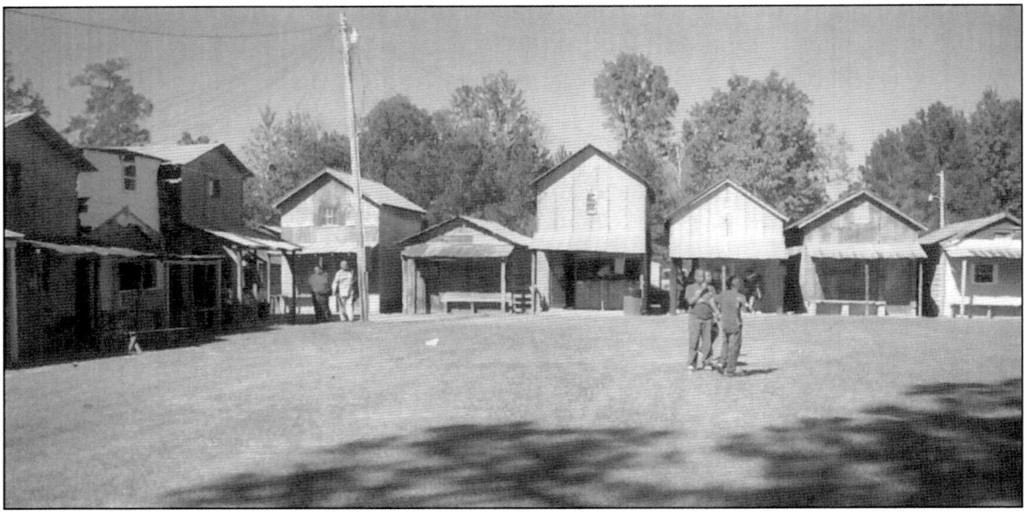

The Shady Grove Campground at one time consisted of a tabernacle or open-air arbor, which was surrounded by small huts or tents that originally had dirt floors. Now, the structures have been modernized to include floors made of either wood or cement. Over the years, the small tents have been replaced with larger buildings, and some have had electricity added. (Courtesy of Lauritza Hill.)

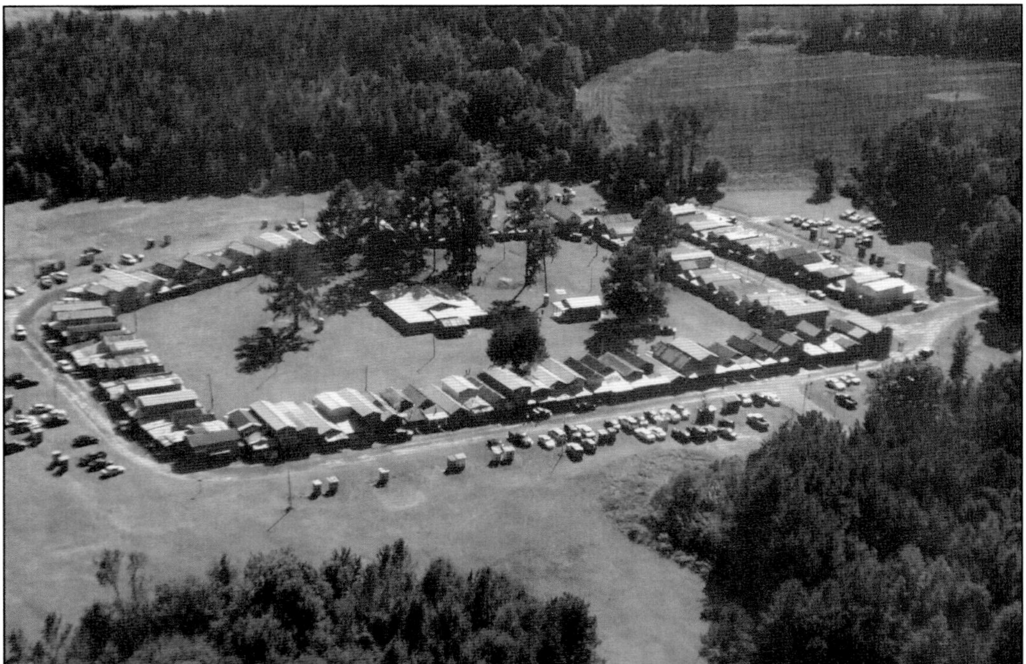

This is an aerial view of Shady Grove Campground, which was and still is a popular place for African Americans to worship once a year. People come from all over the United States for this occasion. The campground started shortly after the Civil War. One way the newly freed slaves expressed their joy and thankfulness to God was through camp meetings. According to local folklore, Caesar Wolfe, an ex-slave, persuaded others to help a rice farmer gather his crop before an approaching storm. The farmer expressed his appreciation by giving them land to be used exclusively for religious purposes. (Courtesy of Rita Newsome.)

Two

EDUCATION AND EDUCATORS

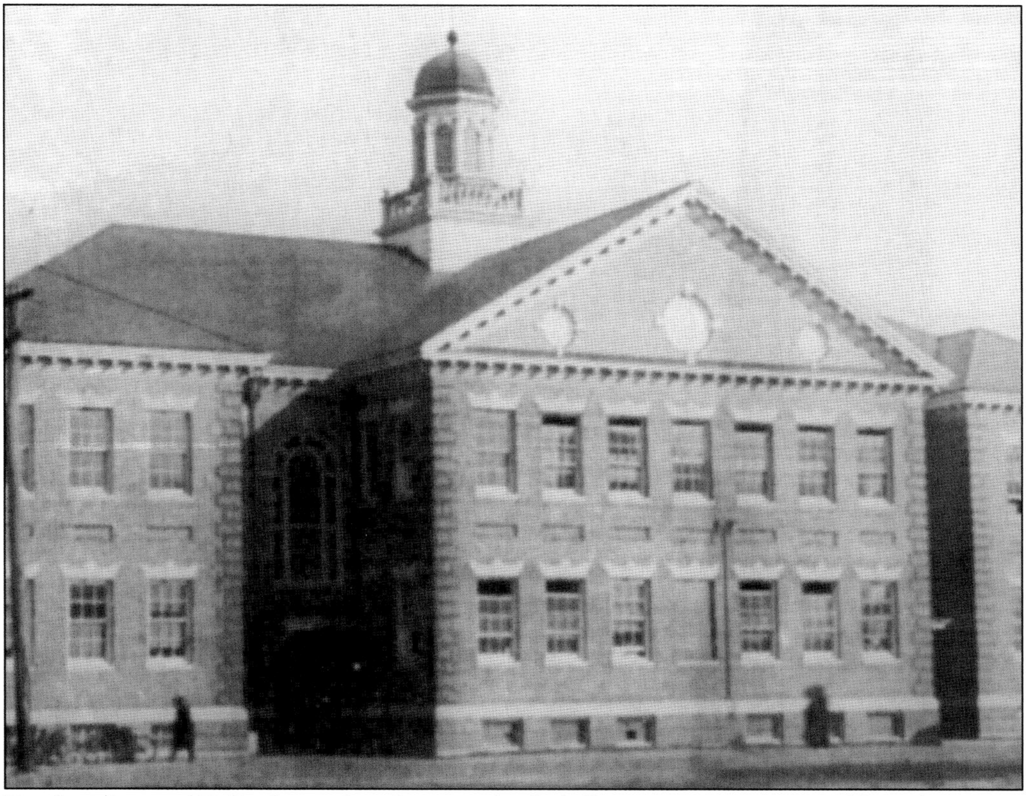

Tingley Memorial Hall is located on the grounds of Claflin University. It is one of five educational buildings constructed between 1898 and about 1915. Founded in 1869, Claflin, the oldest historically black college or university in the state of South Carolina, is located in the city of Orangeburg. Tingley Hall, erected in 1908, is an elegant Georgian Revival composition, with fine proportions and ornate masonry typical of the style. The other four buildings constructed in this time period were Lee Library (about 1900), Trustee Hall (about 1910), Wilson Hall (1913), and the Dining Hall (1913). They have been listed in the National Register of Historic Places since 1983. (Courtesy of Claflin University Archives.)

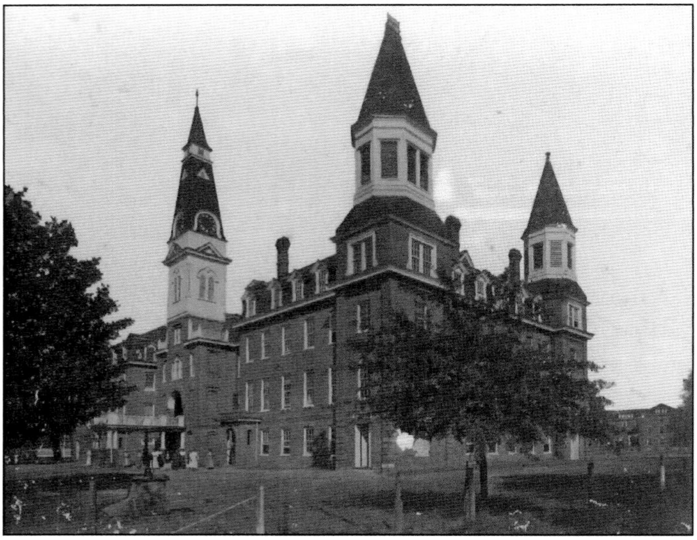

The Fisk Building was a proud monument to Claflin University's growth and progress during its time. The building was designed by Robert Charles Bates, recognized as the first certified black architect in the United States. Bates was a graduate of Claflin and designed several other buildings in Orangeburg. In 1894, a wing, 60 by 83 feet and four stories high, was added to the south end of the main building. (Courtesy of Claflin University Archives.)

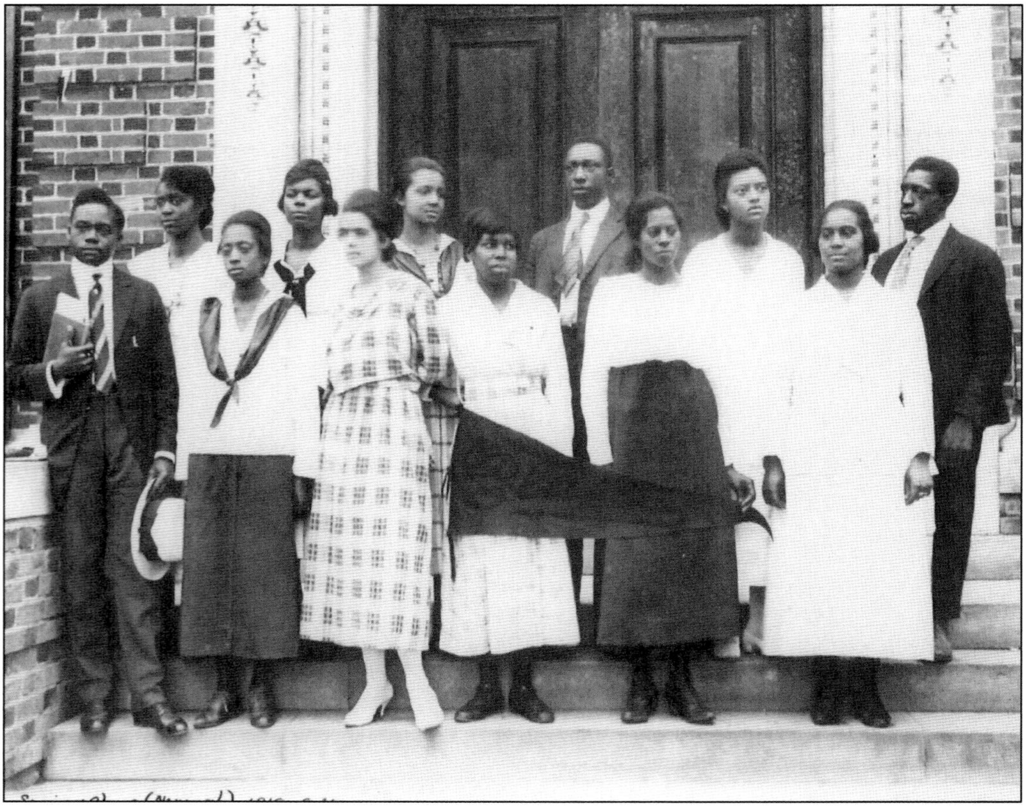

The Claflin College Normal senior class poses for a picture in 1919. At that time, Claflin operated an elementary school and a high school, the latter of which was the Normal school. Claflin College was founded in 1869 by Methodist missionaries to prepare freed slaves to take their rightful place as full American citizens. The university takes its name from two Methodist churchmen, Massachusetts governor William Claflin and his father, Boston philanthropist Lee Claflin, who provided a large part of the funds to purchase the campus. (Courtesy of Claflin University Archives.)

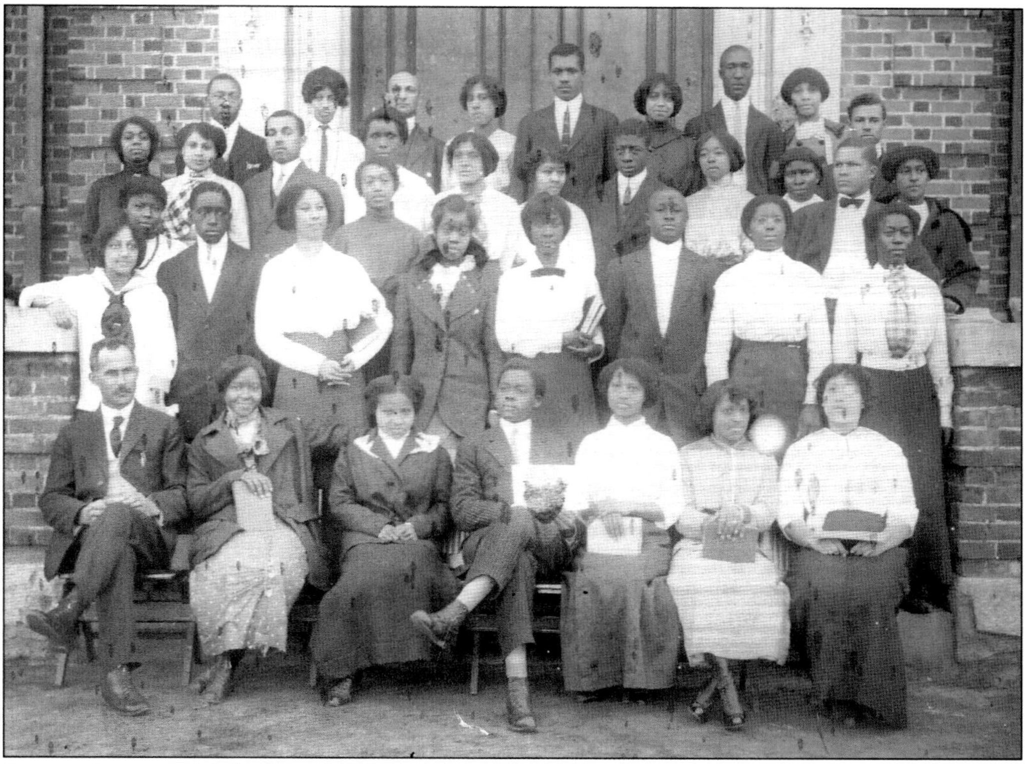

Dunton Memorial School students pose for a class picture in the early 1920s. Menia Steele (first row, second from left) was one of the teachers of the class and is Charles Payne's cousin. (Courtesy of Charles Payne.)

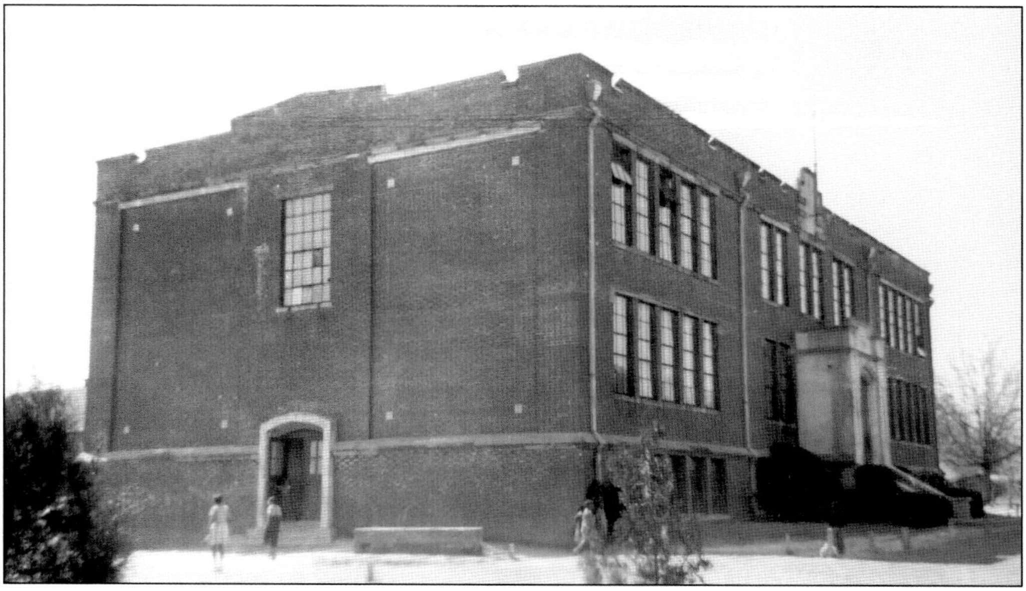

Dunton Memorial Colored School in Orangeburg opened in 1922 on Goff Avenue. Former students recalled that, when Sterling Elementary School on Sunnyside closed, the students and faculty walked from Sterling to the new school on Goff Avenue for the first day of class. (Courtesy of SCDAH.)

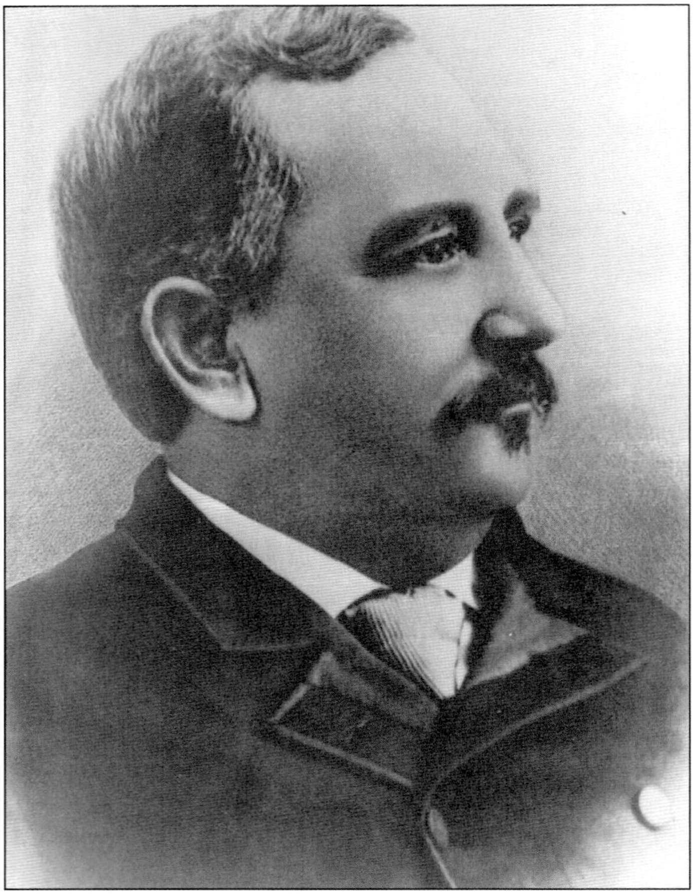

Thomas E. Miller (1849–1938) was a legislator; the first president of the Colored Normal, Industrial, Agricultural, and Mechanical College, now known as South Carolina State University; and the founder of Saint Luke Presbyterian Church, USA. One of the reasons that Miller came to Orangeburg was to found a new Presbyterian church and an institution of higher learning for blacks. He was a graduate of the Presbyterian-related Lincoln University of Chester, Pennsylvania. (Courtesy of Claflin University Archives.)

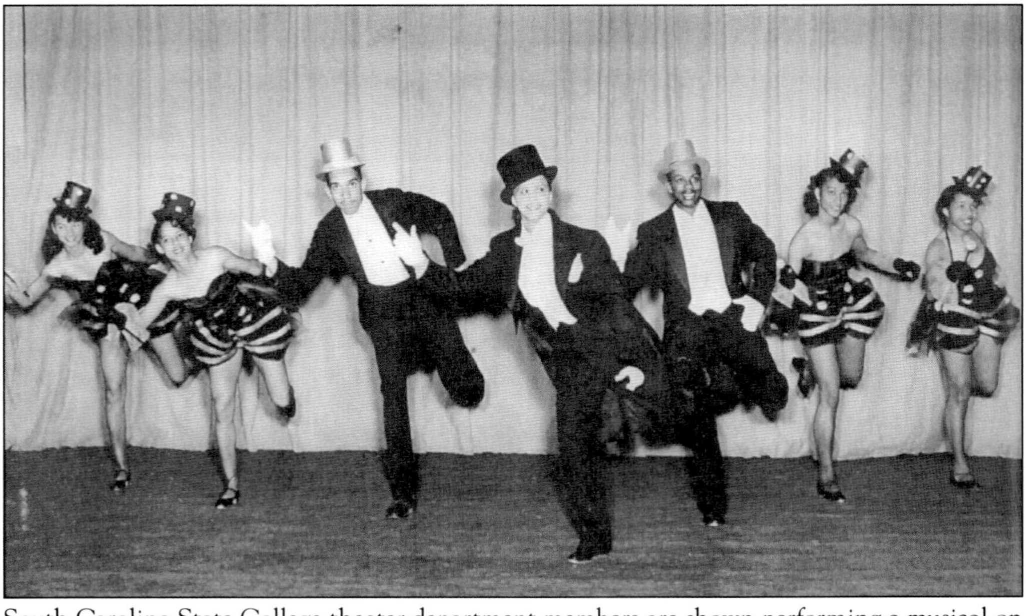

South Carolina State College theater department members are shown performing a musical on campus in 1947. (Courtesy of South Carolina State University Library.)

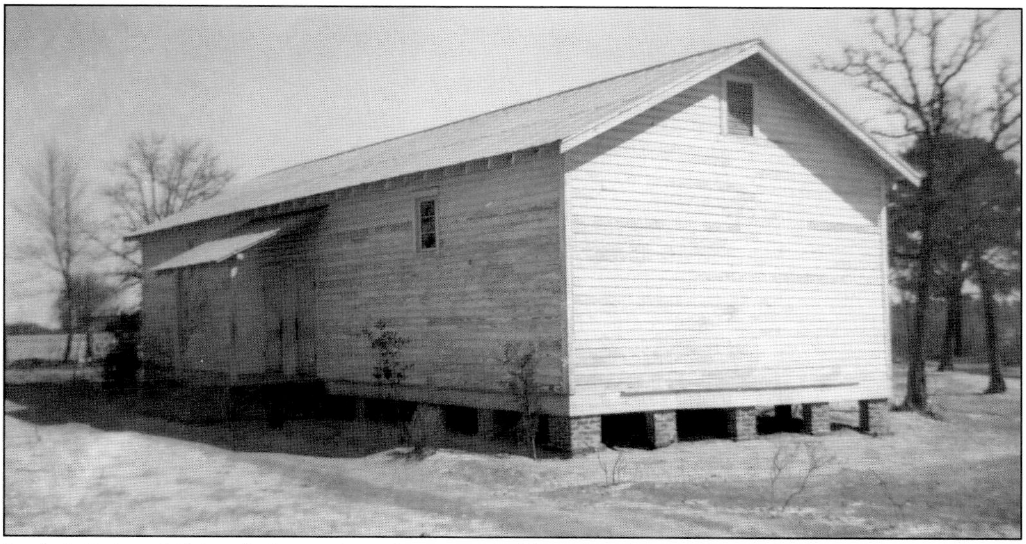

Bethel Colored School, shown here between 1935 and 1950, was located in Livingston, a small rural town within Orangeburg County, during the mid-1930s. (Courtesy of SCDAH.)

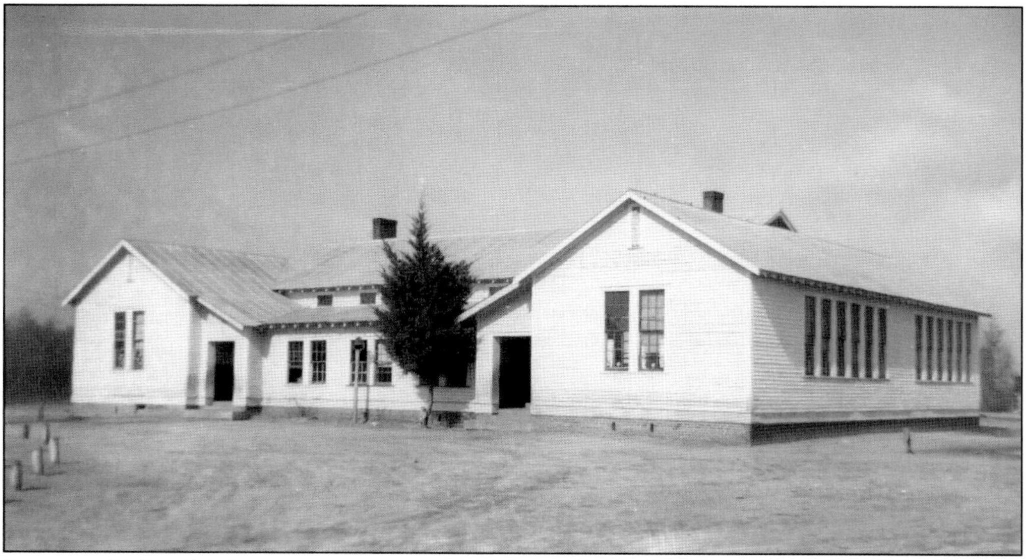

Bowman Colored School, constructed in 1926, was located in Bowman, a rural town within Orangeburg County. The school is shown here between 1935 and 1950. (Courtesy of SCDAH.)

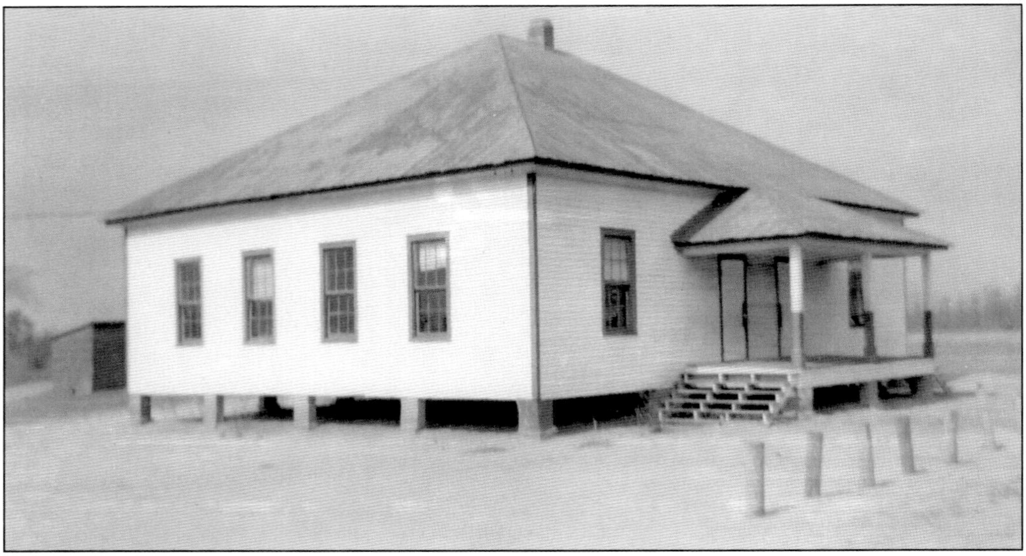

Cope Colored School, shown here sometime between 1935 and 1950, was located in Cope, a rural town in Orangeburg County. (Courtesy of SCDAH.)

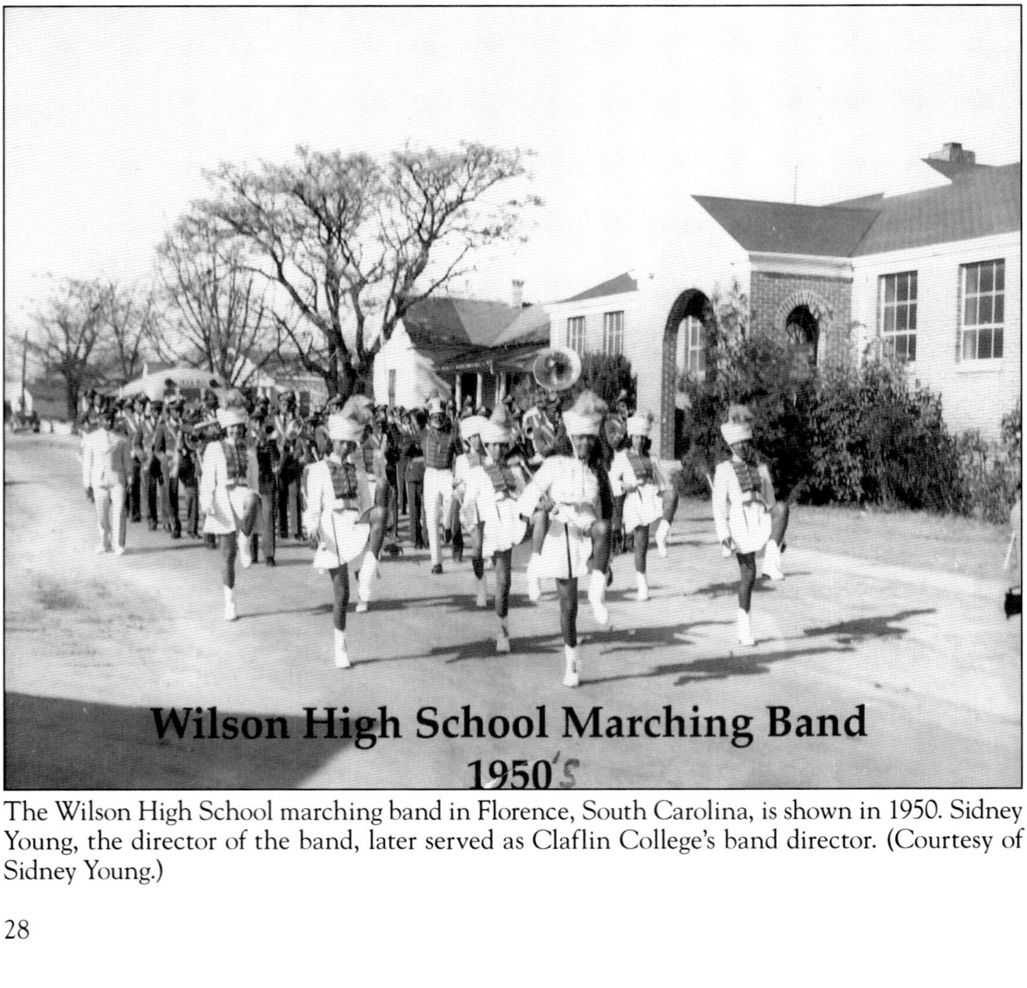

The Wilson High School marching band in Florence, South Carolina, is shown in 1950. Sidney Young, the director of the band, later served as Claflin College's band director. (Courtesy of Sidney Young.)

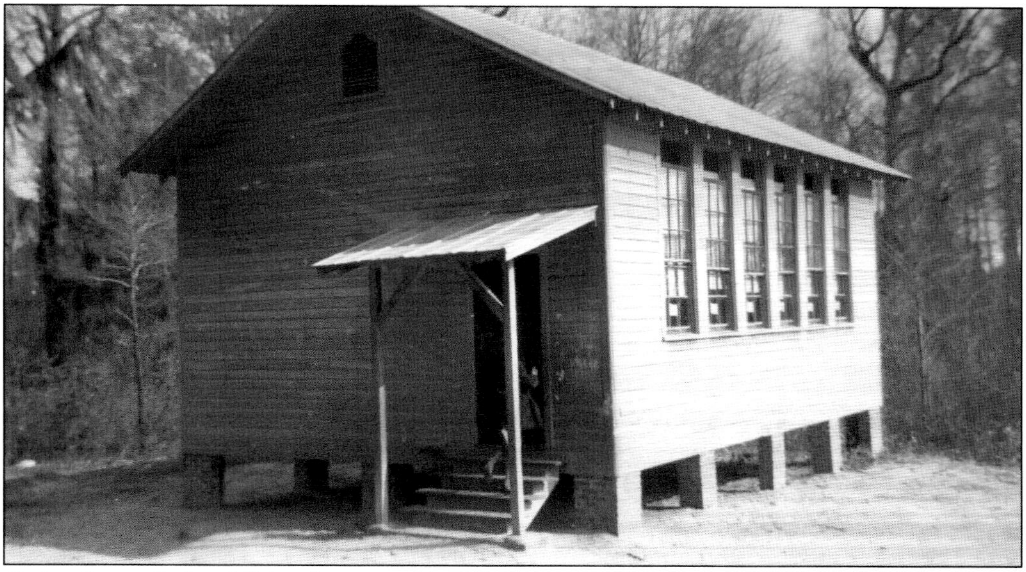

Cedar Grove Colored School, pictured here between 1935 and 1950, was located in Cordova, a town just down the road from the city of Orangeburg. Another school named Cedar Grove was located in the town of Orangeburg. Students later attended George W. Carver Elementary and High School, which was built in 1954. (Courtesy of SCDAH.)

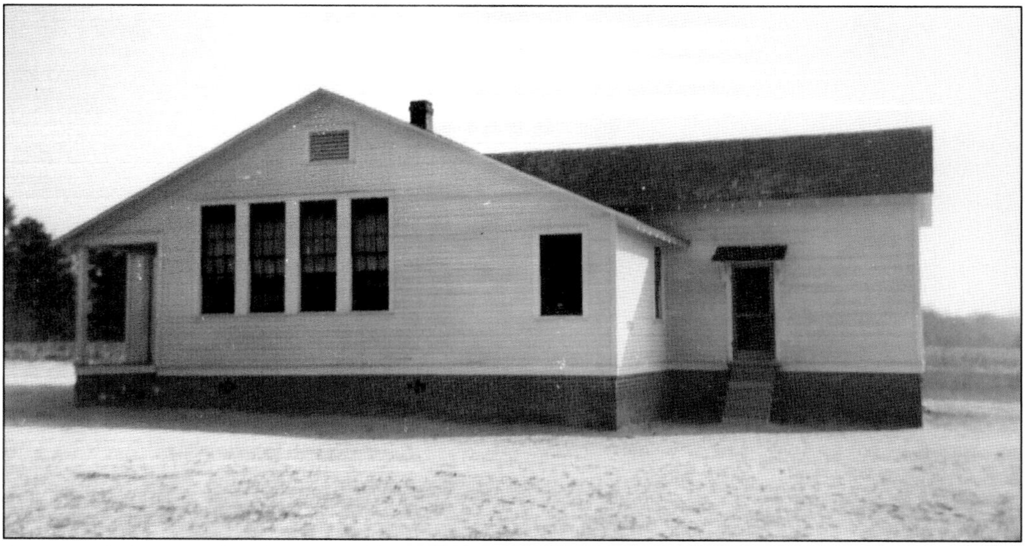

Cordova Colored School, pictured here between 1935 and 1950, was located in Cordova, a rural town in Orangeburg County. Other schools located in the vicinity were Prince Institute, Canaan, Cedar Grove, Emanuel, Old Field, Rocky Pond, Snake Swamp, Edisto Elementary, McMillan Elementary, Wright Elementary, and Turkey Branch. Some schools were known by one name in the African American neighborhood and another by the town. (Courtesy of SCDAH.)

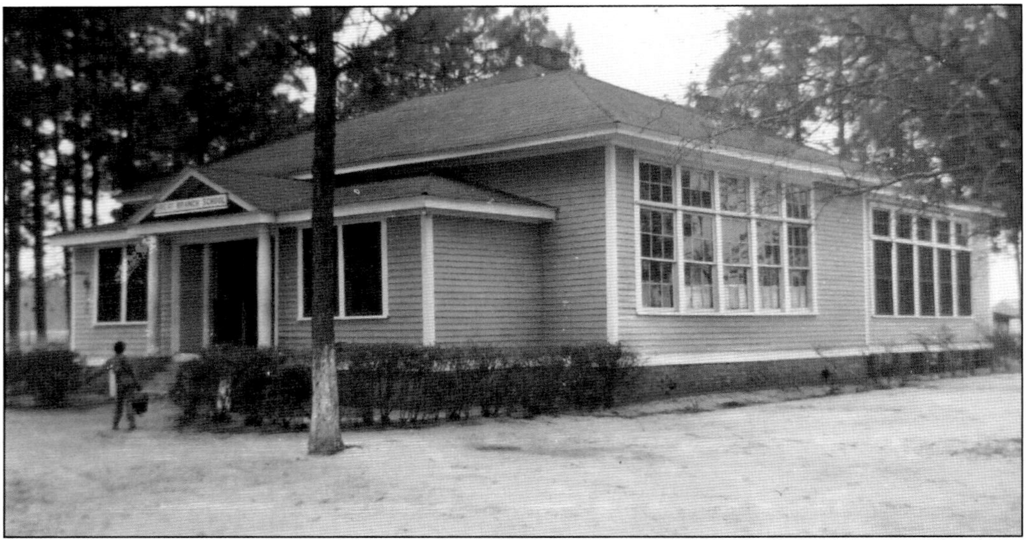

This photograph, taken between 1935 and 1950, shows Great Branch Colored School, located on Neeses Highway in Neeses, a rural town in Orangeburg County. It was built in 1922. The last class at Great Branch had the privilege of being the first to use the newly built G.W. Carver School's name on their diplomas, even though it did not officially open until September 1954. That 1954 class had 12 students. (Courtesy of SCDAH.)

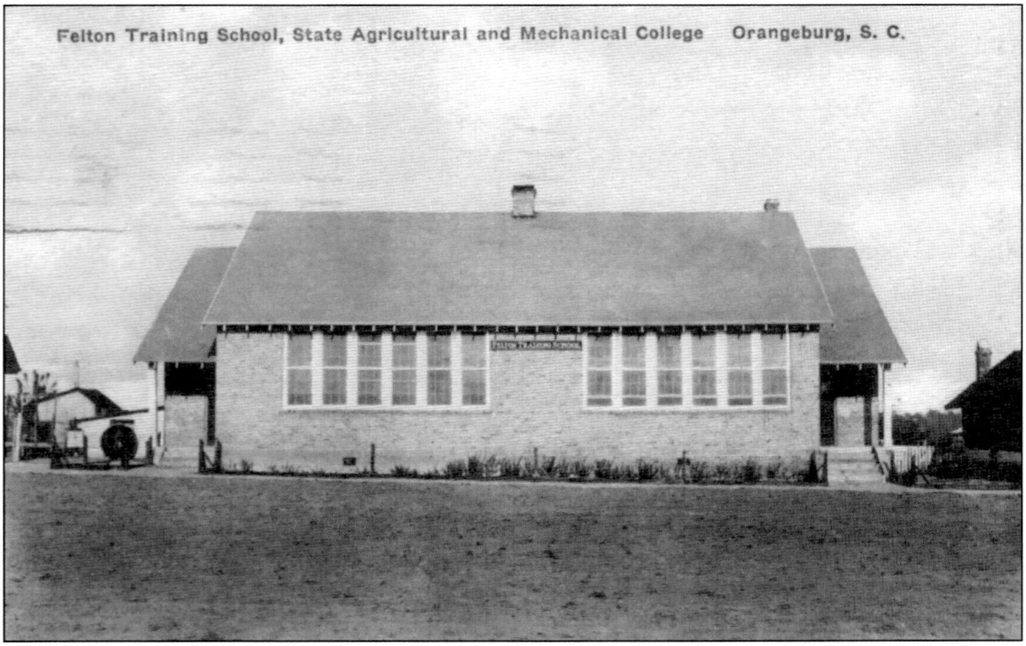

Felton Laboratory School, pictured here between 1935 and 1950, was once called Felton Training School and is still located on the campus of South Carolina State University. It was established in 1920 as a kindergarten and primary school. In 1924, a four room building was donated by the General Education Board and the Rosenwald Fund for teacher education purposes. The school has expanded from kindergarten through the eighth grade. (Courtesy of South Caroliniana Library, University of South Carolina, Columbia.)

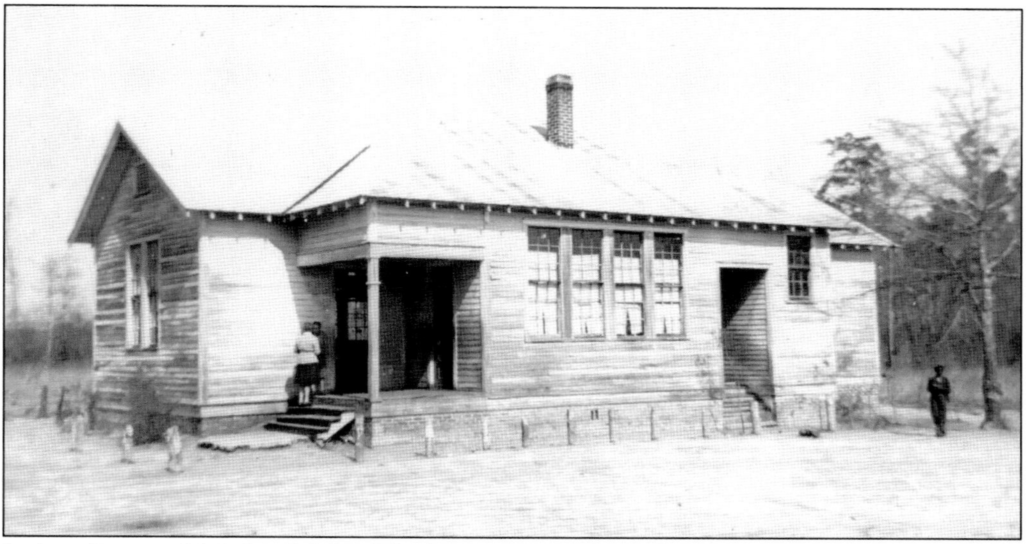

Jenkins Rosenwald Colored School, built in 1928, was located in the town of Bowman. In rural areas, many of these small schools were built by the Rosenwald Organization, which was funded by Chicago philanthropist Julius Rosenwald to help provide schools for African Americans. This photograph is from around 1935. (Courtesy of SCDAH.)

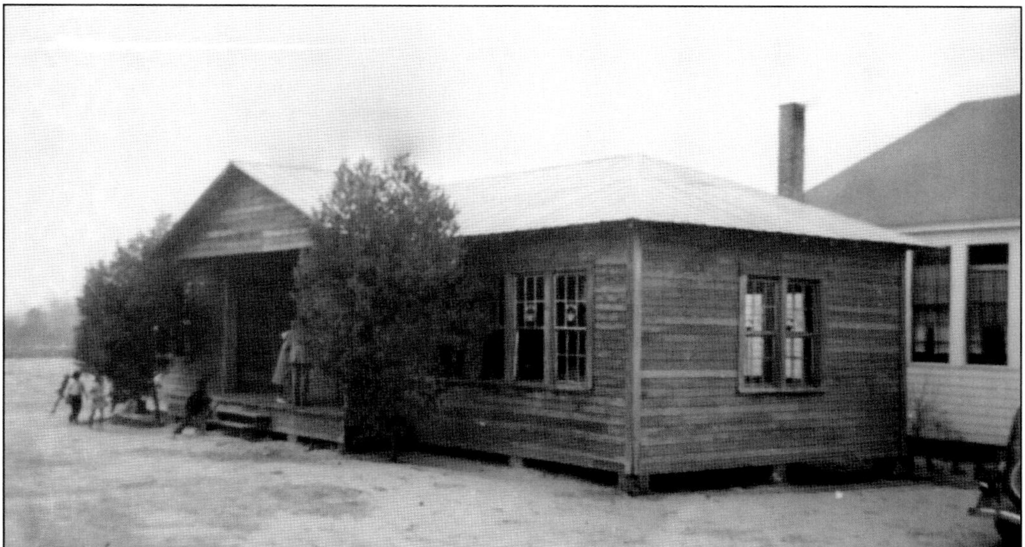

Norway Colored School, pictured here between 1935 and 1950, was located in the rural town of Norway, which is on the western edge of Orangeburg County. (Courtesy of SCDAH.)

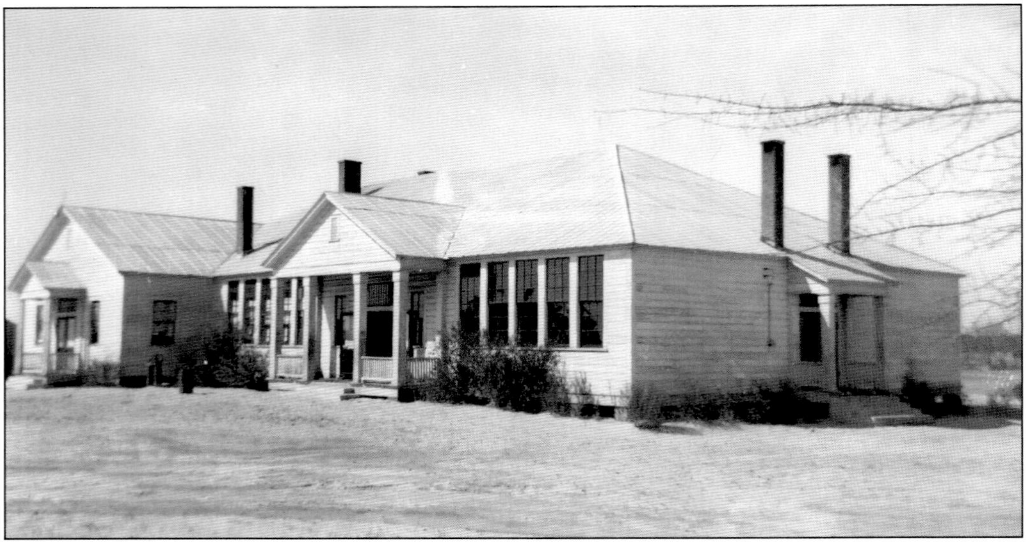

North Colored School was located in North, South Carolina, a rural town near the northwestern border of Orangeburg County. The school is shown here between 1935 and 1950. (Courtesy of SCDAH.)

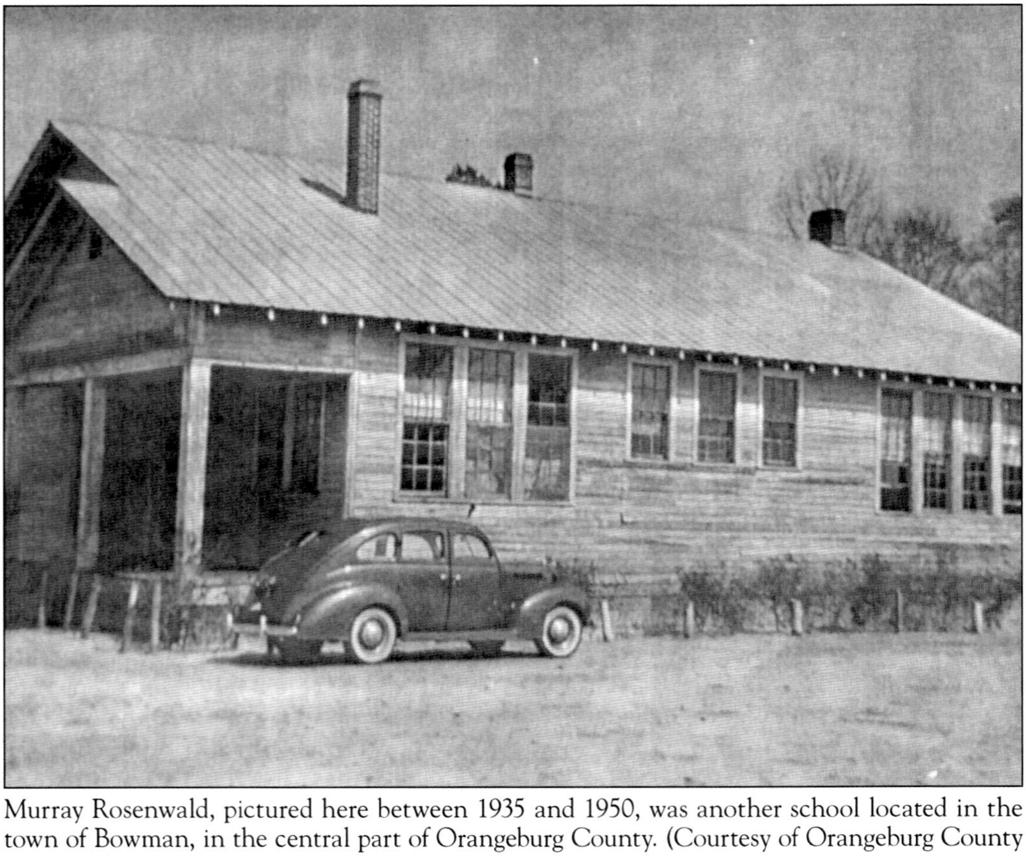

Murray Rosenwald, pictured here between 1935 and 1950, was another school located in the town of Bowman, in the central part of Orangeburg County. (Courtesy of Orangeburg County Historical Society.)

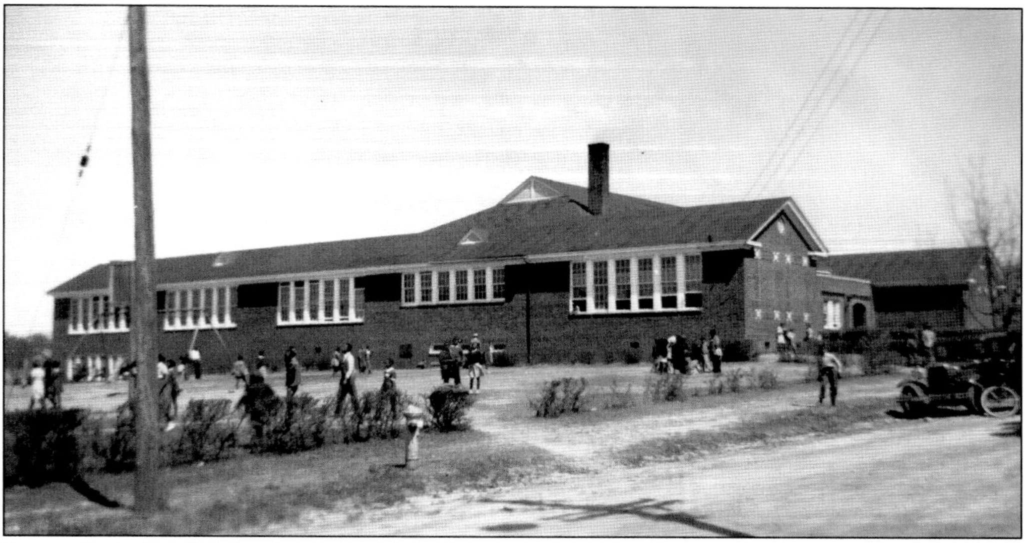

Riverside Colored School, pictured here between 1935 and 1950, was located at the corner of Glover and Maple Streets in the city of Orangeburg. Most of the colored schools in the city were elementary schools. The Riverside Elementary School served area African American students from 1929 until desegregation in 1972. (Courtesy of SCDAH.)

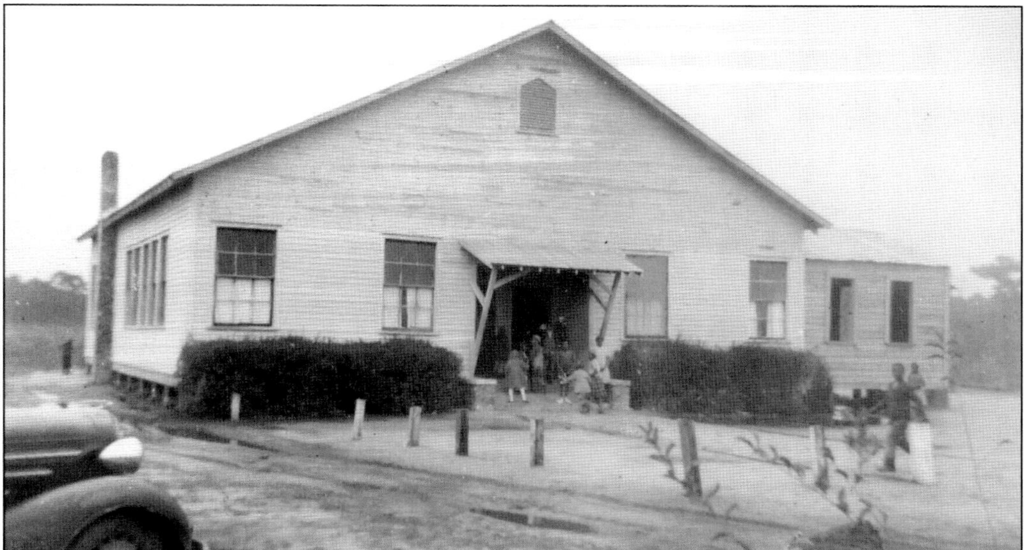

Rowesville Colored School, built in 1920, was in the town of Rowesville. Primarily an agricultural community, Rowesville has changed little since the turn of the 20th century. This photograph was taken between 1935 and 1950. (Courtesy of SCDAH.)

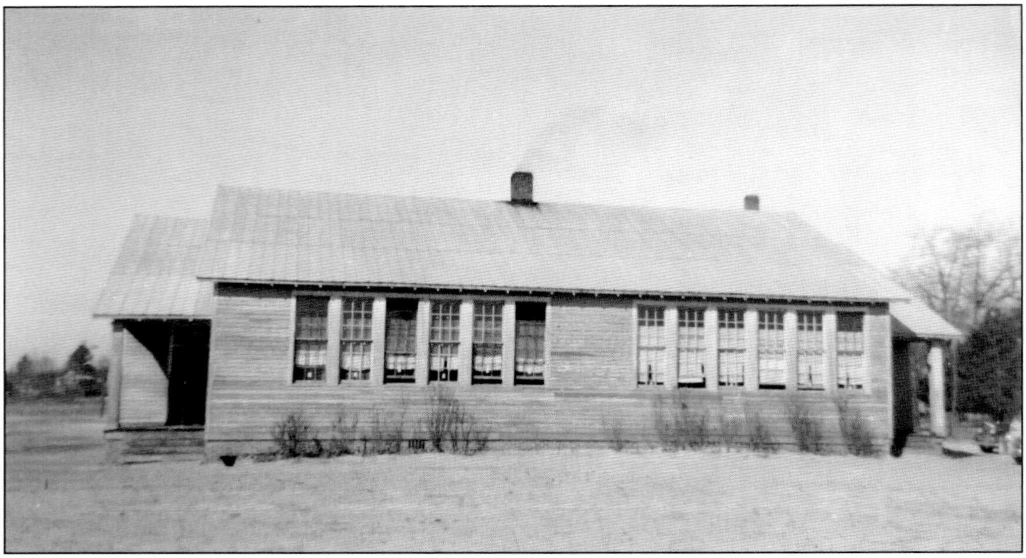

Springfield Colored School, pictured here between 1935 and 1950, was located in the town of Springfield and was built in 1920. Springfield is in the western corner of Orangeburg County. (Courtesy of SCDAH.)

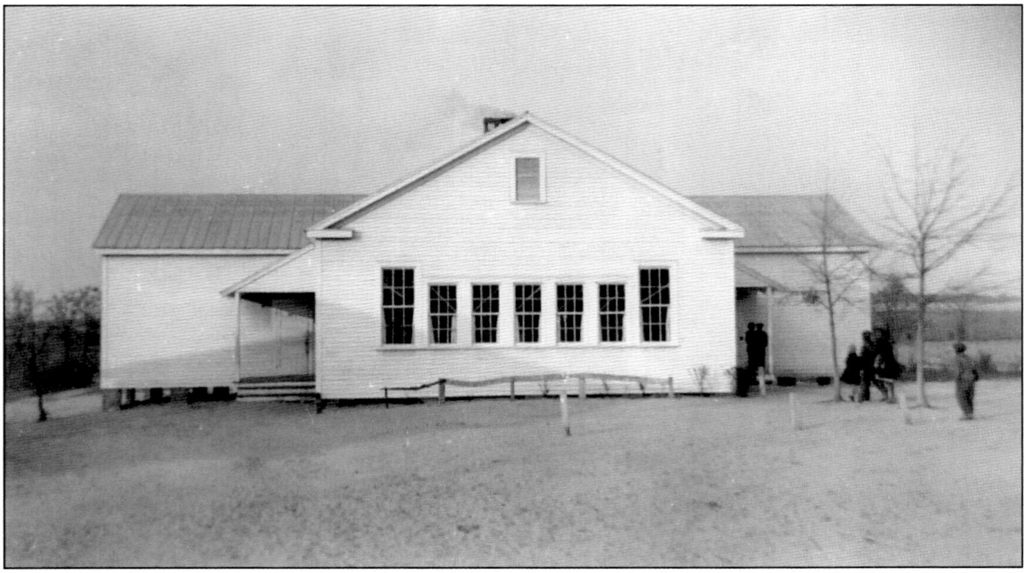

Woodford Colored School, pictured here between 1935 and 1950, was located in Woodford, a small town in Orangeburg County known for the annual Hummingbird Festival in March. (Courtesy of SCDAH.)

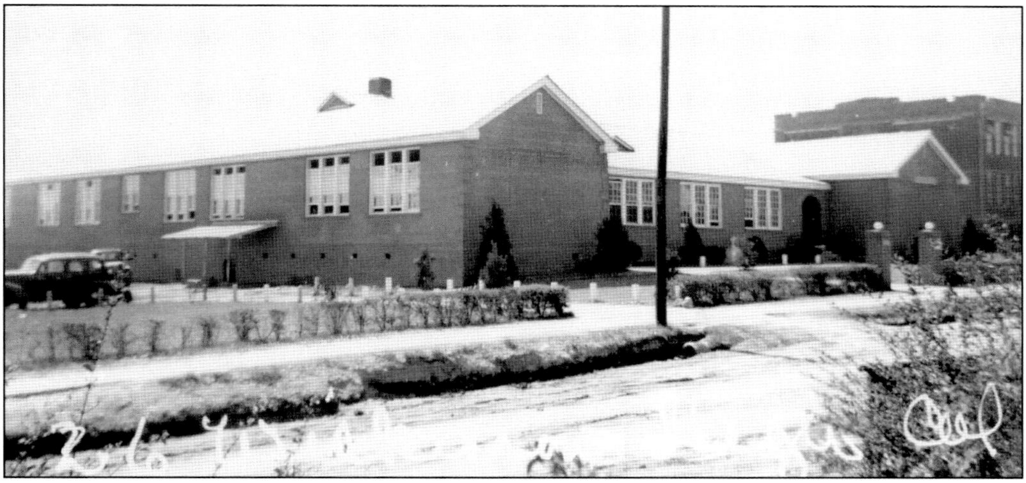

Shown here around 1950, Wilkinson High School opened on Goff Avenue in Orangeburg in 1937, becoming the first African American high school in South Carolina. The school educated students up to the 11th grade. In 1953, Wilkinson on Belleville Road opened as an elementary school and was later renamed Robert E. Howard Middle School. In 1971, when the schools became integrated, Orangeburg High School became Orangeburg-Wilkinson High School and included grades 11 and 12. Wilkinson Elementary on Belleville Road became Orangeburg-Wilkinson for grades 9 and 10. Eventually, a new high school was built for grades 9 through 12. (Courtesy of SCDAH.)

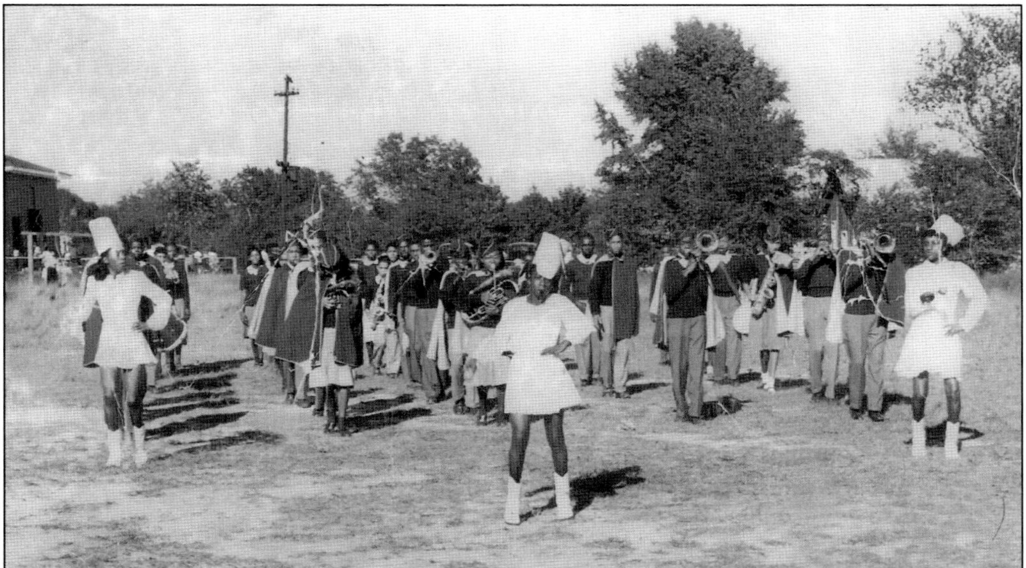

The Wilkinson High School band, shown here around 1948, was started in 1946. The idea for a high school band was originated by Hazel Pierce, the mother of Geraldyne Zimmerman, and Clemmie Webber. James B. Hunt was the first band director. Band members identified here include Barbara Williams Jenkins (majorette on left), who later became dean of the library of South Carolina State College; John C. Williams Jr. (third column, sixth from front); Benjamin Payton (fourth column, front row) who became president of the Tuskegee Institute in Alabama; Paul Webber III, who became a federal judge in Washington, DC; and Charles Thomas (first column, third from front). (Courtesy of John C. Williams Jr.)

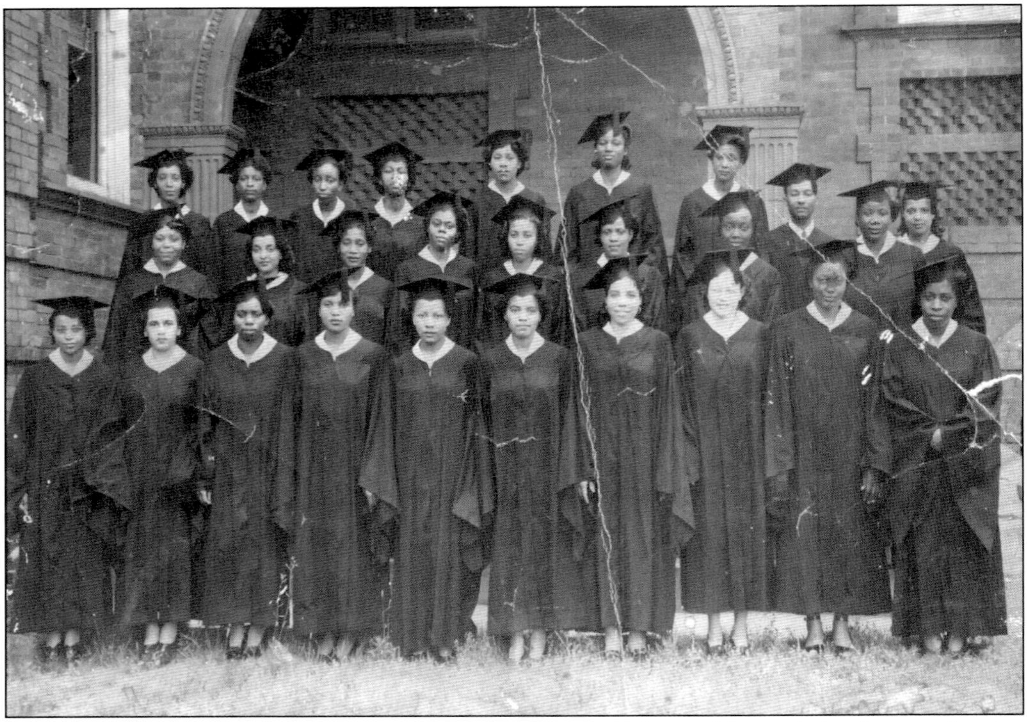

Students of the Claflin College senior class of 1944 pose in front of the arch for their graduation picture. Identified class members are Carmen Sulton Thomasson (second row, second from left), Evangeline Salley Hill (third row, sixth from left), and Gladys Spell (second row, far left). (Courtesy of Evangeline Hill.)

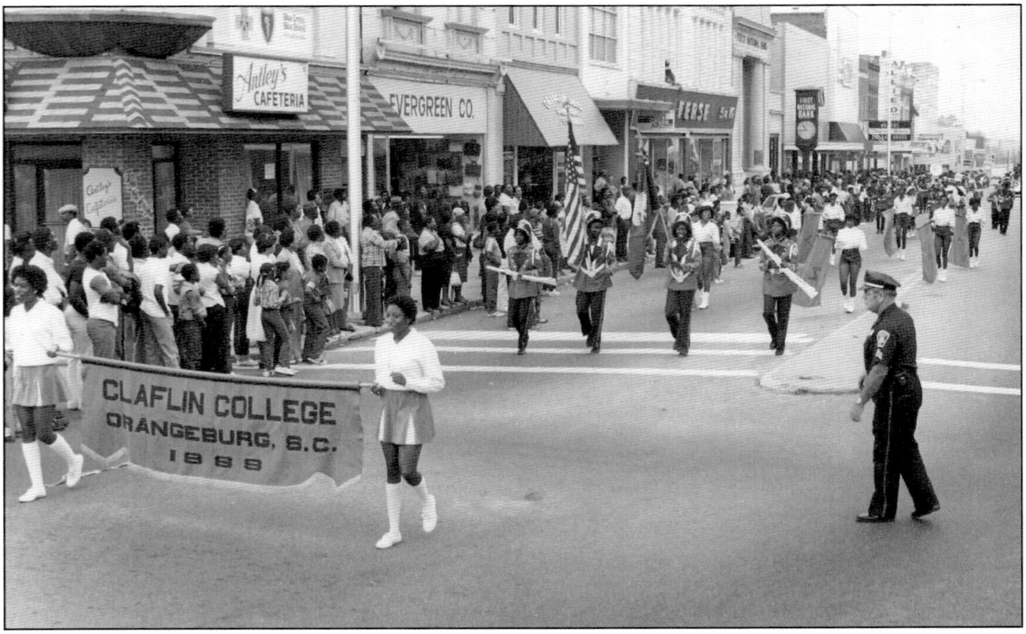

The Claflin University band is shown participating in a parade in 1980. The university's band was small in size compared to that of South Carolina State College, but it was large in sound. (Courtesy of Sidney Young.)

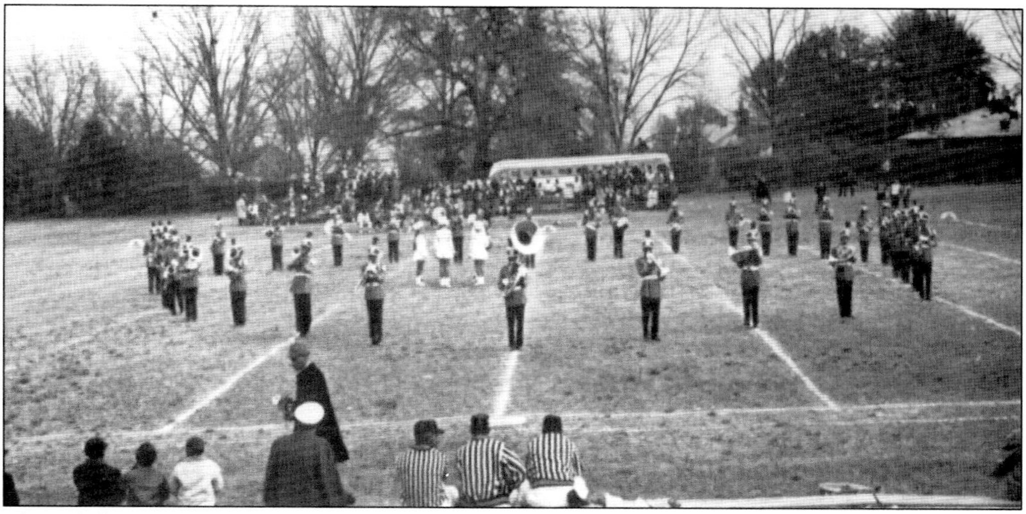

The Claflin College marching band is shown in action on the field in 1965. The band director, Sidney Young, was known for his antics on the sidelines as the band played or marched. (Courtesy of Sidney Young.)

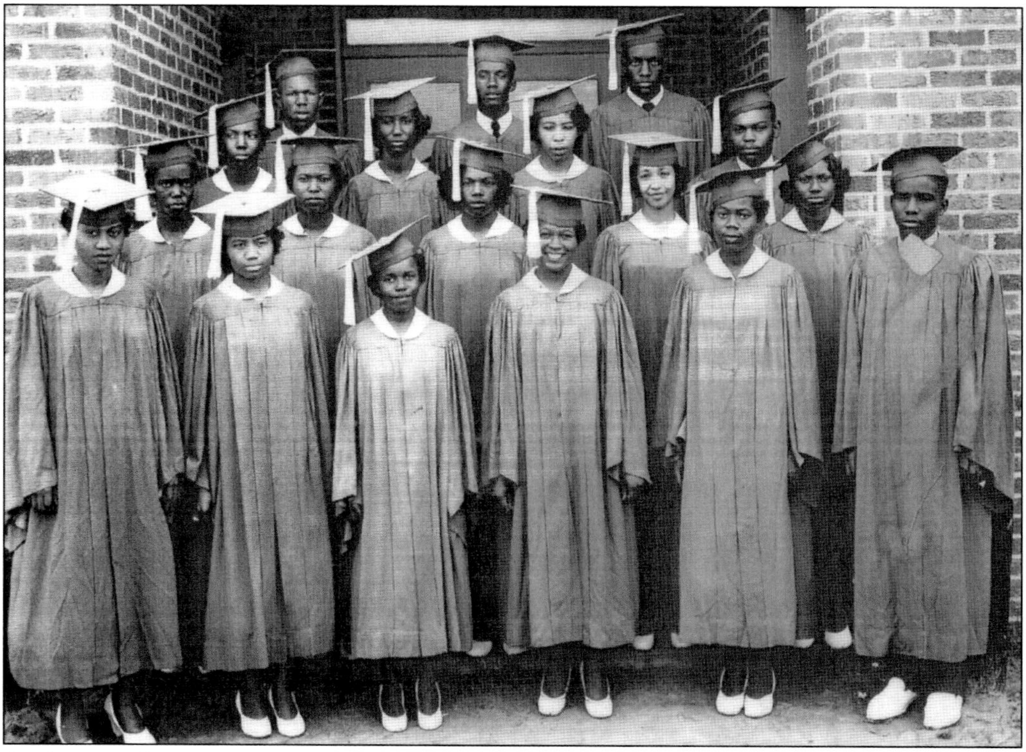

Students in George W. Carver High School's class of 1955 pose for a photograph. In 1954, the George W. Carver Elementary and High School, in Cordova, replaced all of the colored schools in that area. The school district was District No. 4. The students are, from left to right, (first row) Alice Lebby, Inez Izzard, Mary Young, Zelma Tyler, Hester Smith, and Ernest Evans; (second row) Laura Johnson, Catherine Phelps, Lurlene Johnson, Zelma Hoffman, and Earline Johnson; (third row) Alfair Johnson, Janie Summers, Ethel Caine, and Nahaniel Hubbard; (fourth row) Robert Jamison, Paul Jones, and John Walker. (Courtesy of Carver School Reunion Committee.)

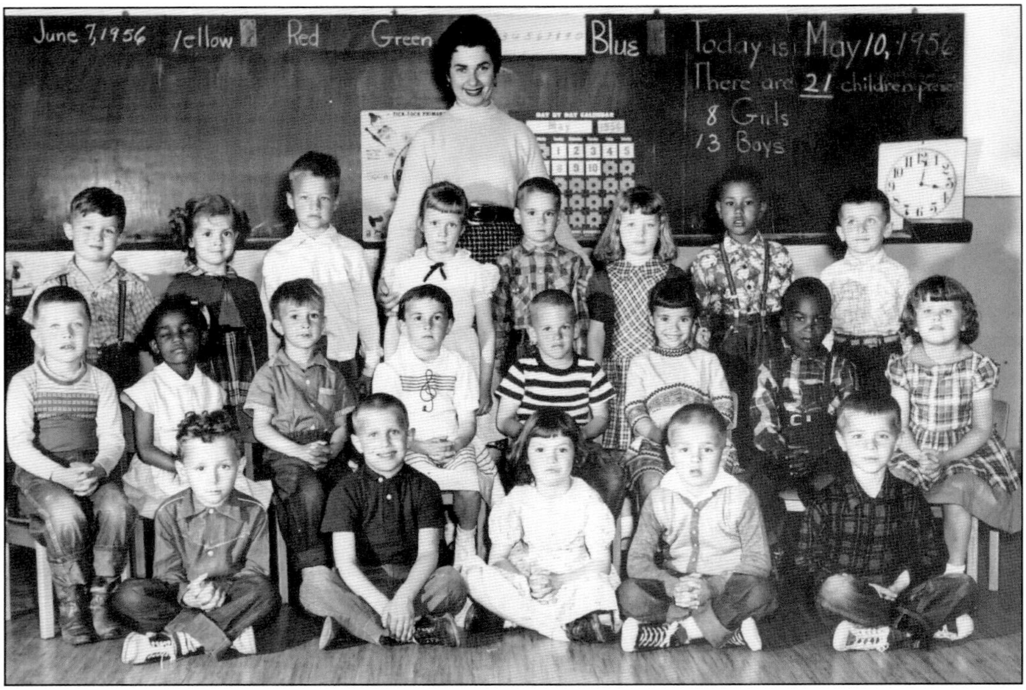

Vandy Gaffney (third row, second from right) and his classmates pose for a photograph at his school in Germany in 1956. He attended school in Germany while his father was stationed there in the US military. Vandy is the son of Capt. Raymond Gaffney Sr. and Lillie Gaffney. (Courtesy of Lillie Gaffney.)

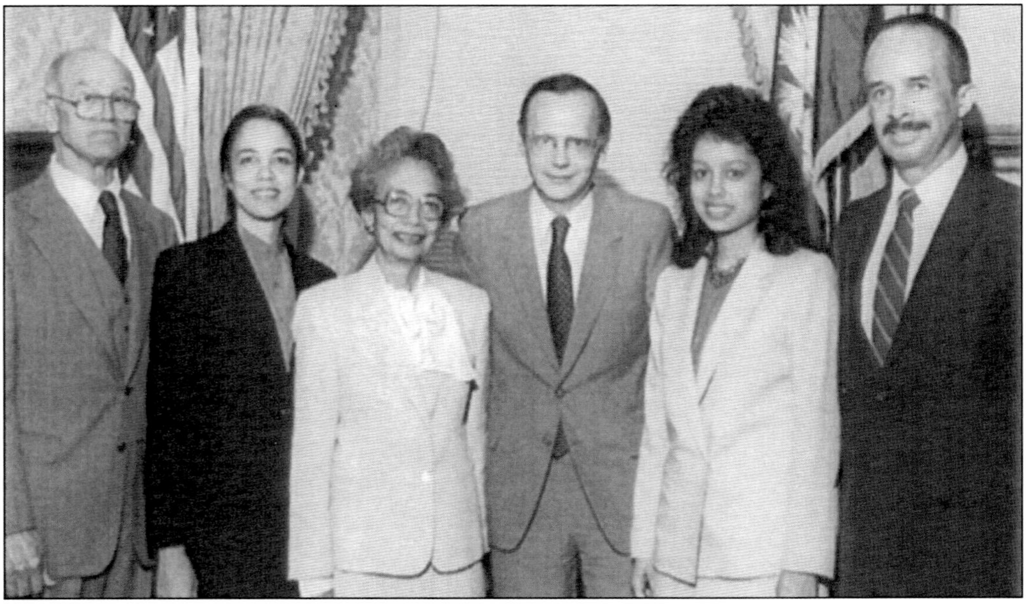

In 1983, Dr. Clemmie Webber of Orangeburg was chosen not only as South Carolina's Mother of the Year, she also had the honor of being chosen National Mother of the Year. Shown from left to right in this 1983 photograph are Paul Webber Jr., Dr. Carolyn W. Thomson, Dr. Clemmie Webber, South Carolina governor Richard Riley, Sheryl W. Washington, and Judge Paul Webber III. (Courtesy of the Webber family.)

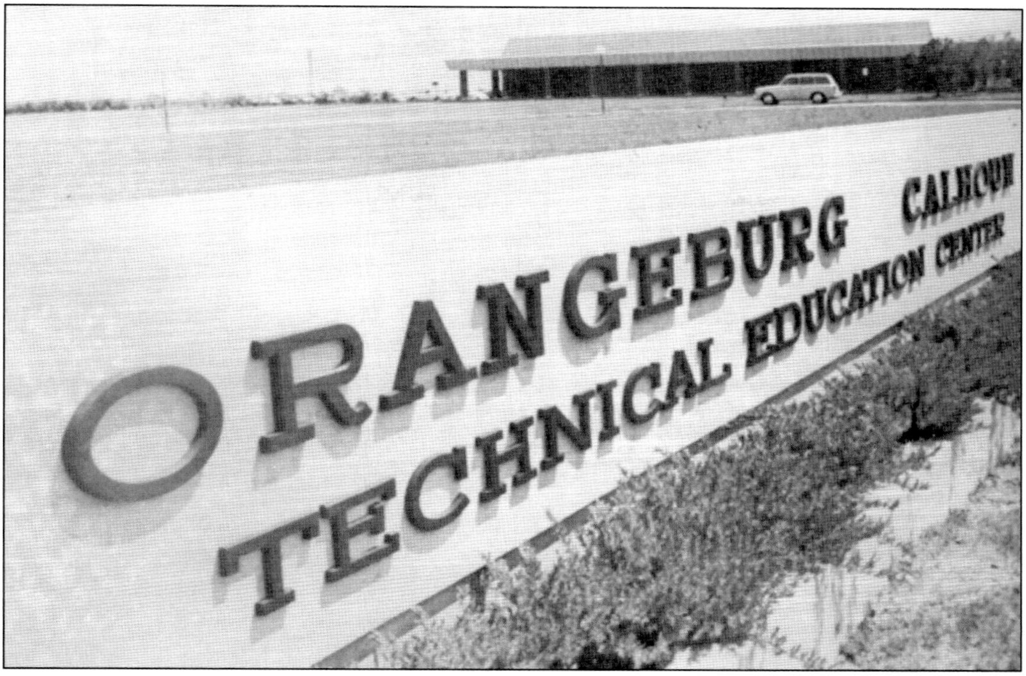

The Orangeburg-Calhoun Technical College, shown here around 1971, was established in 1968 and the official dedication ceremonies were held in 1969. Prior to 1974, it was known as Orangeburg-Calhoun Technical Center. (Courtesy of Orangeburg-Calhoun Technical College.)

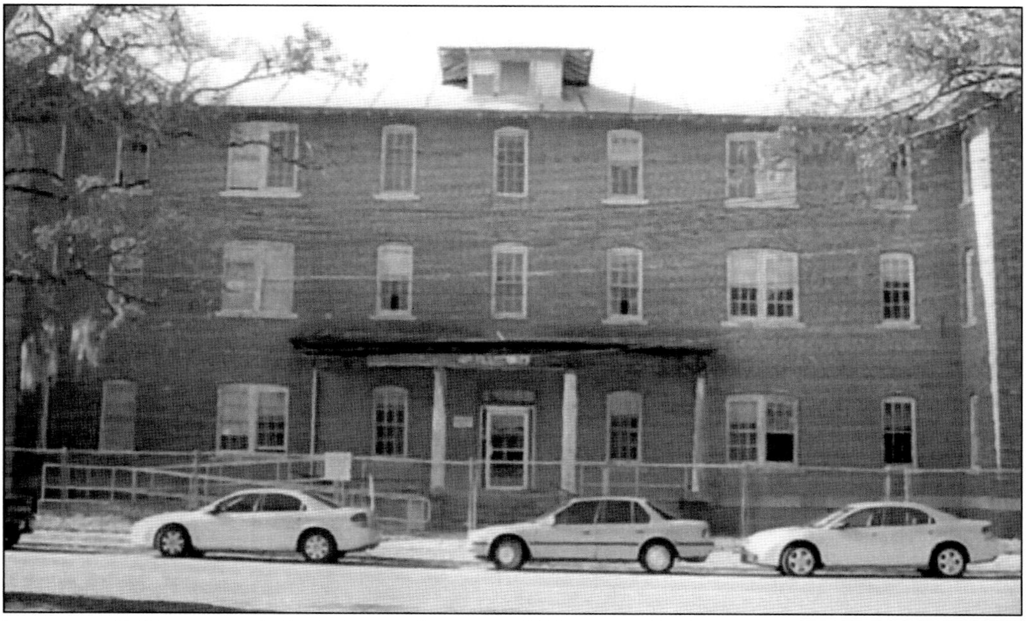

Lowman Hall, originally built by students in 1917 as a male dormitory, is one of the oldest buildings on the South Carolina State University campus. This building was one of the first designs of architect Miller F. Whittaker, who was then on the college staff. Whittaker was an African American architect in South Carolina who helped set standards for students aspiring to the architectural profession. The hall, listed in the National Register of Historic Places in 1985, is one of the few remaining original buildings on campus. (Courtesy of SCDAH.)

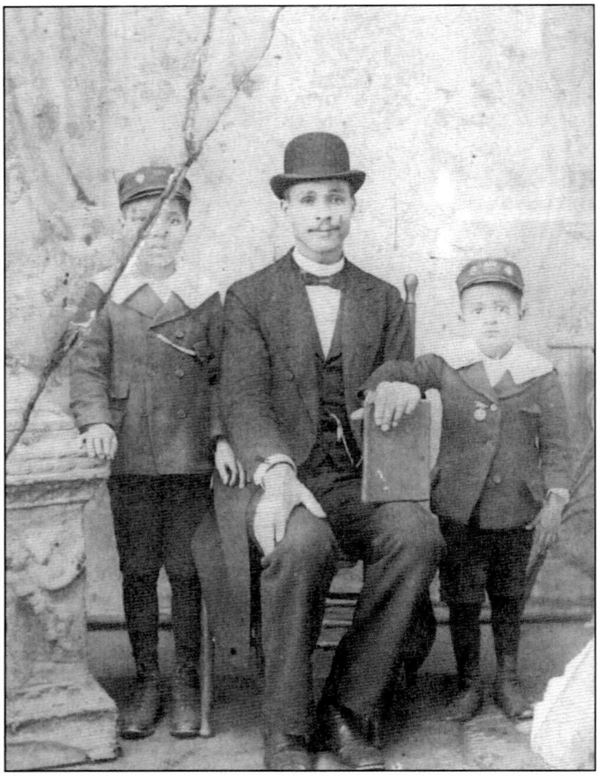

James A.S. Pinson (center) is shown with his two sons, Ira David Pinson (left) and Sylvester Pinson. James Pinson lived for a time in Altoona, Pennsylvania. Ira graduated from Benedict College, Yale, and Colgate Divinity. He taught German and philosophy at Morris College in Sumter, South Carolina; coached the baseball team; and, eventually, became president of the institution in 1930. He was killed in an automobile accident at South Hill, Virginia, in 1939. Ira was Eugene Pinson's father. Sylvester also graduated from Benedict College in Columbia and Meharry Medical College in Nashville. He practiced medicine in Philadelphia for many years. (Courtesy of Eugene Pinson.)

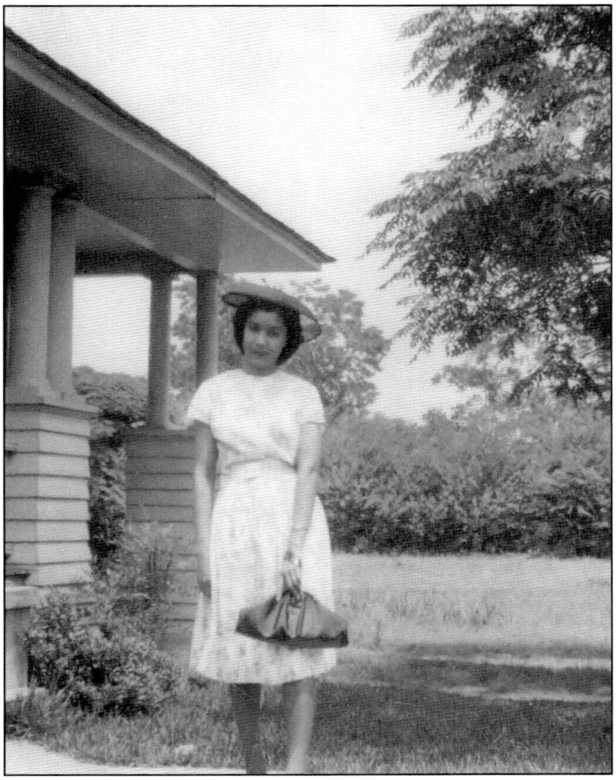

Yvonne Disher Pinson (1927–2009), an educator, was married to Eugene Pinson. She graduated from South Carolina State College and began her teaching career at the Elloree Training School in Elloree, South Carolina. She taught in the Darlington School System from 1948 to 1967. Pinson was employed in the Calhoun County school system and taught at St. John Elementary School in 1968 and at John Ford Elementary School in St. Matthews, South Carolina. (Courtesy of Eugene Pinson.)

From left to right, Joy Barnes, Dr. Maceo Nance Jr., Julie Nance, and George Barnes are shown in the early 1980s around Christmas. Dr. Nance was the fifth president of South Carolina State College, serving from 1968 to 1986. (Courtesy of Joy Barnes.)

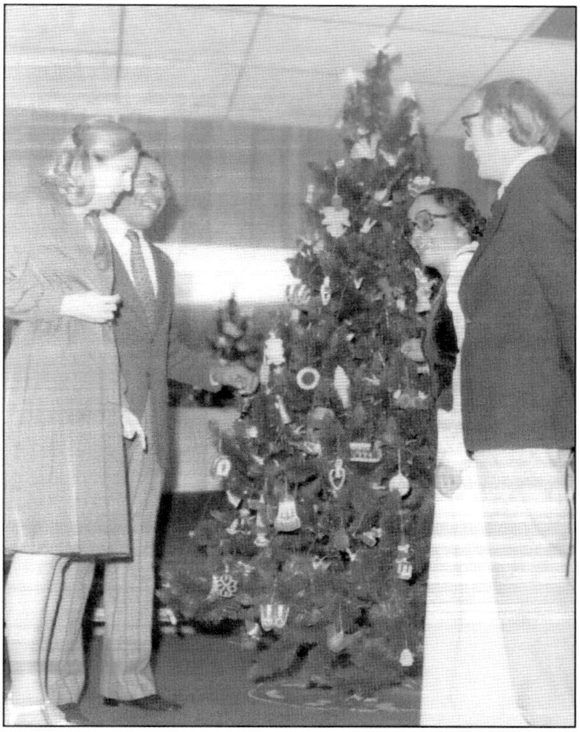

Students are shown on a field trip at the statehouse in 1988 with then state senator Strom Thurmond. The students, from Bennett Middle School (now William J. Clark Middle School), pose in Thurmond's office. Shown are, from left to right, Francine Franklin, April Dantzler, Secenario Jones, Thurmond, Richard Duncan, Shanna Lambert, and Deloris Frazier (teacher). (Courtesy of Deloris Frazier.)

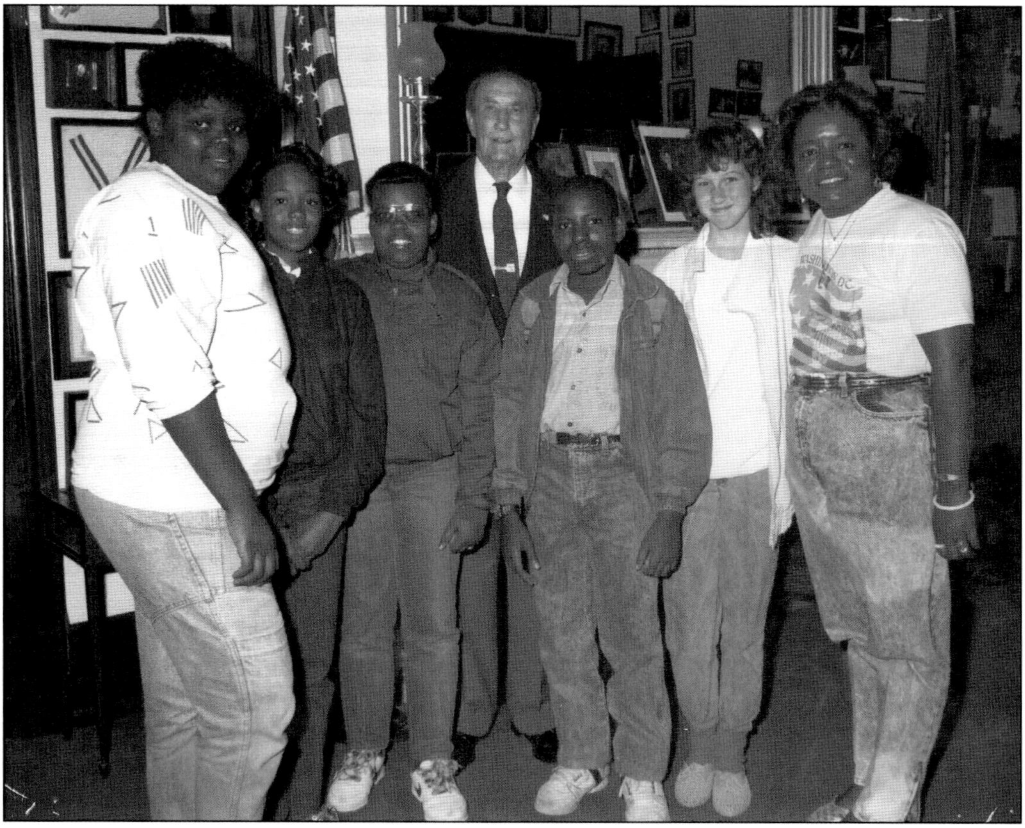

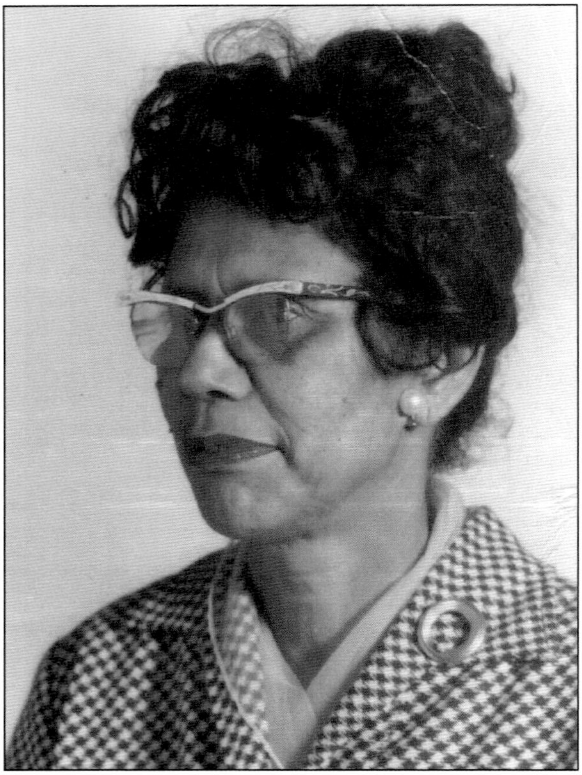

Annie Lou Crummel Glover, of Orangeburg, was an educator and businesswoman. She attended North Elementary School, Claflin University Elementary School, and Claflin College, where she received a degree in home economics and a bachelor's degree in elementary education. She completed further studies at South Carolina State College. Glover taught in the public schools of Florence, Clarendon, Lexington, and Orangeburg Counties, retiring in 1975 after 45 years as a teacher. She was also a mother to many young girls who lived in her home while they attended one of the colleges. Her home was in close proximity to both colleges, and the girls could walk to school. She was a member of Trinity United Methodist Church. (Courtesy of Vera Glover.)

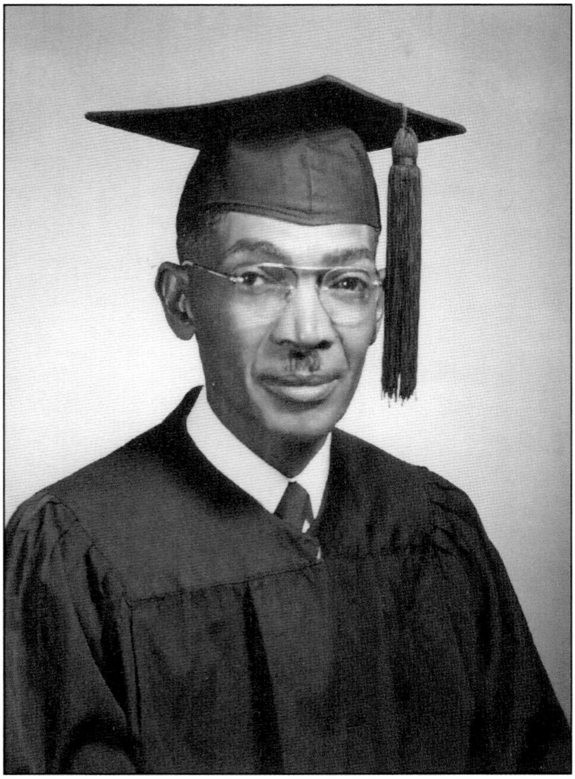

Shown here about 1950 is Orangeburg native Oscar E. Glover Sr., an educator, businessman, and farmer. He was principal of Dover Elementary School in North. He and his son, O.E. Glover Jr., owned and operated a gas station on Russell Street and a farm. Glover, a graduate of Claflin College, was married to Annie Lou Glover. (Courtesy of Vera Glover.)

Francis Frederick (1922–2011) of Orangeburg was an educator and World War II veteran. He graduated from Claflin College and South Carolina State College. Frederick was principal of several schools, including Turkey Branch, Cedar Grove, and Prince Elementary Schools, as well as Great Branch and G.W. Carver High School in the Edisto School District. (Courtesy of the G.W. Carver Reunion Committee.)

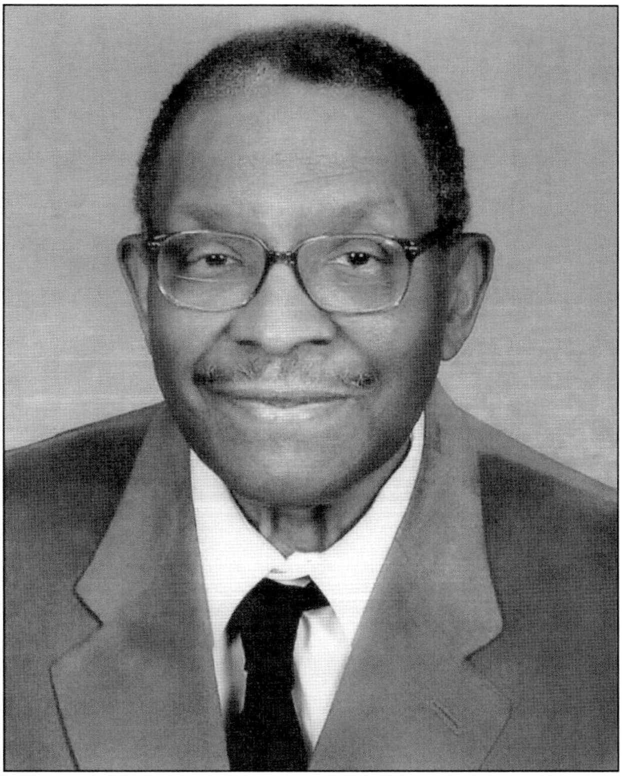

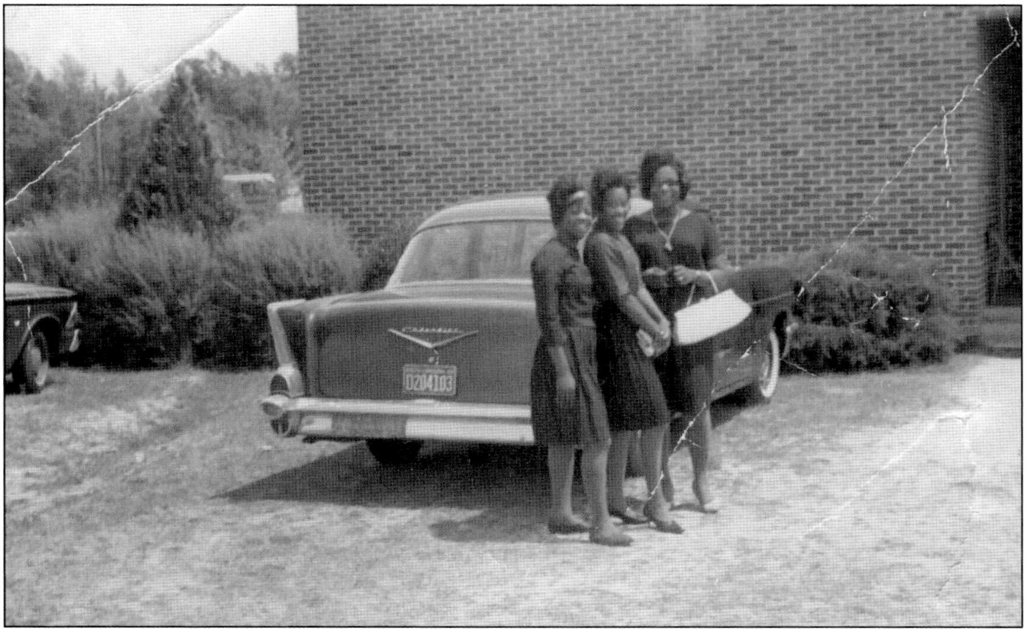

Students pose with a staff member, Ms. Blount, on the grounds of George W. Carver High School in Cordova around 1962 after a special event. Shown from left to right are Ellen Simpson Mosley, Ella Mae Waymer, and Beatrice Simpson Blount. When George W. Carver opened in 1954, the existing schools in Cordova and surrounding areas were closed. Students could attend G.W. Carver Elementary and High School. (Courtesy of Beatrice Blount.)

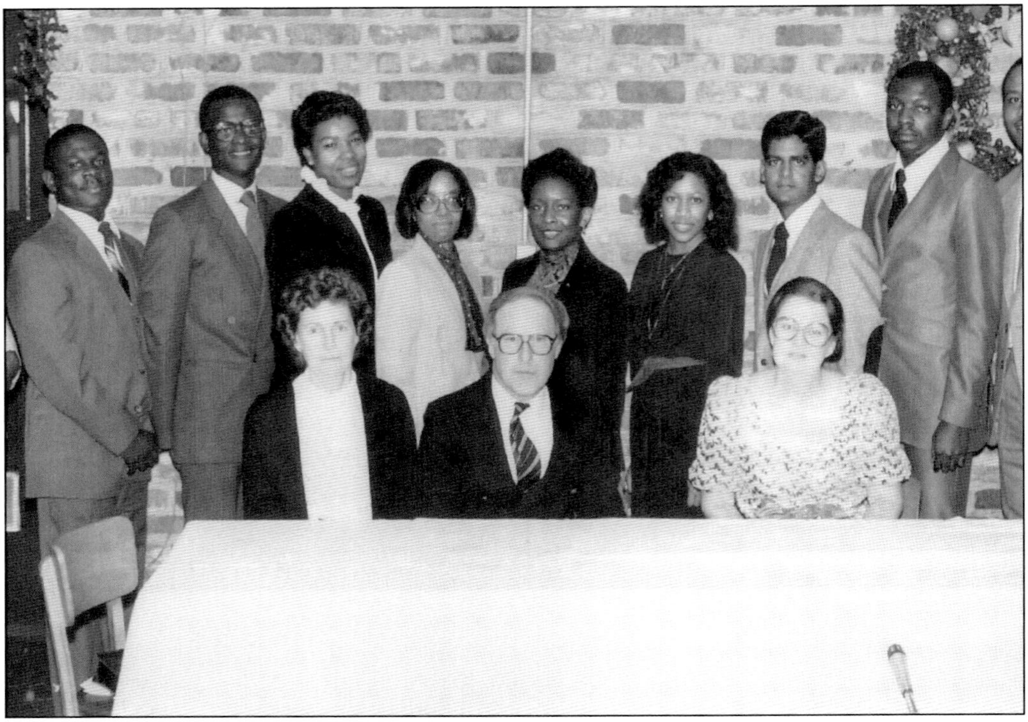

Burrell E. Workman Jr. Memorial Scholarship recipients pose with their donors, George and Joy Barnes, at the popular Berry's On the Hill restaurant for the scholarship's 10th anniversary celebration. The restaurant was a very popular place during the 1980s. (Courtesy of Joy Barnes.)

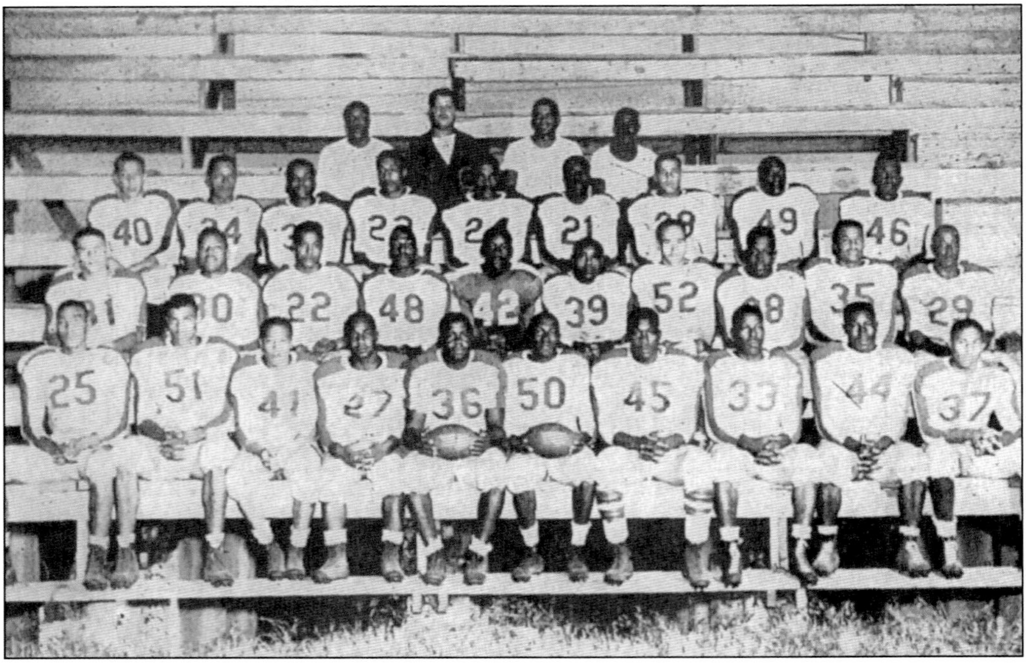

South Carolina State football team members pose for a photograph in 1947. The team was undefeated that year, said to be the best season in its history. Oliver Dawson was the head coach. The football stadium is named in his honor. (Courtesy of South Carolina State University Library.)

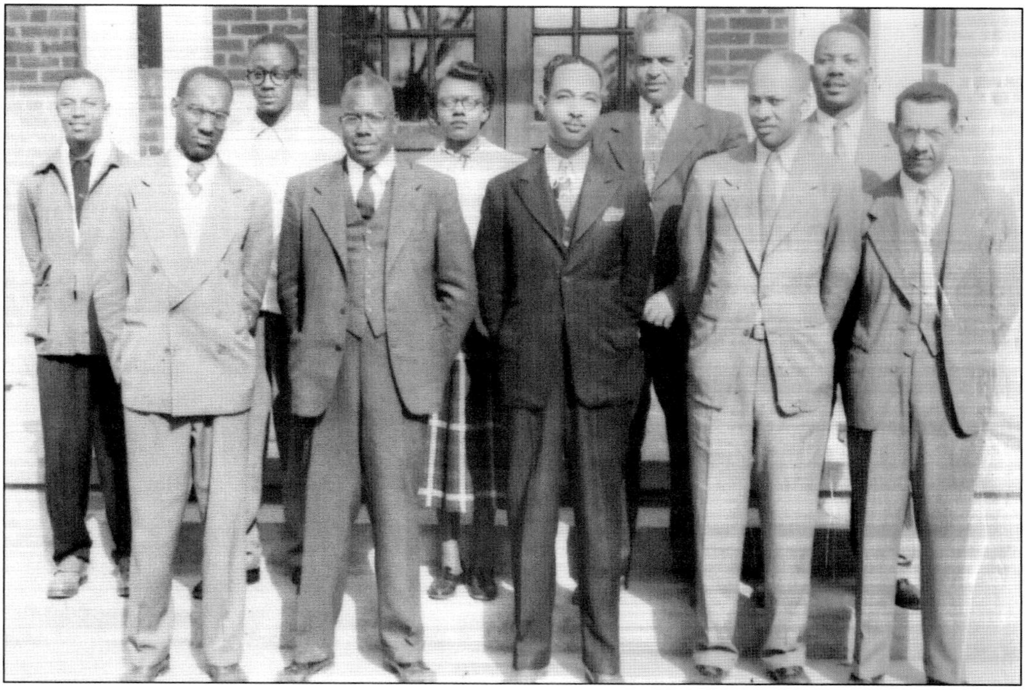

The Claflin College athletic staff poses for a photograph during the 1949–1950 school year. Ernest A. Finney Sr. (first row, far right) is the father of South Carolina Supreme Court justice Ernest Finney Jr., who was a graduate of Claflin College. (Courtesy of Claflin University Archives.)

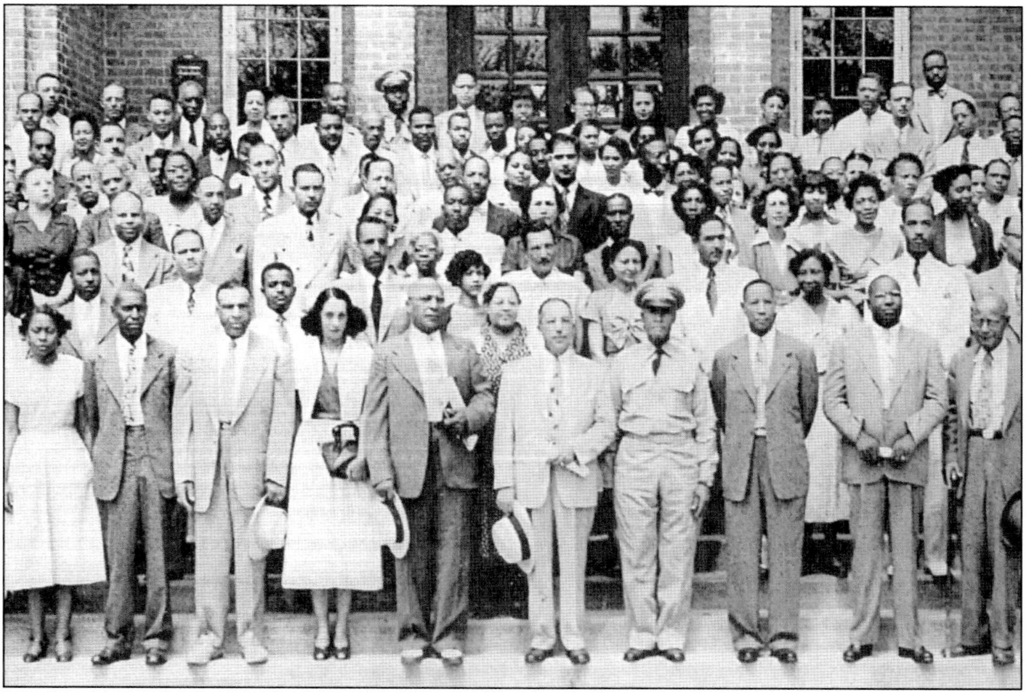

South Carolina State College staff members pose for a photograph during the 1950–1951 school year. Benner C. Turner (first row, sixth from left) was the president of South Carolina State at that time. (Courtesy of South Carolina State University Library.)

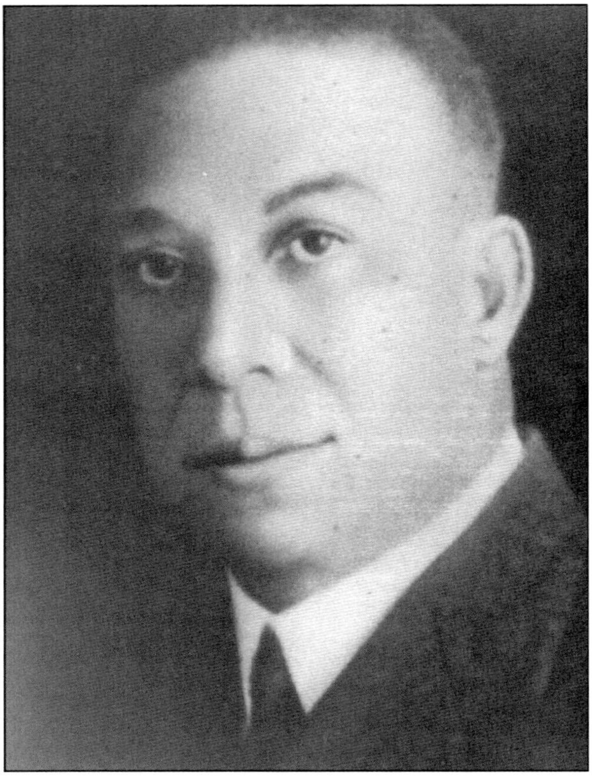

Joseph Benjamin Randolph was the first African American to serve as president of Claflin College (1922–1945). He received his early education from schools in Mississippi. In 1898, Randolph matriculated at New Orleans University, where he was awarded an AB degree in 1902 and an MA degree in 1905. He also attended Harvard during the summers in 1907–1911. Among his achievements are the founding of the Vocational Guidance and Career Opportunity Program, Freshman Orientation week, the *Claflin Panther*, formation of the Claflin University String Quartet, enclosure of the basketball court, promotion of intramural sports, purchase of *The Back Water* painting by Henry O. Tanner, recruitment of an all-black faculty, and initiation of Negro History Week. (Courtesy of Claflin University Archives.)

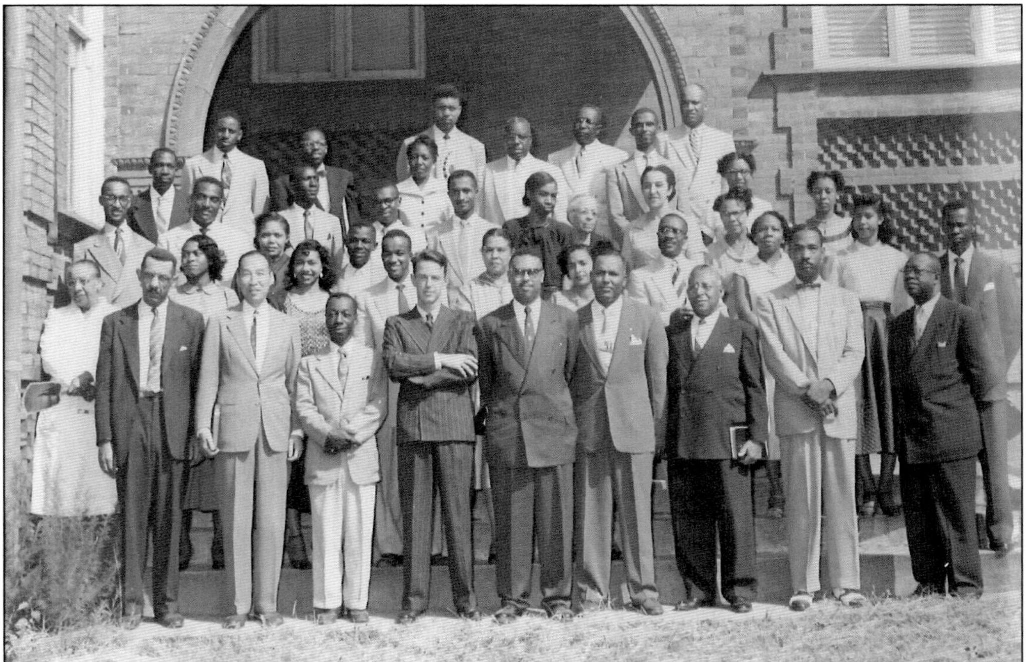

Claflin College staff members pose for a picture during the 1953–1954 school year. Florella Fordham (second row, far left) was the college nurse. In 1903, Fordham became the first African American registered nurse in Orangeburg. (Courtesy of Claflin University Archives.)

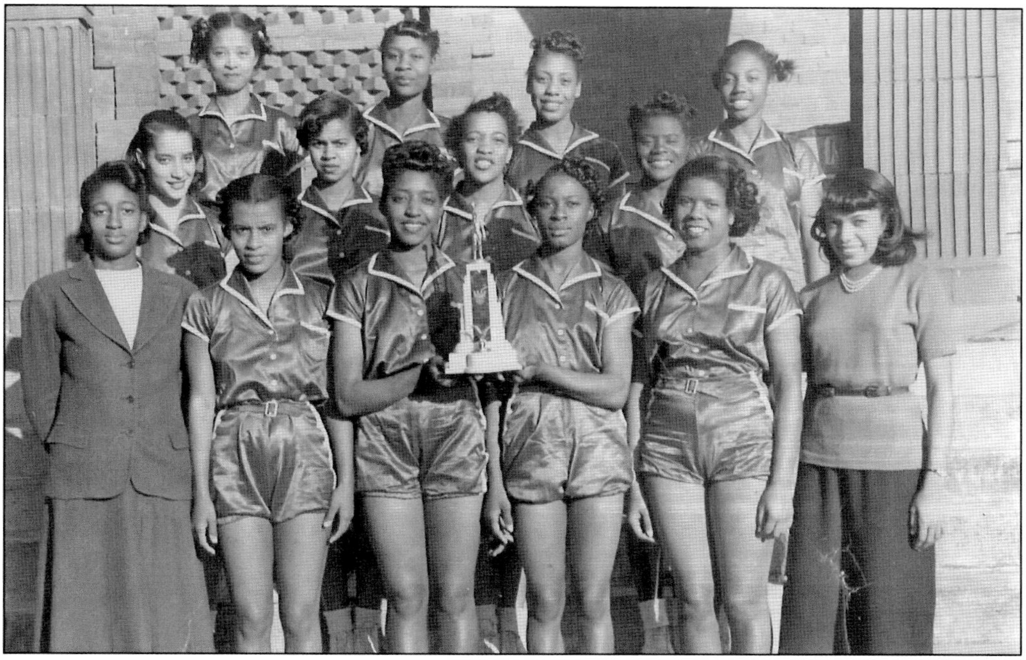

This 1940 photograph of the Claflin girls basketball team includes Elizabeth Rose (first row, second from left). A graduate of Claflin, Rose later became an instructor there. She was married to Arthur Rose, also a Claflin alum, an art instructor at Claflin, and a noted artist in Orangeburg. (Courtesy of Claflin University Archives.)

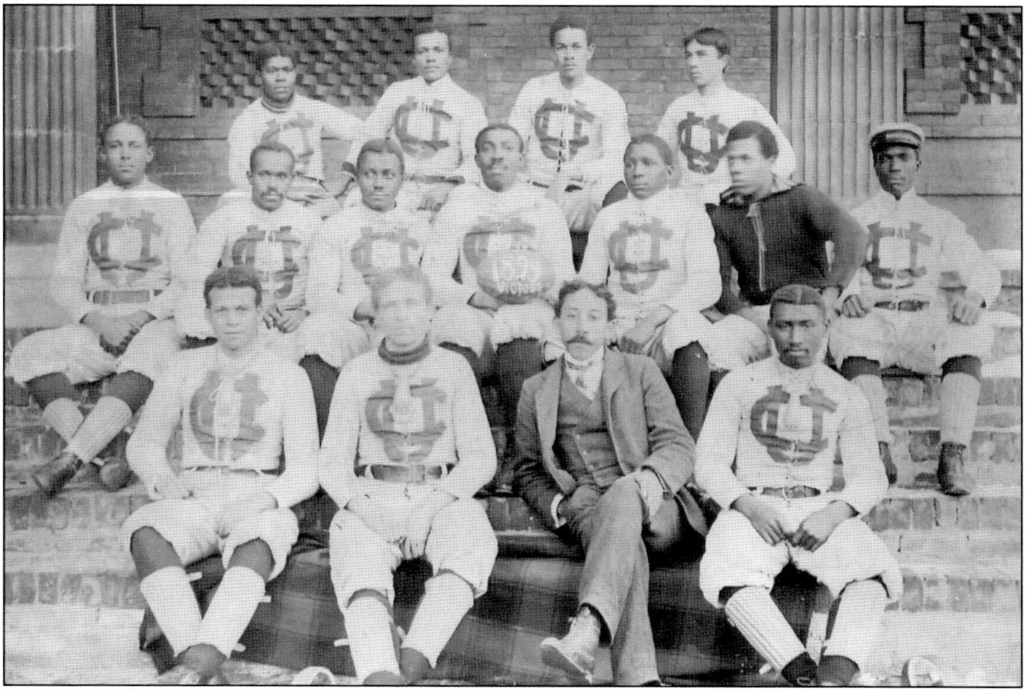

The Claflin College football team is shown here in 1920. In that era, games between Claflin College and South Carolina Agricultural and Mechanical College were big events at the fairgrounds. (Courtesy of Claflin University Archives.)

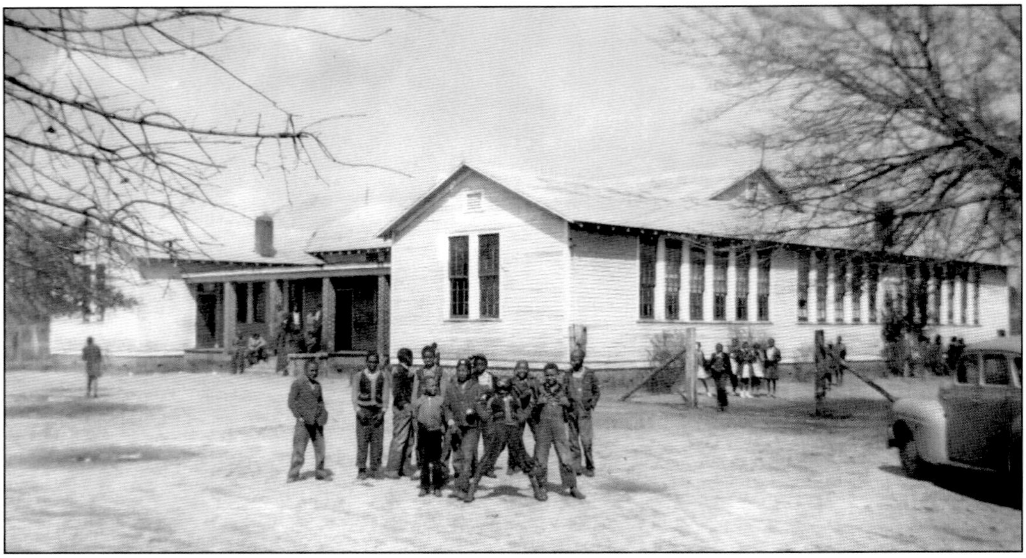

Holly Hill Colored School, shown here around 1935, was located in Holly Hill. The first school for blacks, founded in 1892, was called Hickory Bend (Holly Hill School District No. 14), and was located on Highway 176. Years later, the school was moved to State Street and called Holly Hill Colored School. It was moved again in 1926 and was later called Holly Hill Rosenwald School. In 1946, the school was destroyed by fire and was not replaced until 1953 by the Roberts School, which was named in honor of J.S. Roberts, who was principal from 1929 until 1955. (Courtesy of SCDAH.)

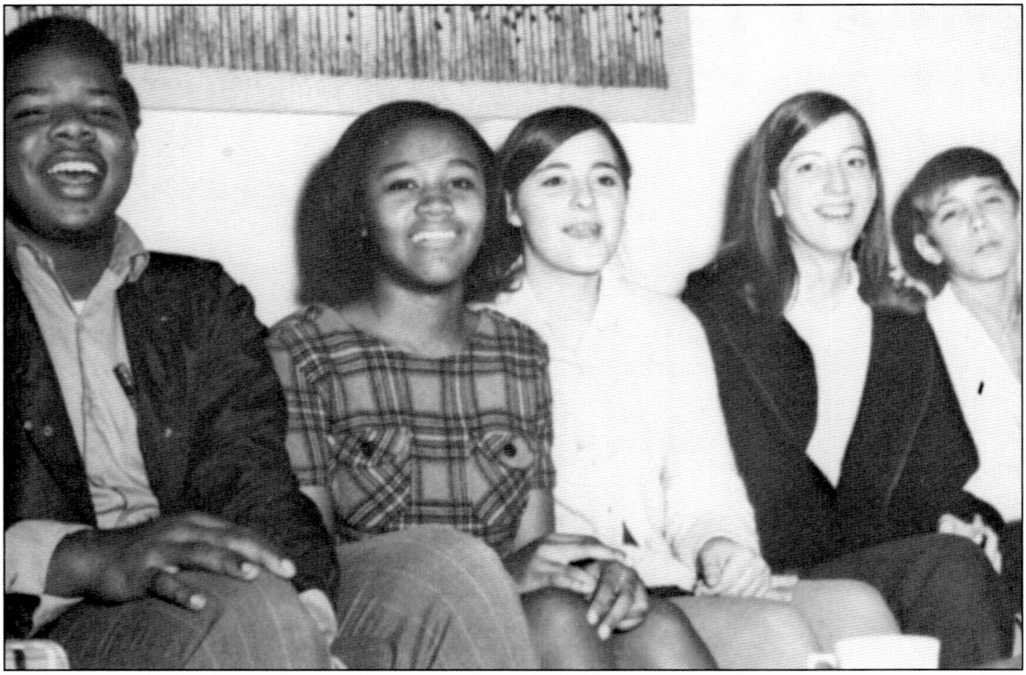

Gwendolyn Wright-Barksdale (second from left) was one of the first African American students to integrate the Holly Hill School District in 1971. Her father was Rev. John W. Wright. She follows in her father's footsteps as president of the Holly Hill NAACP. (Courtesy of Gwendolyn Wright-Barksdale.)

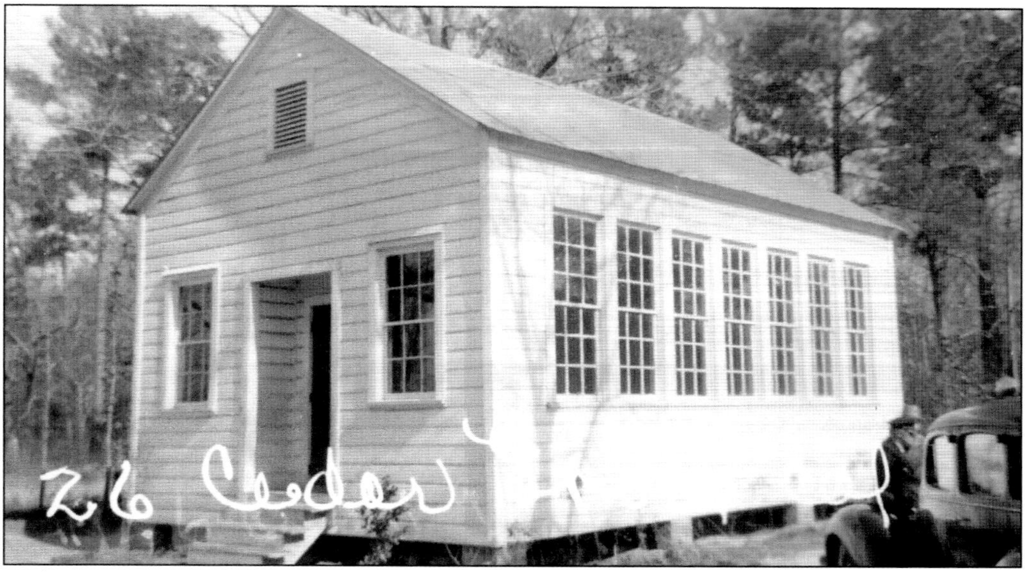

Cedar Grove Colored School was located in Orangeburg in the mid-1930s. There was another school called Cedar Grove in Cope, a rural town in the county of Orangeburg. (Courtesy of SCDAH.)

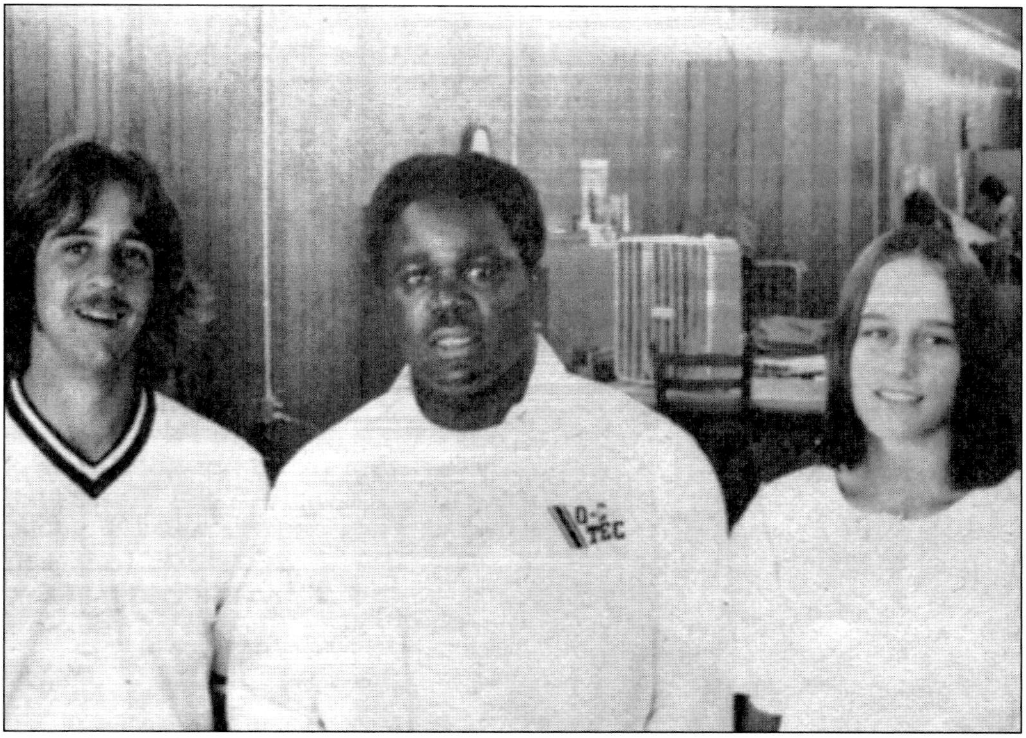

Alexander "Bubba Son" Gardner Jr. (center), a native of Orangeburg, was a South Carolina State University graduate and top football player in the late 1950s. Gardner was a two-time All-SIAC and a 1958 small-college All-American who signed with the Oakland Raiders. Gardner, shown here with members of the tennis club at Orangeburg-Calhoun Technical College in 1970, was a college recruiter. (Courtesy of Orangeburg-Calhoun Technical College Library.)

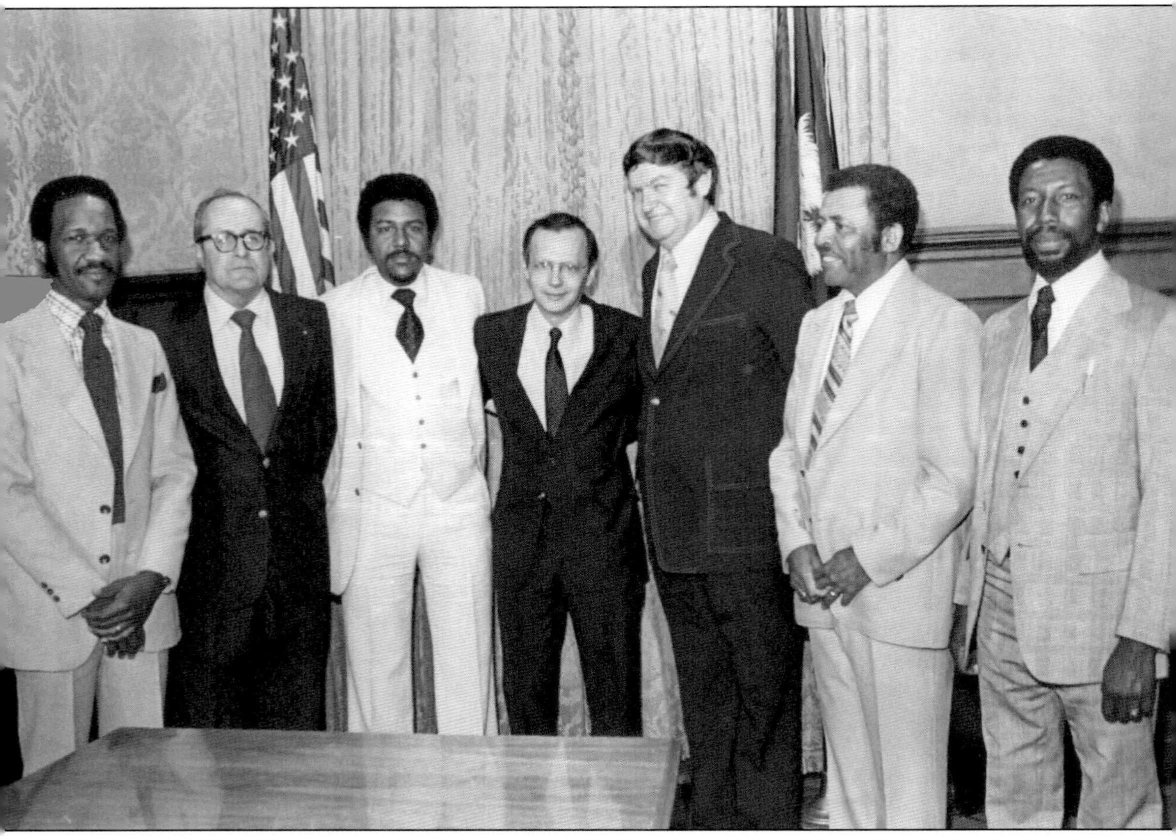

In this c. 1979 photograph, the Bowman School District No. 2 school committee meets with Gov. Richard Riley to seek funding for a vocational shop for Bowman School District No. 2. Shown are, from left to right, John W. Matthews Jr. (now a state senator), Lawrence Weathers, Melvin Crum, Governor Riley, Julian Boland (then mayor of Bowman), Quincy J. Smith, and Joseph W. Rice Jr. (superintendent of Bowman School District No. 2). (Courtesy of Joseph Rice Jr.)

Three

Businesses and Organizations

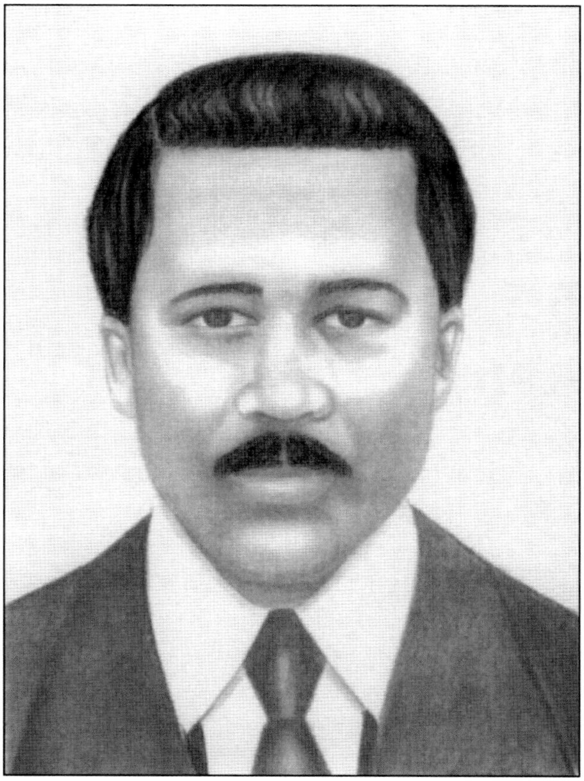

John William Little (1876–1931) was a farmer, agri-businessman, landowner, and freemason. He was born in Bowman, South Carolina, to an Anglo-European American father and an African American mother. Little became a self-made man and a leader in the African American community. He purchased 160 acres of land and a farm, and owned and operated several businesses including a grocery store, cotton gin, logging transport, rental property, and a coffin manufacturer. He also had shares in the Bowman Colored Fair. This picture was drawn by a portrait artist from an original photograph. He was about 52 years old when the photograph was taken. (Courtesy of John D. Spells.)

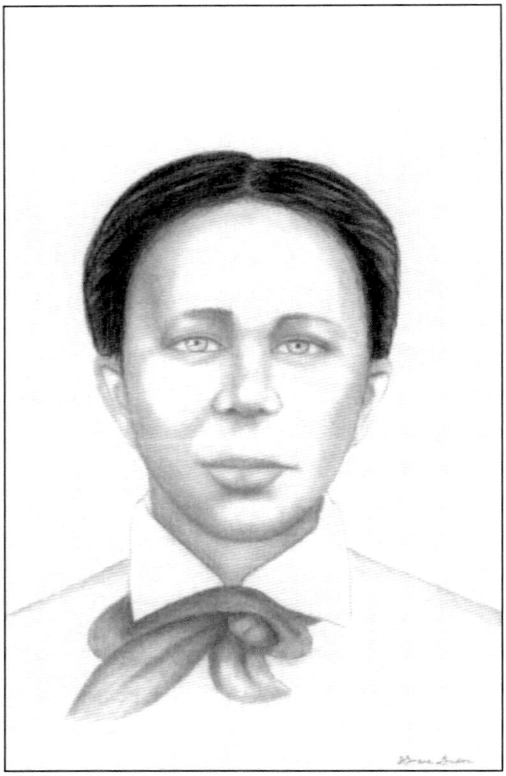

Ada Berry Little Fersner (1880–1972) of Branchville, South Carolina, was married to John William Little. They had nine children: William, Wesley, James, Maggie, Fred, Ida, Earlean, Mary Ruth, and Minnie Bell Little. After John's death, she managed the farm and family businesses. After all of her children were adults and married, Ada Little married Reddick Fersner, a local farmer. She lived to be 92 years old. At the time of this portrait, she was about 48. (Courtesy of John D. Spells.)

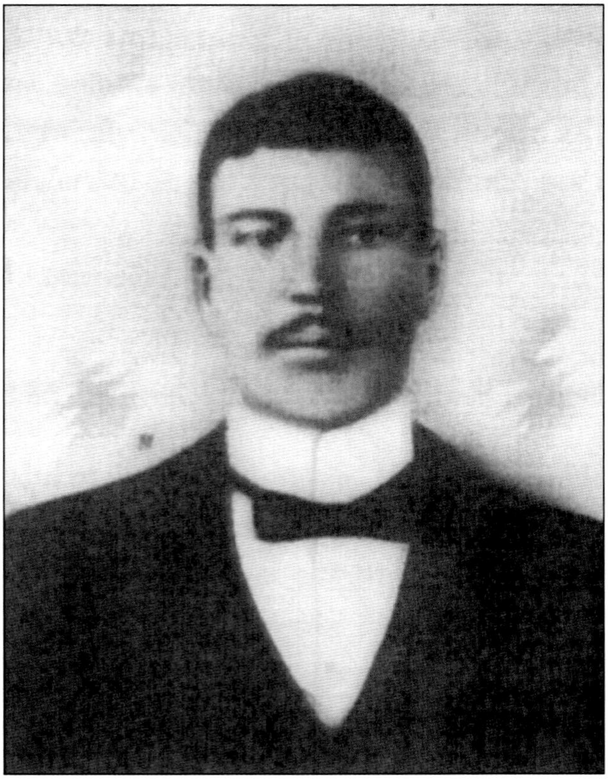

James V. Summers (1871–1927) was a carpenter, farmer, and minister from Branchville in the late 1800s, who owned over 40 acres of land. The family's primary income was farming and livestock. The family had tenant sharecroppers to keep up with the farm. According to an agriculture schedule in the 1880 census, some of the crops farmed included corn and cotton. As the children in the family got older, the men went away to work in northern factories while the women remained and worked on the farm. (Courtesy of Horace Byrd.)

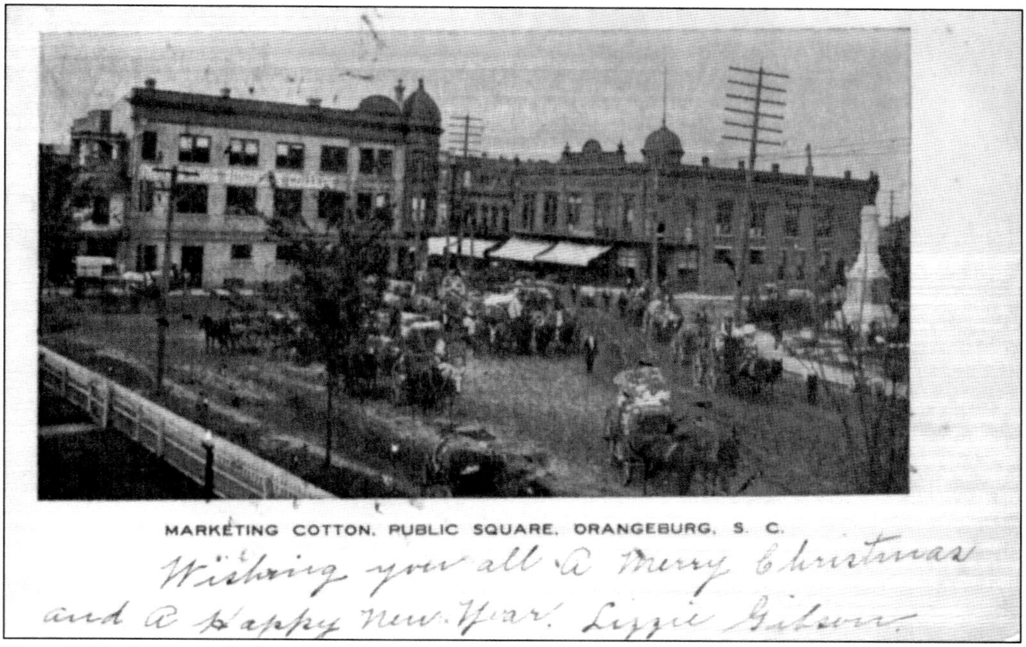

This 1908 photograph shows cotton being marketed in the town square in Orangeburg. This was a common activity during the early and mid-1900s. (Courtesy of South Caroliniana Library, University of South Carolina, Columbia.)

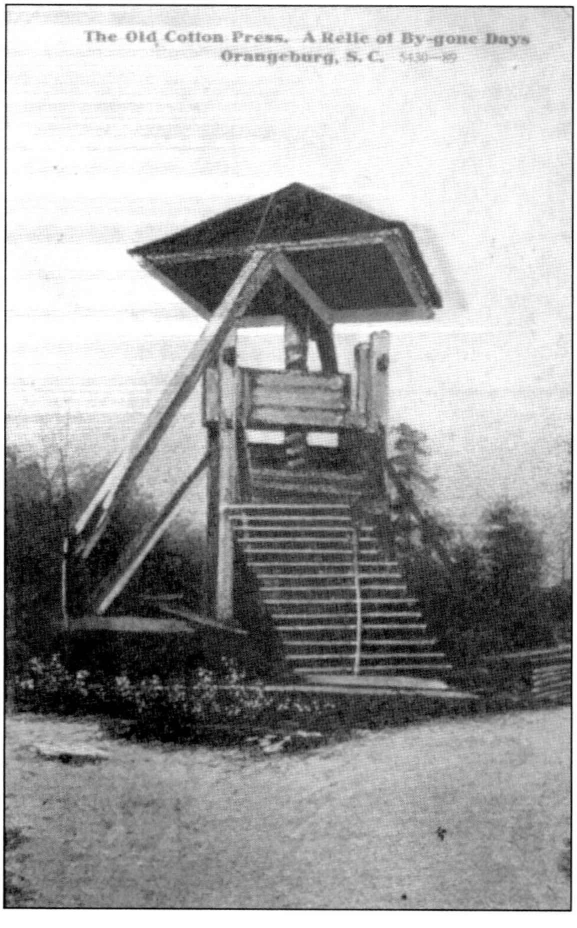

The Old Cotton Press in Orangeburg is a relic of the past. This postcard has a postmark of 1910. Orangeburg had two cotton mills, the Orangeburg Cotton Mill and the Orangeburg Manufacturing Company. They were two of the county's largest manufacturing employers during this time. (Courtesy of South Caroliniana Library, University of South Carolina, Columbia.)

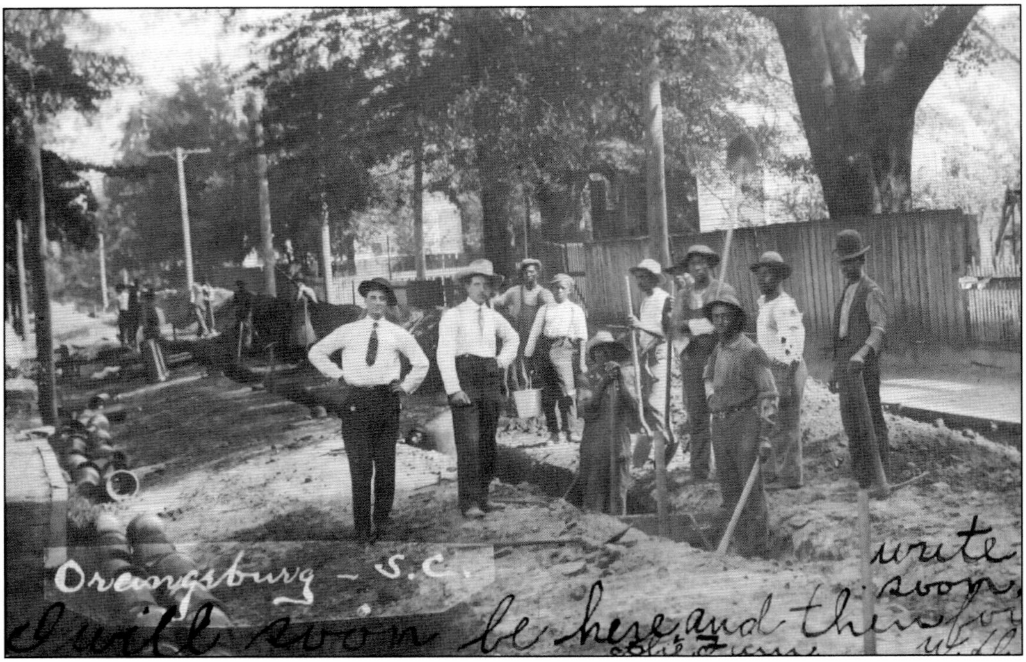

Changes were happening in the city of Orangeburg, as evidenced by this group of men laying pipes on Doyle Street in 1907. (Courtesy of South Caroliniana Library, University of South Carolina, Columbia.)

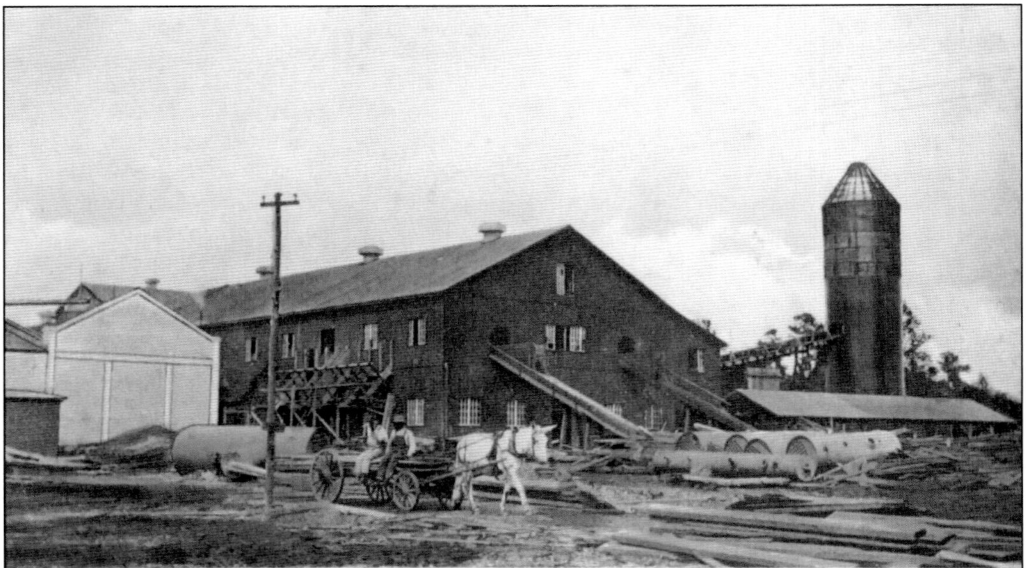

Ferguson Lumber Mill, shown here around 1907, was located in the town of Eutawville. This was a large lumber mill that employed many and was operated by the Beidler Lumber Company of Chicago. A town named Ferguson was built around it for the workers. The mill closed in 1912 and the area was gradually deserted. (Courtesy of South Caroliniana Library, University of South Carolina, Columbia.)

Earl Middleton (right), of Orangeburg, is shown standing in front of his office welcoming a customer in 1968. He operated an insurance business, and expanded into real estate. (Courtesy of Joy Barnes.)

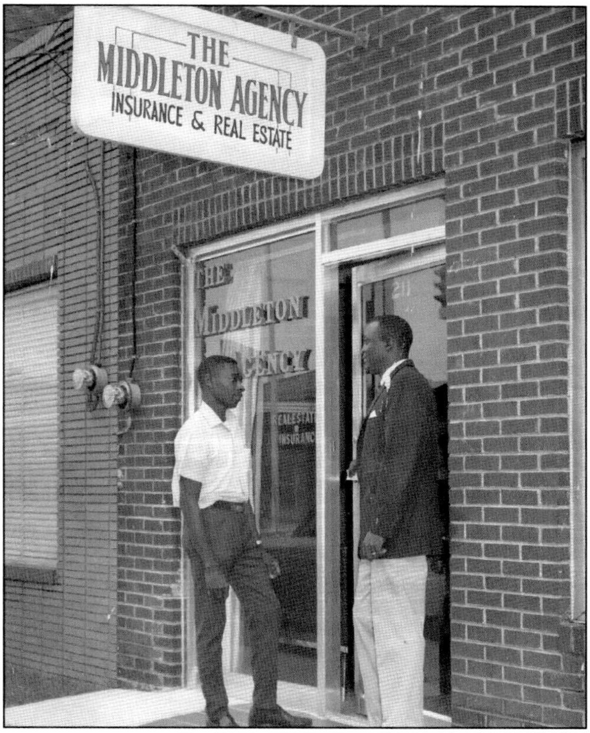

EdAiken (left) and Ozie Bell Aiken (right) are pictured around 1945 celebrating their 25th wedding anniversary with granddaughter Joyce (second from left) and daughters Louise (center) and Rose Marie. The Aikens operated a restaurant on the lower end of Russell Street in Orangeburg for 46 years. (Courtesy of Lillie Gaffney.)

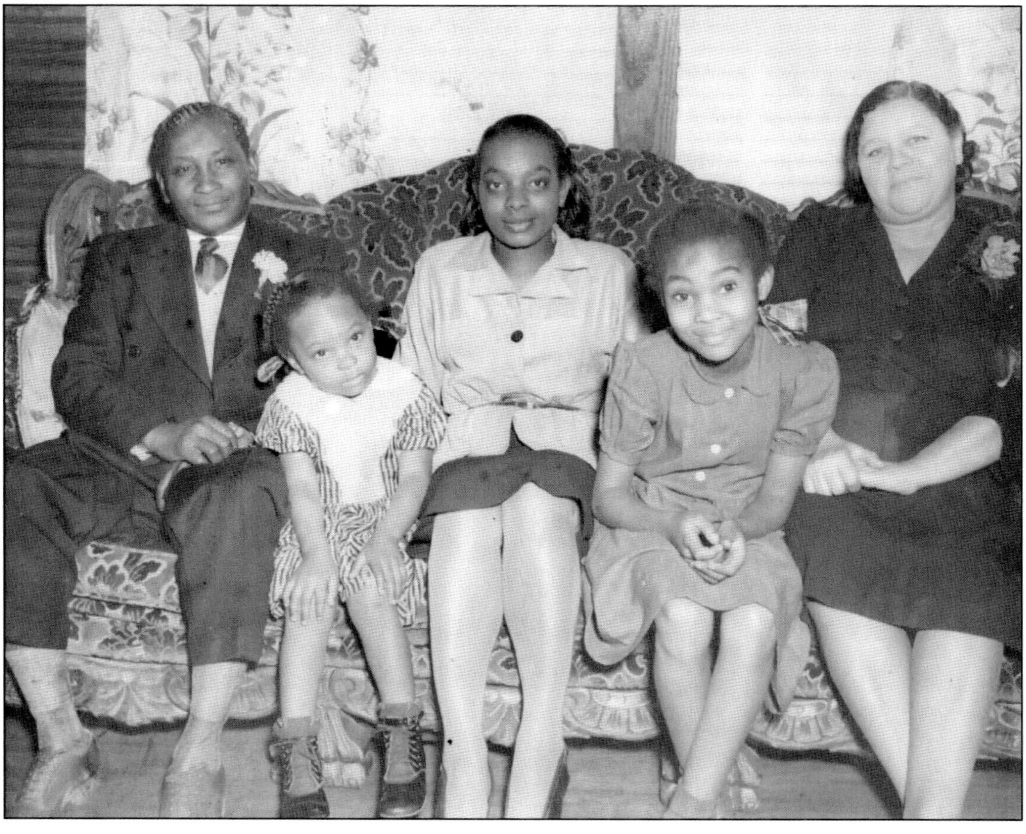

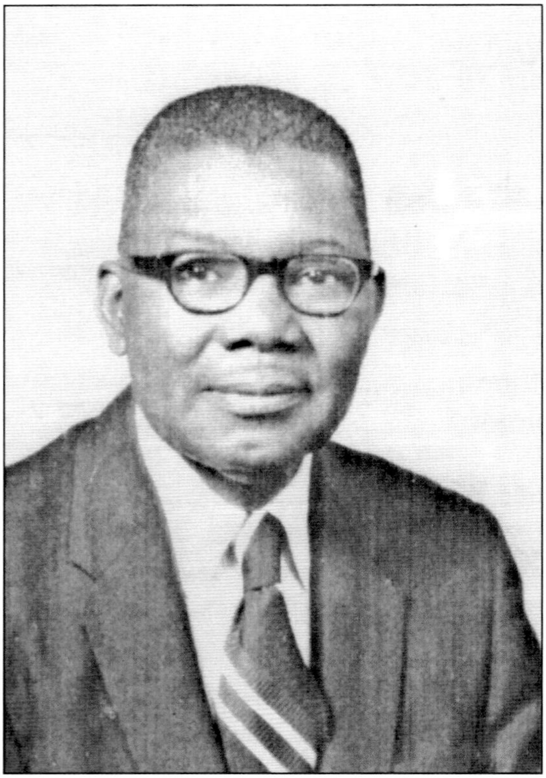

Milton Boyd of Orangeburg operated a dinette on Russell Street for over 38 years. At one time, it was a popular place to dine. (Courtesy of Helen Reid.)

Dantzler Drug Store, operated by a black pharmacist named Alexander Dantzler, was located on Russell Street, next door to what is now the Department of Public Utilities. The building is still standing today. (Courtesy of Richard Reid.)

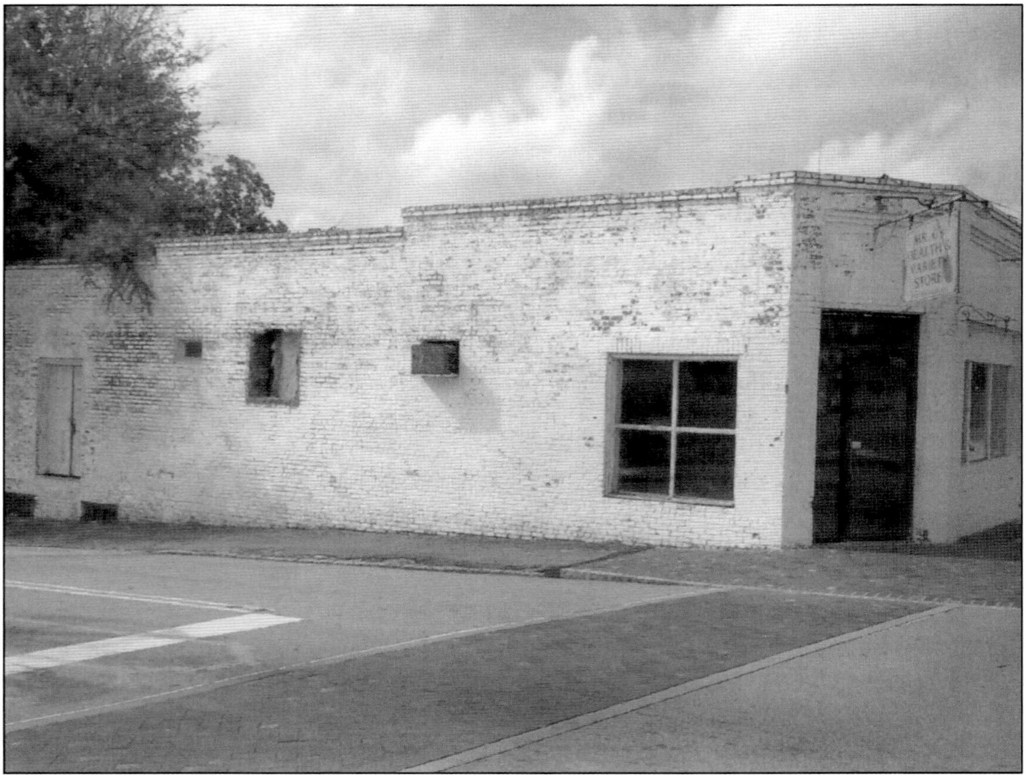

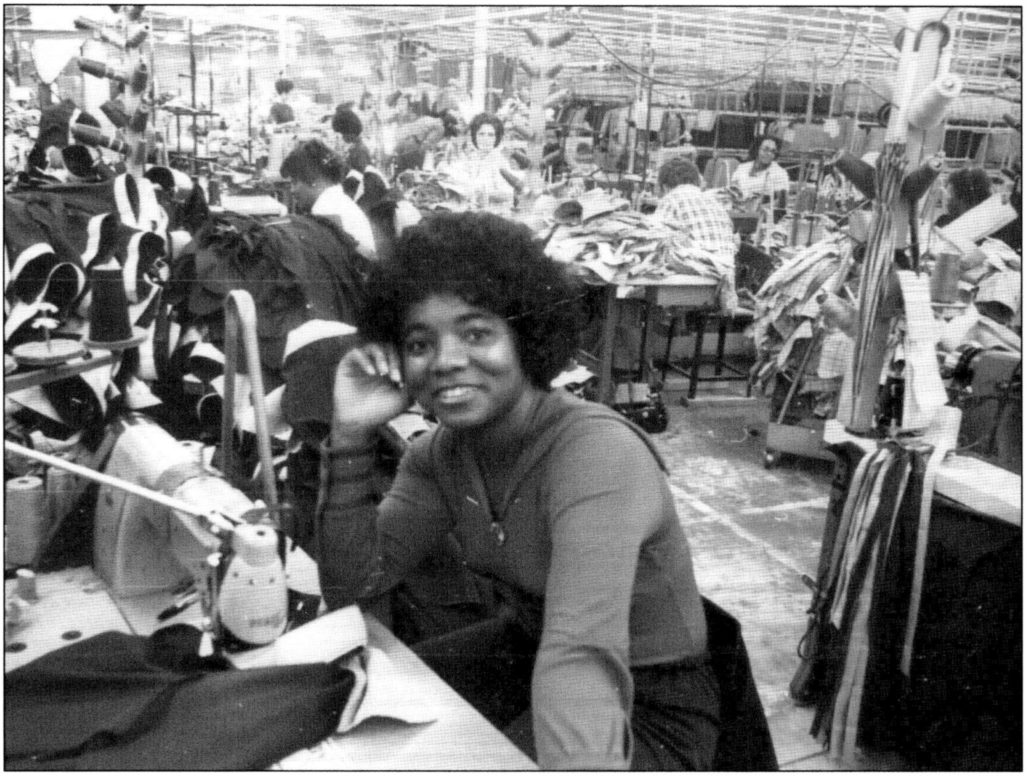

Deloris Frazier of Orangeburg is shown sitting at the sewing machines at Amblers Industries in 1974. Amblers Industries was a sewing manufacturing company that employed over 900 people with a majority of blacks in the 1970s and 1980s in Orangeburg. Frazier later went on to college; she is now a retired educator. She has traveled extensively in the United States, in many countries in Africa, and elsewhere. (Courtesy of Deloris Frazier.)

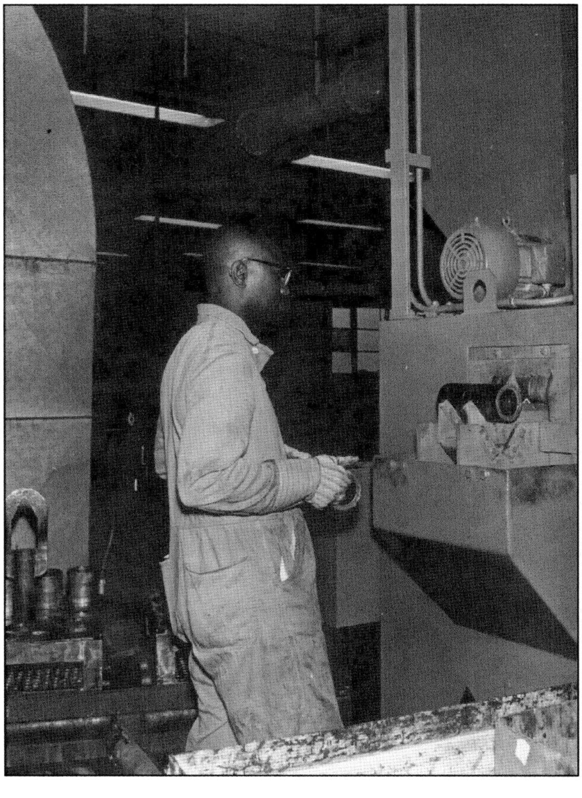

Julius Harrison of Orangeburg was a minister who served many churches. This photograph shows him at the Savannah River Plant (E.I. Dupont, Aiken, South Carolina), where he was employed until 1987. He and other men from the city of Orangeburg who worked at the Savannah River site often carpooled together. He was the husband of Ruth Harrison. (Courtesy of Ruth Harrison.)

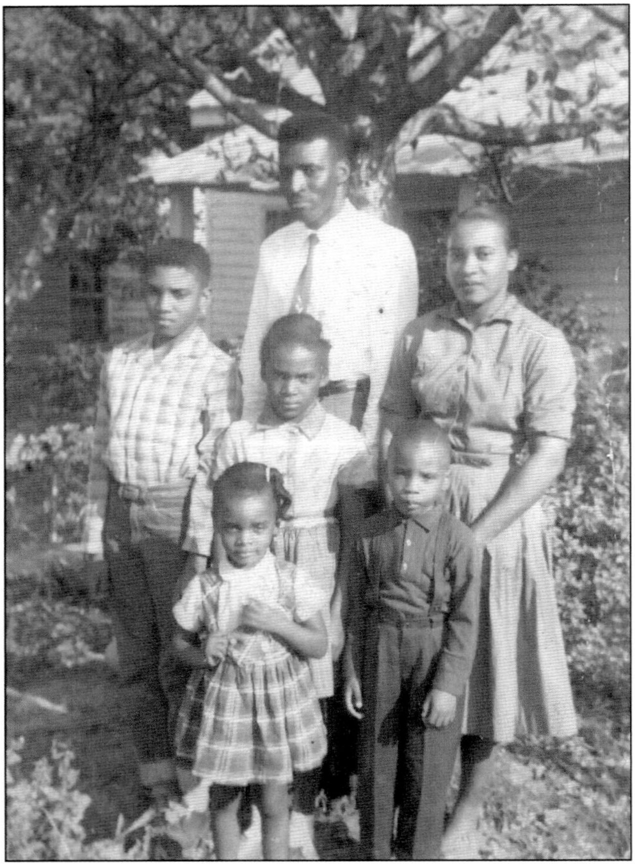

David Phillips of Orangeburg is shown with his family in 1963. Starting in 1951, and for the next 42 years, he was employed by the Savannah River Plant, formerly called Westinghouse. He was also the only barber for 45 years in the town of Norway. He was usually open on Fridays and Saturdays or as his time would permit. Phillips is chairman of the deacon board at Mount Pisgah Baptist Church. (Courtesy of David and Catherine Phillips.)

Sulton Brothers Lumber was one of the oldest businesses in Orangeburg. This truck and trailer, shown between 1915 and 1918, was the first mechanized transport for lumber east of the Mississippi. It was owned by the J.J. Sulton & Sons Lumber Company, which was founded in 1825 by John Sulton. The driver was E. Benjamin McTeer, who later became a dentist in Orangeburg. (Courtesy of Miriam Abernathy.)

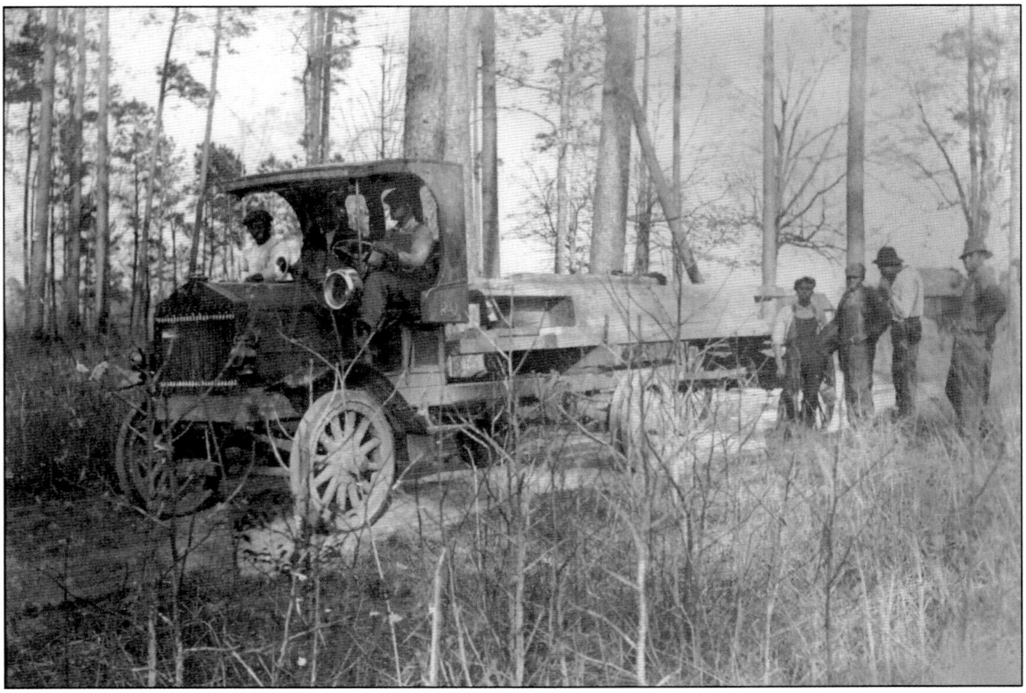

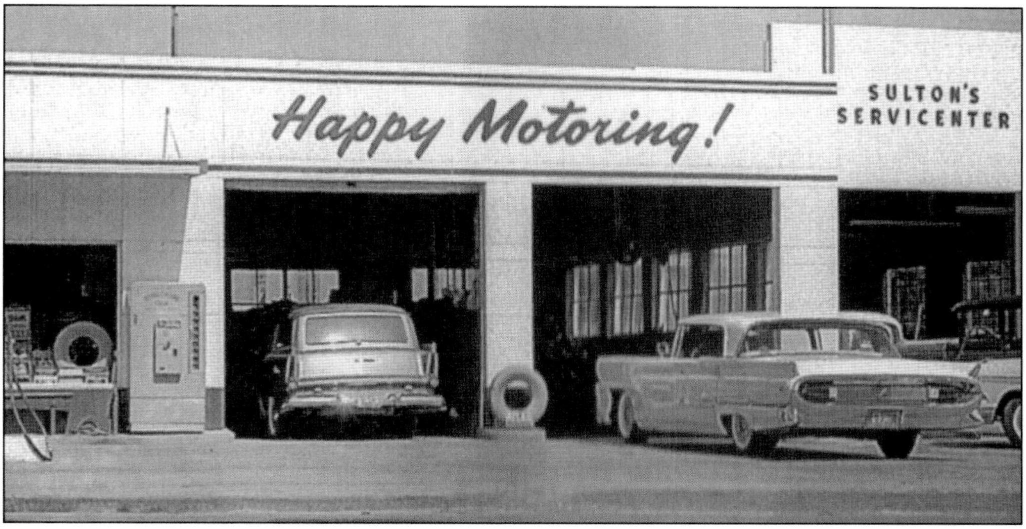

The Esso gas station was located on East Russell Street in Orangeburg in the heart of the black community. It was owned by civil rights activists James E. Sulton Sr. and his brother, Roy Sulton. The business was victimized many times for the brothers' efforts in getting signers for the school integration petition. Gasoline suppliers and soft drink bottlers stopped making deliveries when the Sultons refused to stop their efforts. (Courtesy of Cecil Williams.)

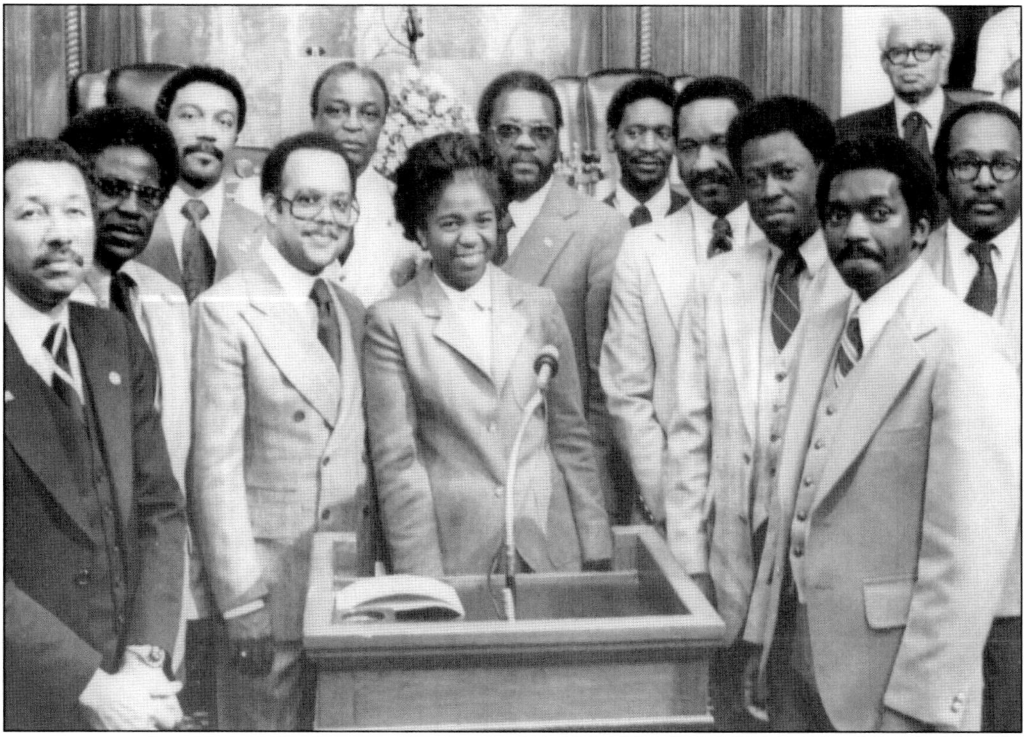
Legislative Black Caucus members gather after a meeting in 1980. The group is made up of black legislators in South Carolina and was formally organized in 1975, although it had been in existence since 1973. Former representative Earl Middleton (second row, fourth from left) and state senator John Matthews (second row, third from right) are shown representing Orangeburg County. (Courtesy of Joy Barnes.)

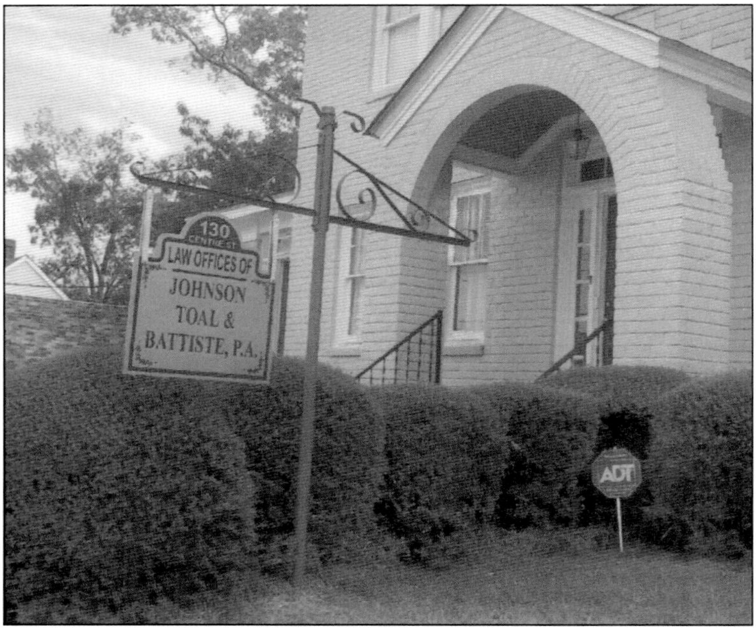

The Johnson Toal & Battiste law firm in Orangeburg was chartered in 1975 by the trio of I.S. Leevy Johnson, William T. Toal, and Luther J. Battiste III. It is an outgrowth of the sole proprietorship founded in 1968 by Johnson. The firm also has an office in Columbia, the capital of South Carolina. (Courtesy of Johnson Toal & Battiste Law Firm.)

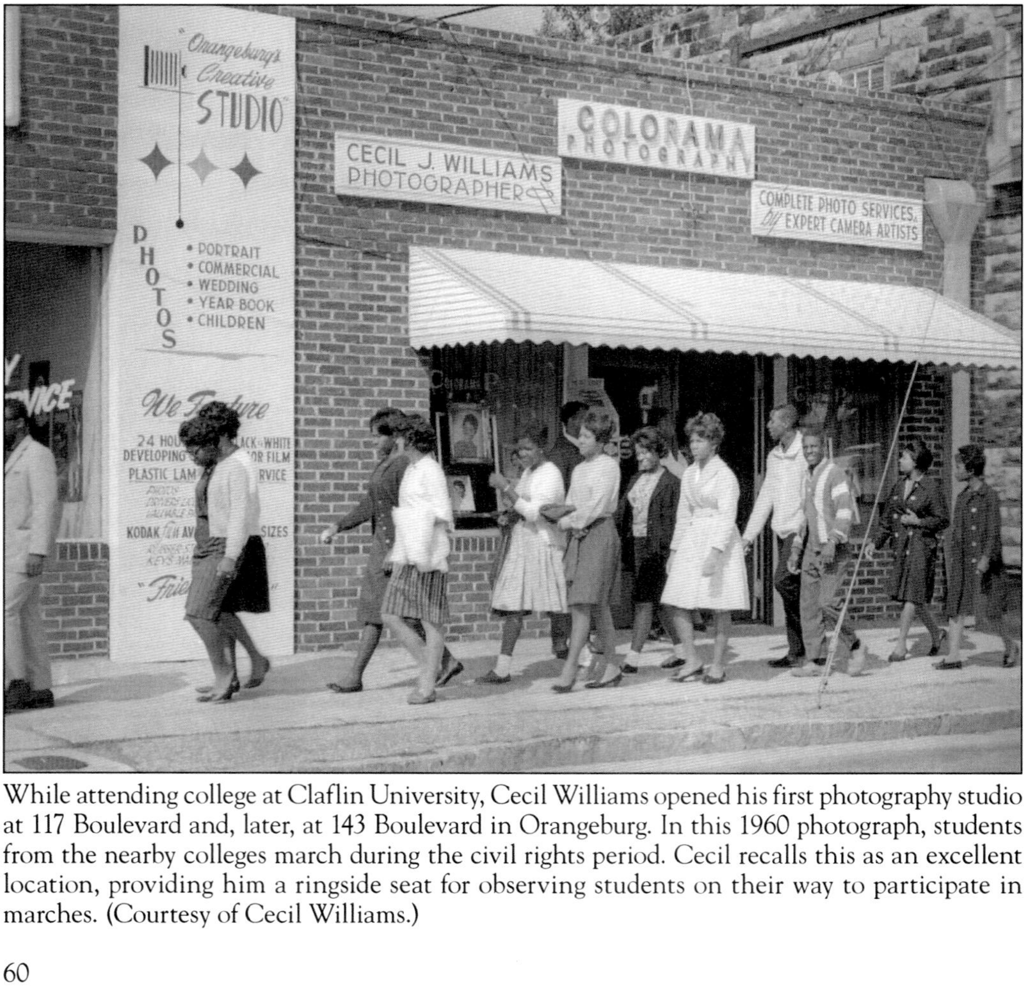

While attending college at Claflin University, Cecil Williams opened his first photography studio at 117 Boulevard and, later, at 143 Boulevard in Orangeburg. In this 1960 photograph, students from the nearby colleges march during the civil rights period. Cecil recalls this as an excellent location, providing him a ringside seat for observing students on their way to participate in marches. (Courtesy of Cecil Williams.)

E. Benjamin McTeer was born in Orangeburg County and was a graduate of Claflin University and Meharry Medical College in Nashville, Tennessee. He later became a dentist in Orangeburg and practiced for 45 years. He and his family posed for this photograph in 1949 after celebrating his son William's graduation from medical school. Shown are, from left to right, (seated) E.B. McTeer and his wife, Claudia; (standing) daughter Miriam and son William. William was later employed as a doctor at the Veteran's Administration Hospital in Tuskegee, Alabama. Tragically, he died suddenly after working as a doctor for only 10 years. (Courtesy of Miriam Abernathy.)

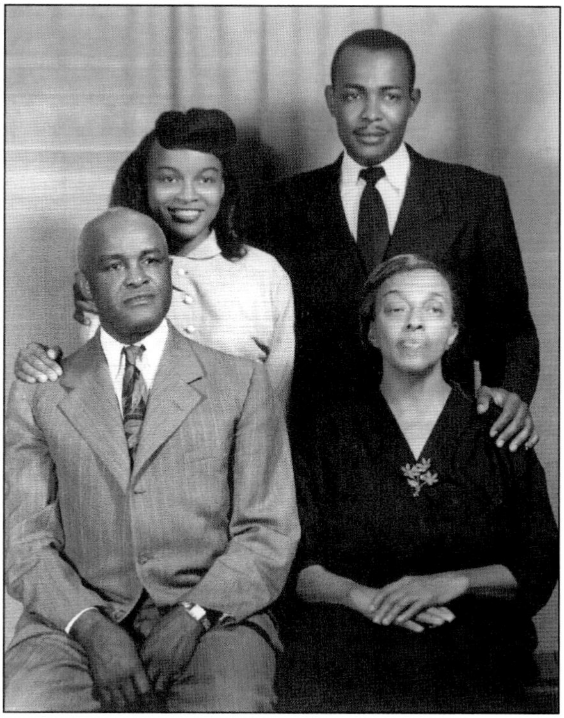

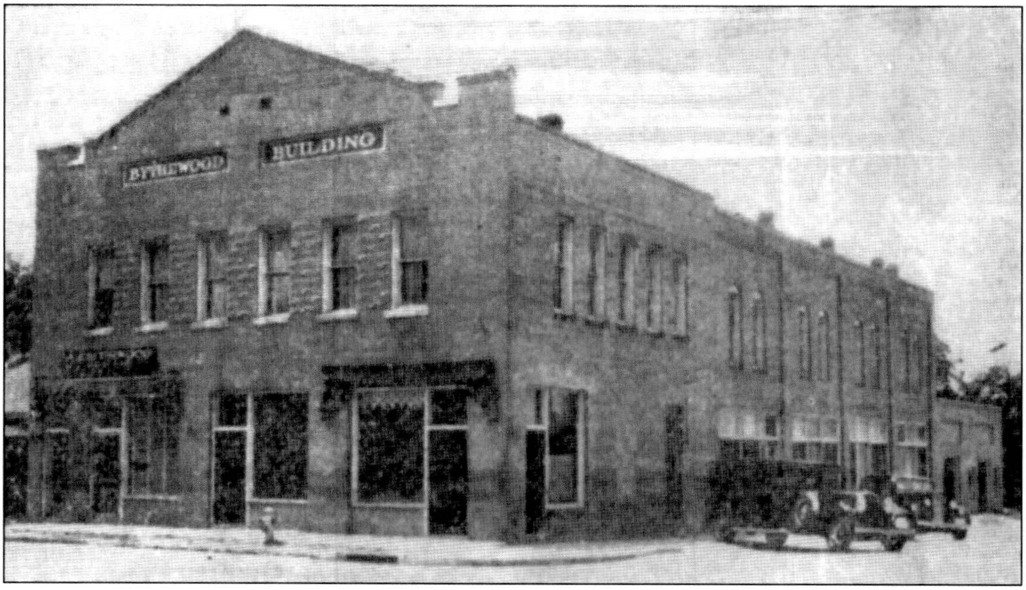

Bythewood Funeral Home was one of the first funeral homes for African Americans in Orangeburg and was started in 1907 by Alton Bythewood Sr. Shown here around 1937 on the corner of Amelia and Middleton Streets, this building was erected in 1917 to replace a wooden building destroyed by fire. An extension was added in 1923 to provide more space for the enlarged equipment and the facilities needed to give African Americans mortuary service. (Courtesy of John F. Lessane, Jr.)

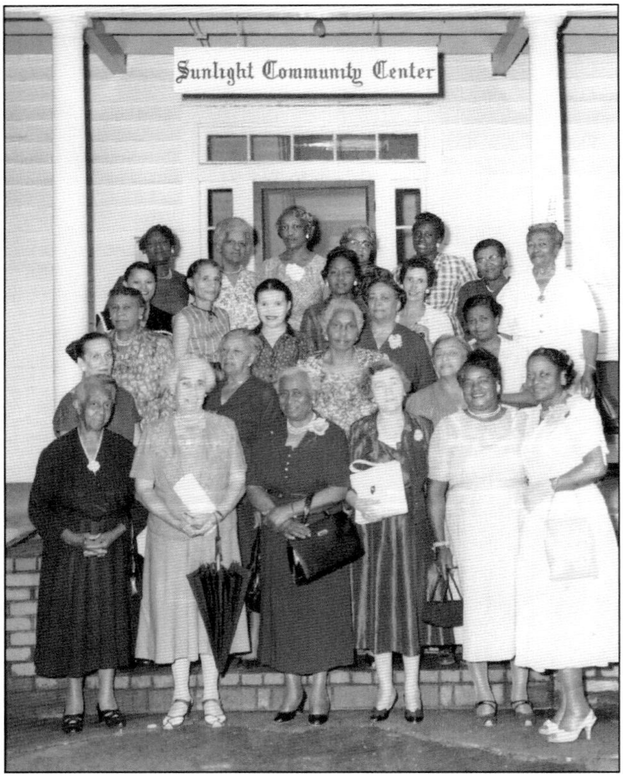

Sunlight Community Center Club members pose for a photograph in the early 1950s. Founded in 1910, it was the first African American club established to help that community's most needy. Marian Birnie Wilkinson (wife of Robert Shaw Wilkinson, a former president of South Carolina State University), was president and one of the founders. (Courtesy of Lillie Gaffney.)

Members of Cosmetologists of Orangeburg are shown in 1955. The Cosmetology Association was a nationwide organization made up of African American cosmetologists. Hairdressers, as they were called in the early days, sometimes set up shop in their homes. (Courtesy of Malqueen Kennerly.)

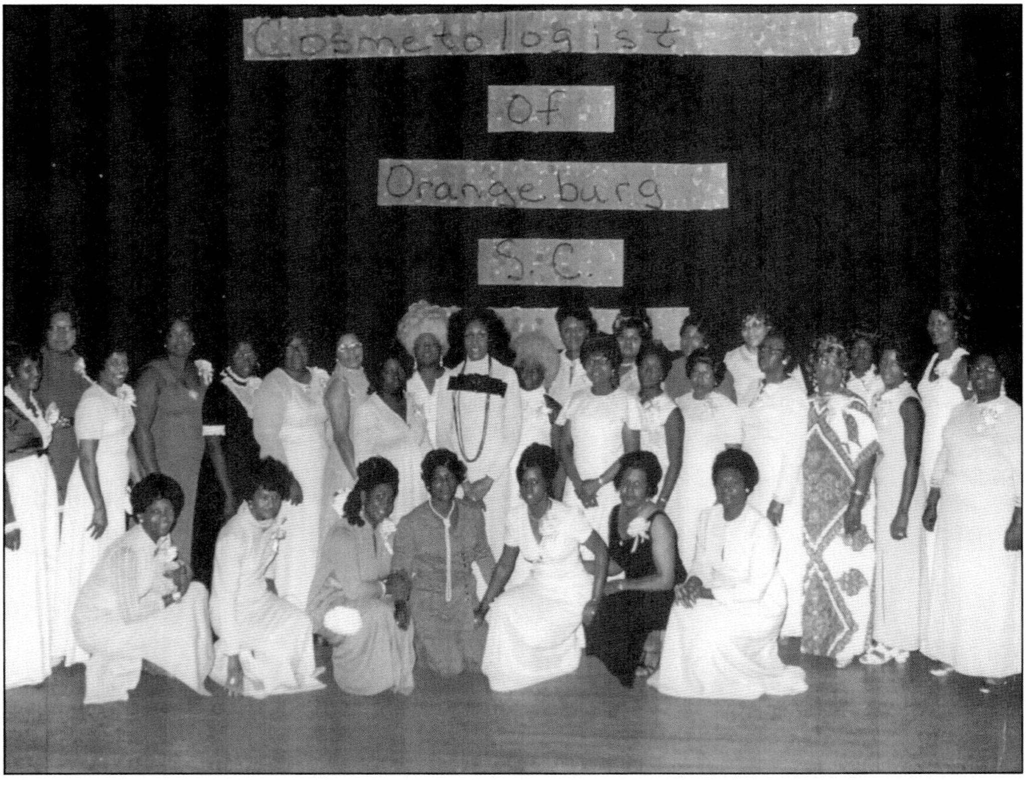

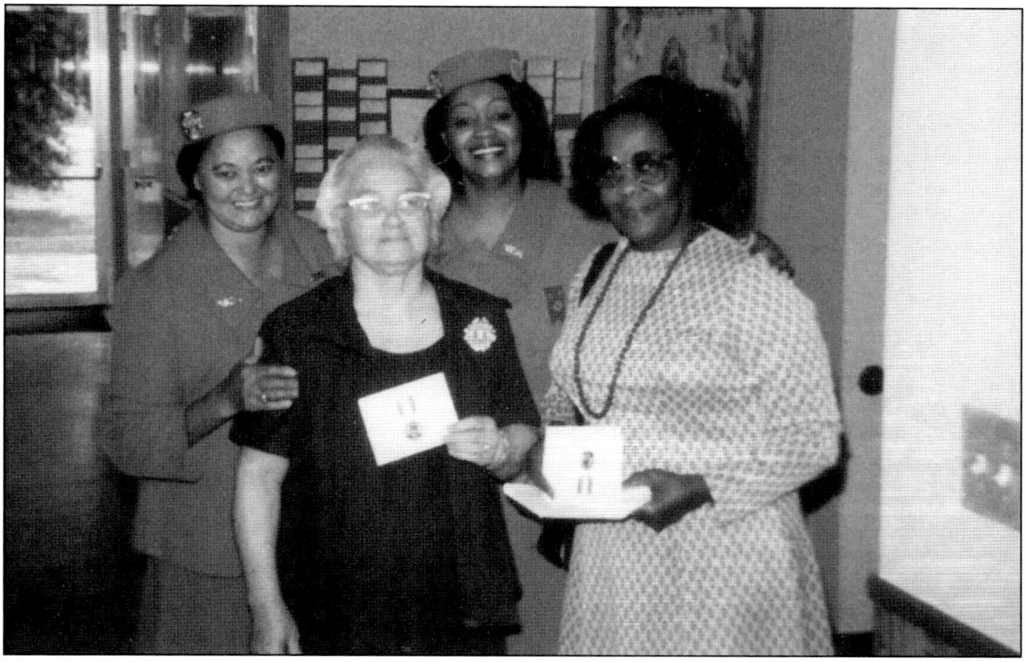

Veterans of Foreign Wars (VFW) Ladies Auxiliary members, including Lillie Gaffney (left) and Ermine Kennerly (right), are shown in the early 1960s greeting a representative from the state department. The VFW was located on Treadwell Street at that time. It is now located on Amelia Street in Orangeburg. (Courtesy of Lillie Gaffney.)

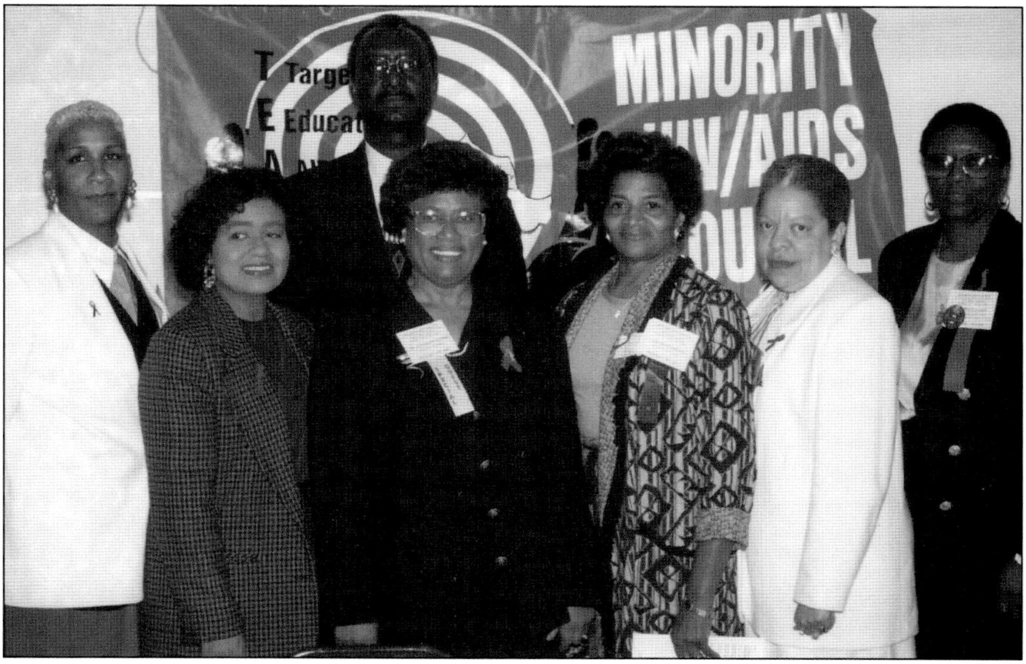

The Minority AIDS Council is shown in 1994 following a program in which former surgeon general Jocelyn Elders was the featured speaker. From left to right are Bambi Sumpter, Janice McCollum, Calvin Wright (rear), Elders, Clarice Green, Brenda Williams, and Shirley James. (Courtesy of Shirley James.)

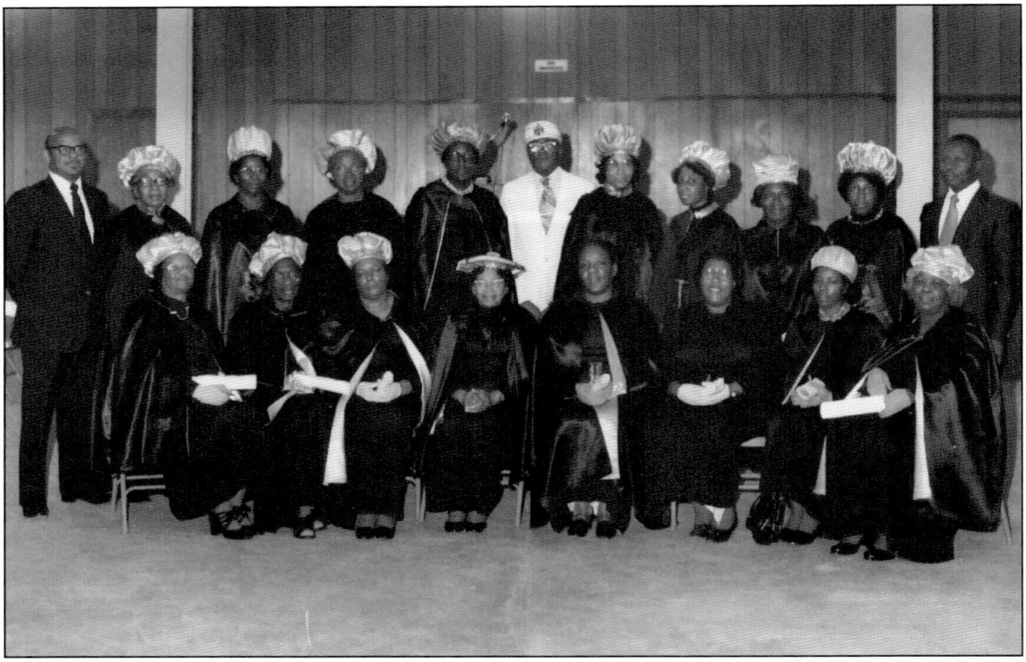

Members of the Royal House of William Grand Lodge, Rose Sharon, the last house of the Eastern Stars, pose for their annual portrait at the Masonic Lodge in the early 1980s. Ruth Harrison is in the second row, third from left. Julius Harrison, her husband, is at far right in the second row. (Courtesy of Ruth Harrison.)

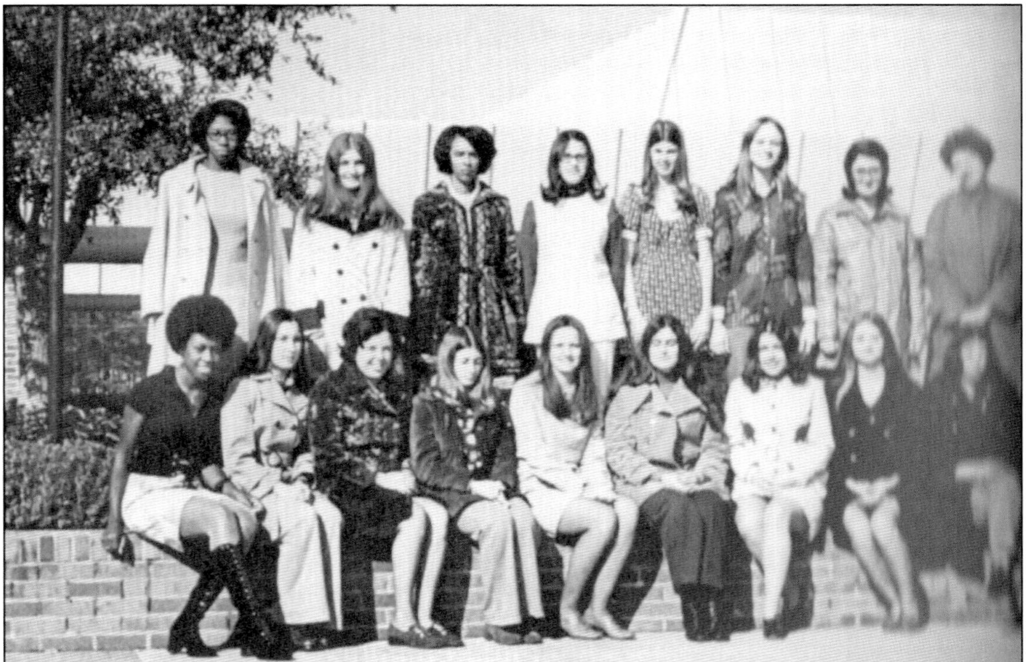

These future secretaries, students of the secretarial science curriculum at Orangeburg-Calhoun Tech, now known as Orangeburg-Calhoun Technical College, pose for a photograph in 1973. (Courtesy of Diane Floyd.)

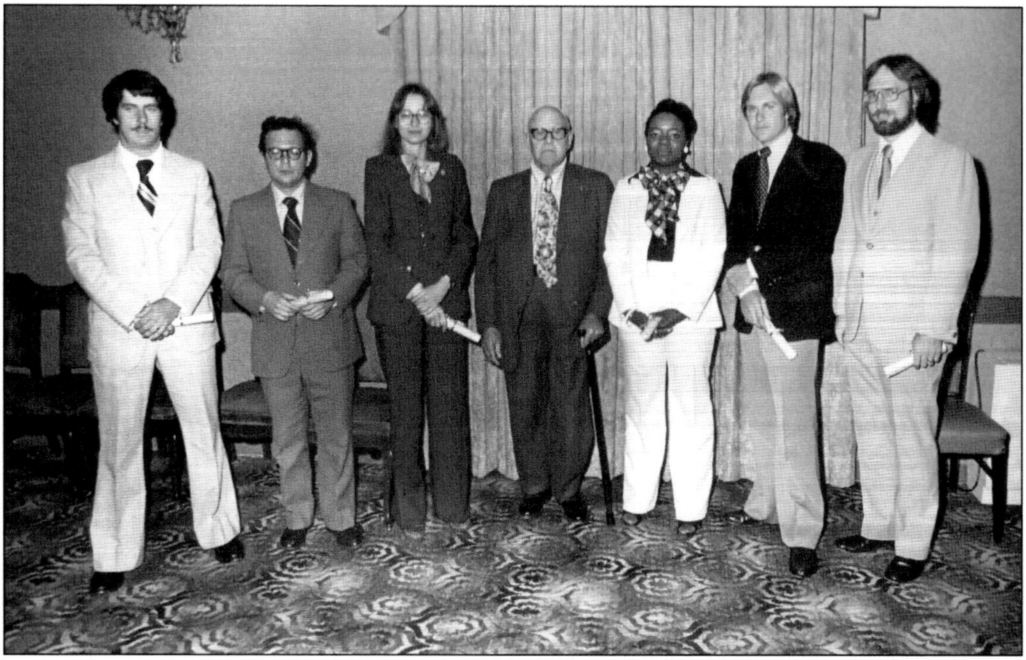

Deloris Frazier Haigler (third from right) was the first African American to participate in a ten-month internship in the Field Services and Organization Department Intern Program, sponsored by the AFL-CIO in Washington, DC. Haigler, shown with other members of the union, was able to travel to various states as a union organizer for the AFL-CIO. (Courtesy of Deloris Frazier.)

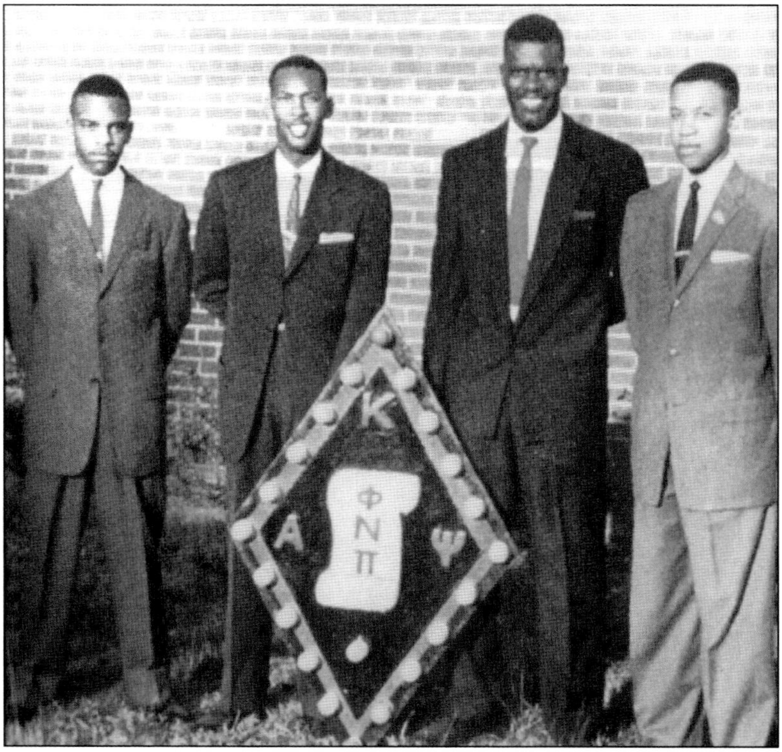

Kappa Alpha Psi brothers pose at South Carolina State College in 1957. Col. Richard Singleton stands second from left. Kappa Alpha Psi was founded in 1911 at Indiana University to foster brotherhood among young black college men. (Courtesy of Richard Singleton.)

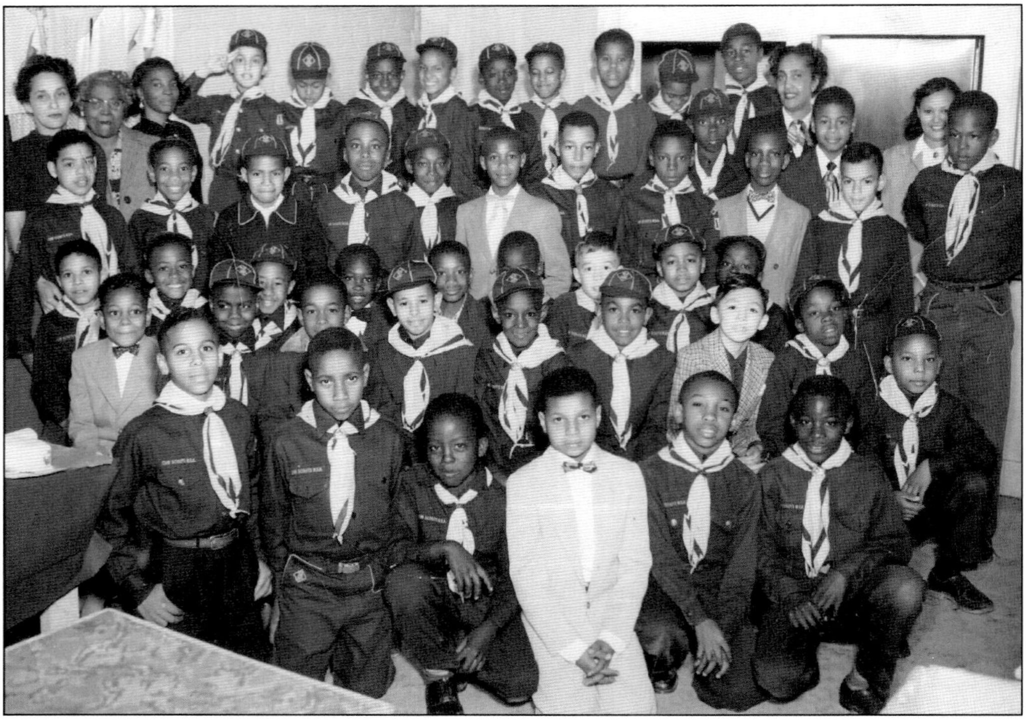

Cub Scouts pose for a photograph after a meeting in 1954. There were four or five dens in Orangeburg. Sometimes, when the scoutmaster visited from Columbia, all of the dens would come together as a group and meet at the Catholic school. Benner C. Turner, president of South Carolina State College, was the speaker for this occasion. Lillie Gaffney, a den mother, is in the last row at far right. (Courtesy of Lillie Gaffney.)

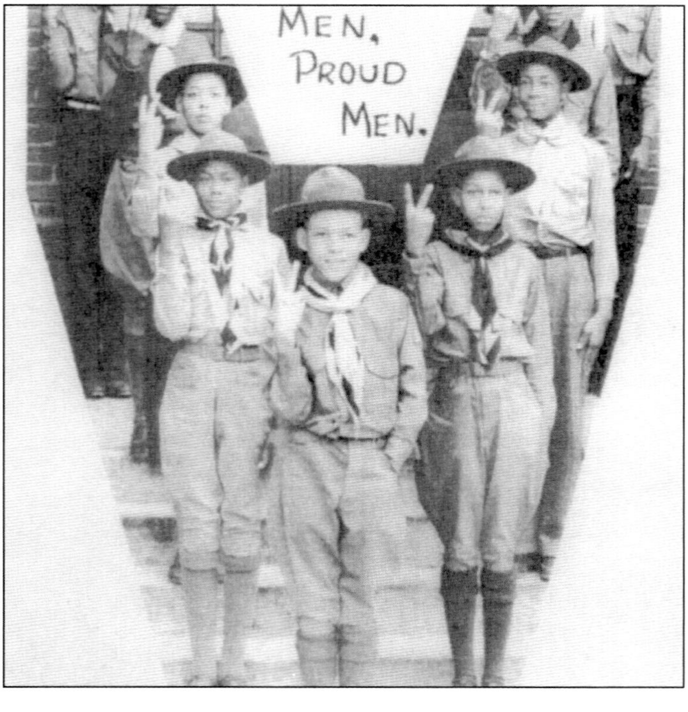

Members of the Cub Scouts pose for a photograph after their meeting in 1943. (Courtesy of Agnes Glover.)

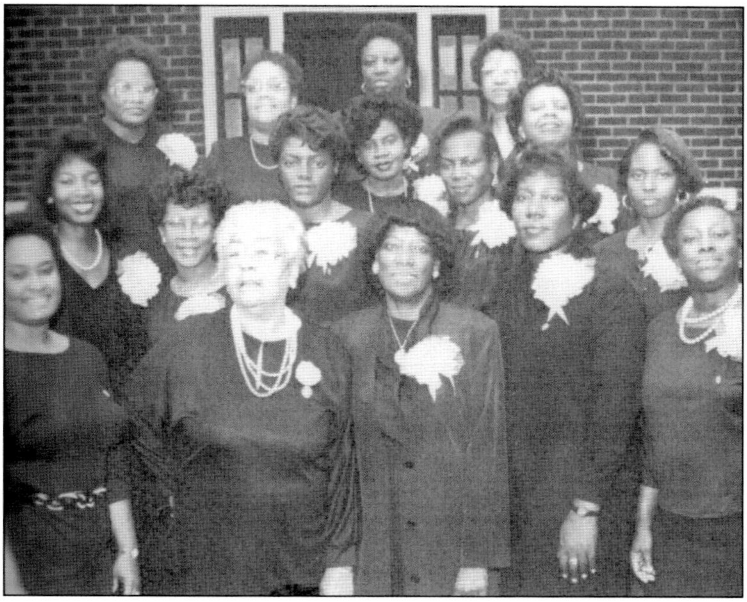

The Xi Eta chapter of Chi Eta Phi sorority was organized in Orangeburg on October 14, 1989. Shown are 12 area nurses welcomed by national officers at South Carolina State College. (Courtesy of Shirley M. James.)

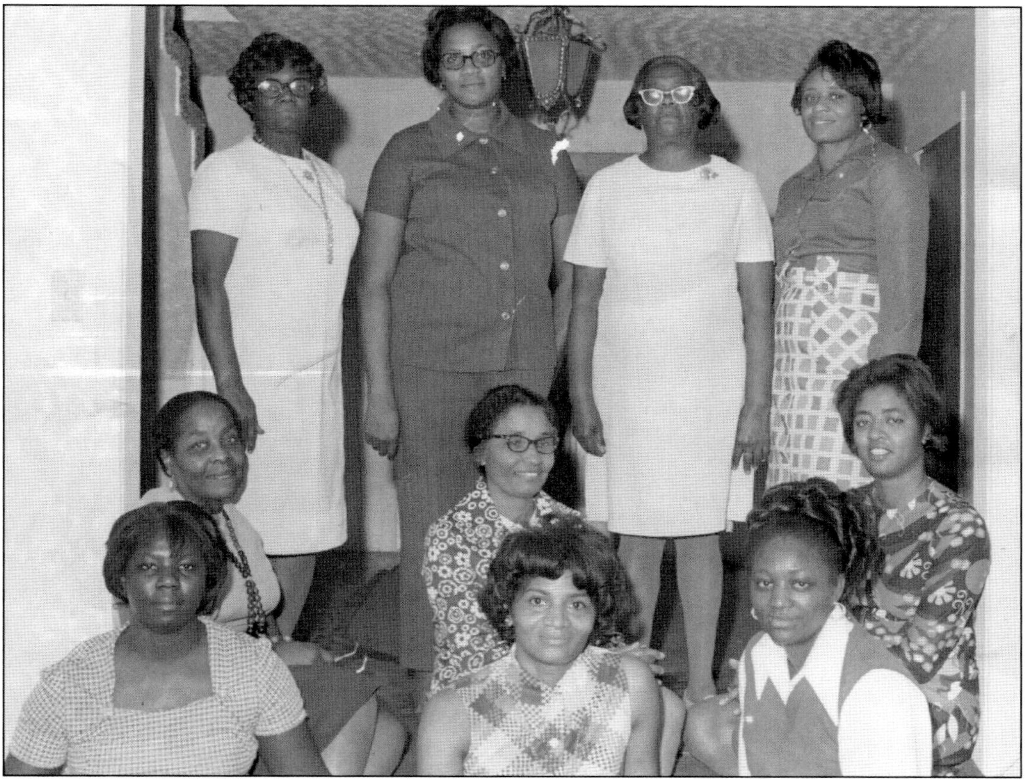

The Ebony Nurses Club was founded in 1973 in Orangeburg. Posing for a photograph after a meeting are, from left to right, (first row) Thelma Glover, Clarice Green, and Shirley James; (second row) Ermine Kennerly, Ida Dash, and Judy Bradley; (third row) Flossie Holmes, Gusella Brown, Maggie Kennerly, and Eartha McNeal. Maggie Kennerly, an LPN, was employed for 30 years at the Orangeburg Regional Hospital when it was located on Carolina Avenue. (Courtesy of Shirley James.)

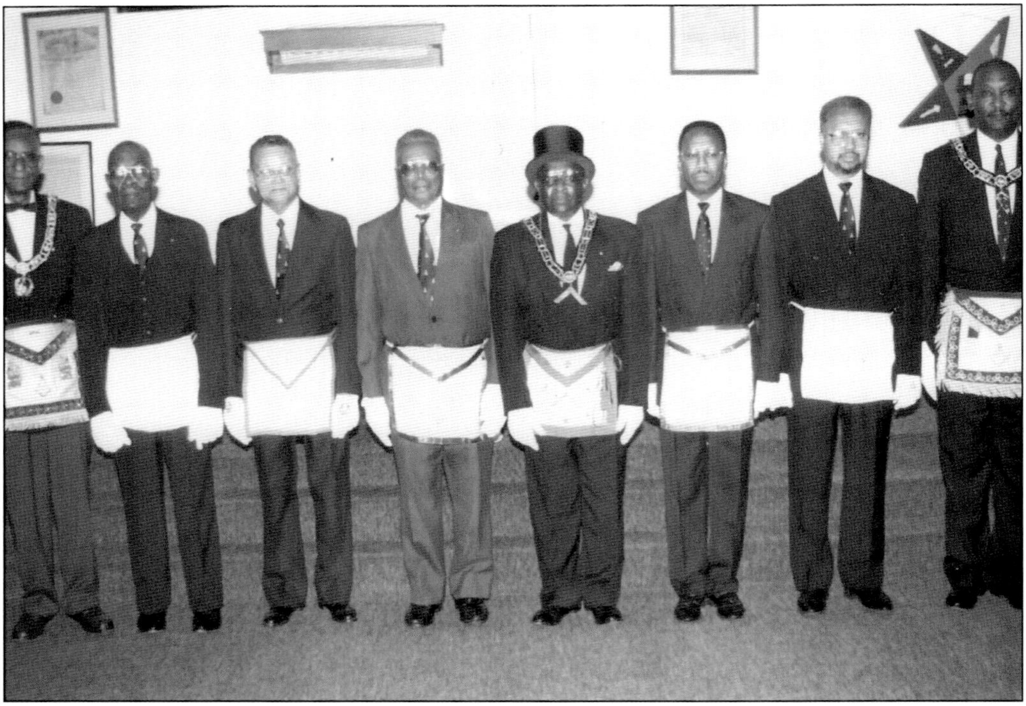

Pictured are past masters of Edisto Masonic Lodge No. 39 on Mingo Street in Orangeburg. From left to right are W. Newton Pough, Carl Kennerly, Walter Miller, I.C. Gillespie, Howard Williams (worshipful master), John Rivers, John F. Lessane Jr., and Curtis Carter. (Courtesy of Carl Kennerly.)

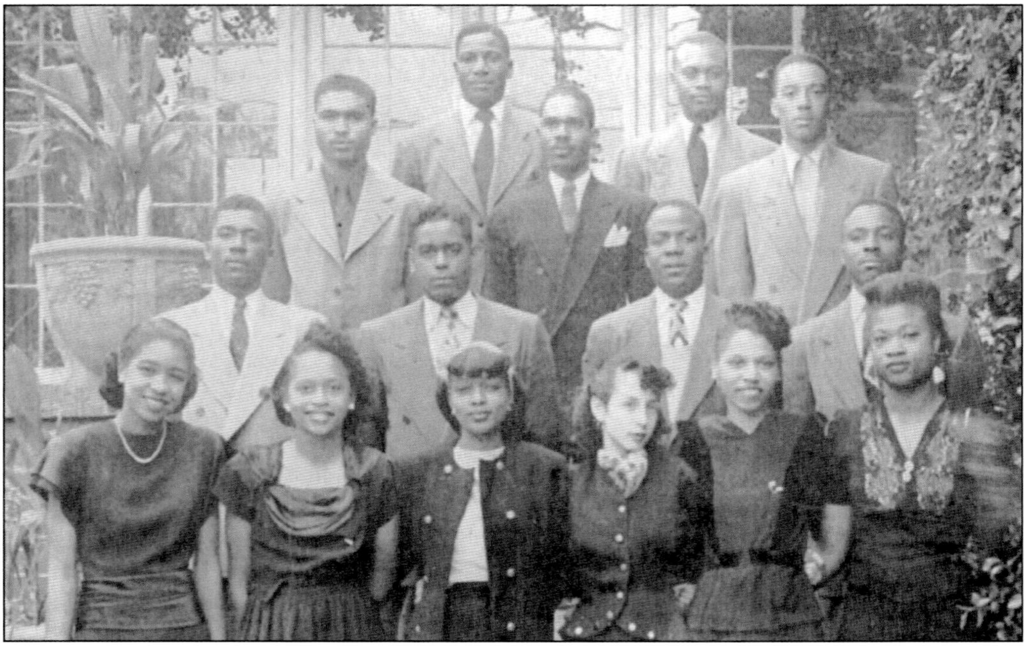

The Pan-Hellenic Council of South Carolina State College takes time to pose for a photograph on the campus in 1953. The council is made up of representatives from all of the sororities and fraternities on campus. (Courtesy of South Carolina State University Library.)

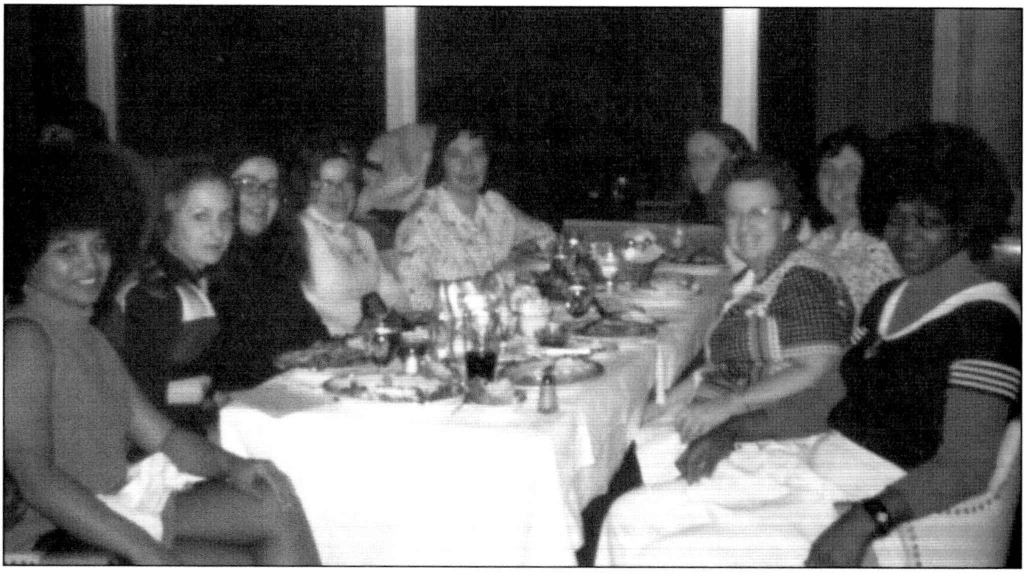

Nurses from all over the nation pose for a photograph at the Newark, New Jersey, airport after completing the nurse practitioner program in 1973. This training was the beginning of the concept of nurse practitioners for South Carolina. (Courtesy of Shirley James.)

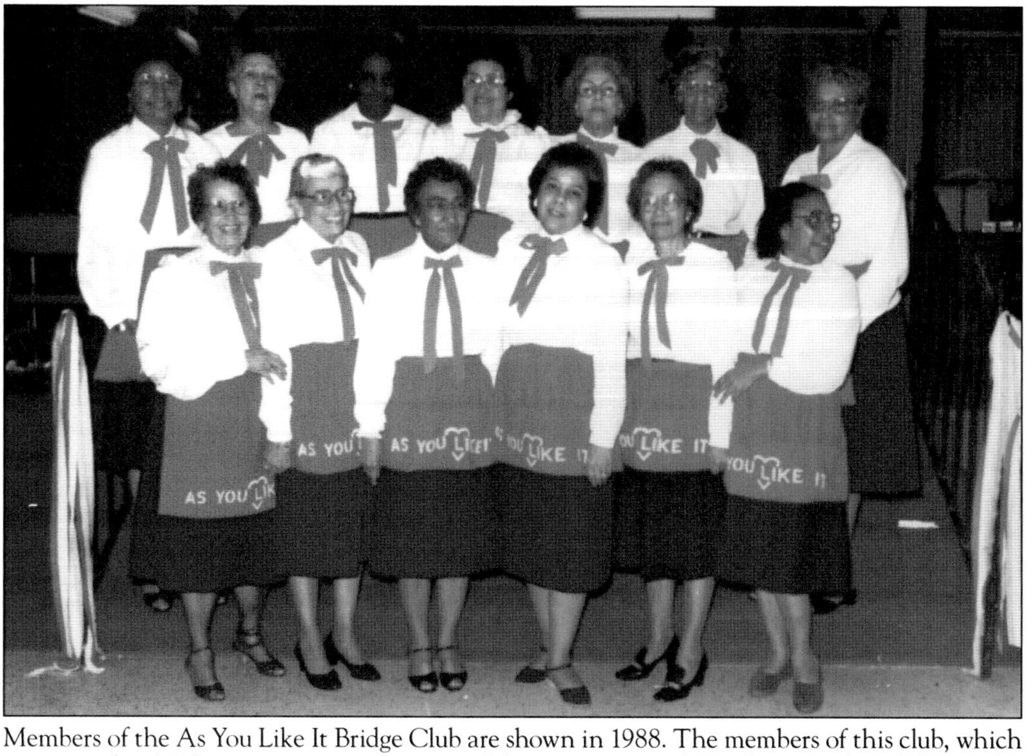

Members of the As You Like It Bridge Club are shown in 1988. The members of this club, which was started in 1938, were prominent citizens of the community. Shown here are, from left to right, (first row) Bertha Williams, Marie Fraser, Flossie Clinkscales, Alba Lewis, Clemmie Webber, and Rossie Caldwell; (second row) Evelyn Hartzog, Geraldine DeCosta, Dorothy Middleton, Nettie Parler, Ursala Frasier, Emma Jane Castleberry, and Geraldyne Zimmerman. (Courtesy of D. Malone Zimmerman.)

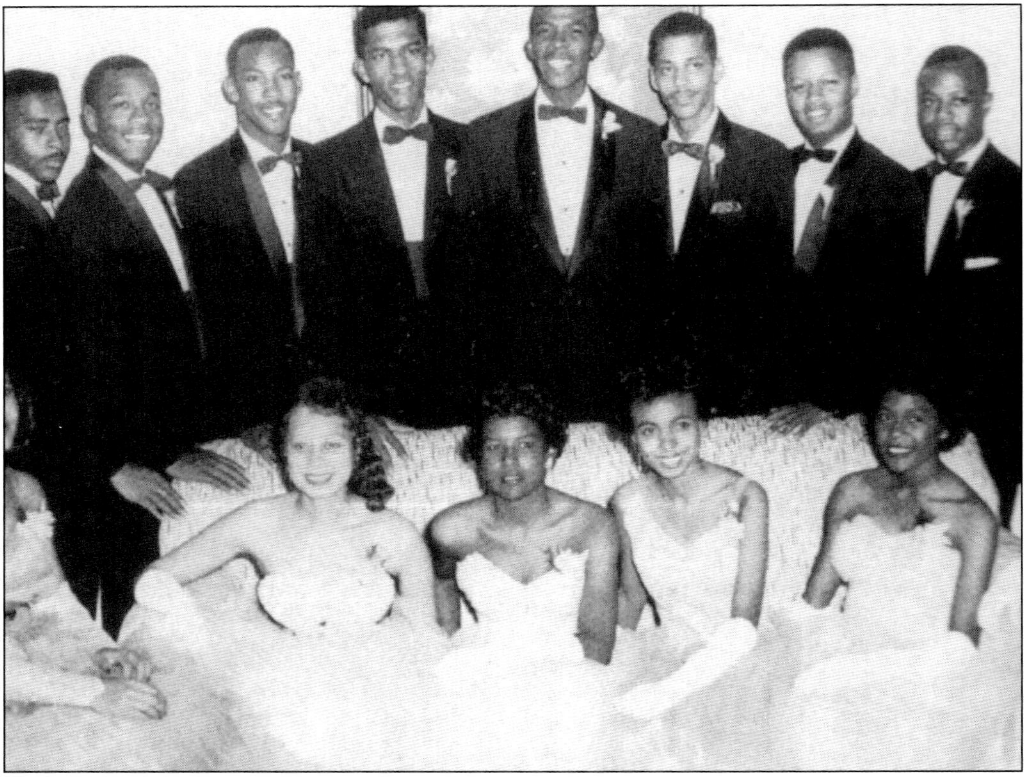

Members of the Delta Psi Omega Honors Club pose after an event at South Carolina State College in 1957. Richard Singleton is in the second row, third from left. (Courtesy of Richard Singleton.)

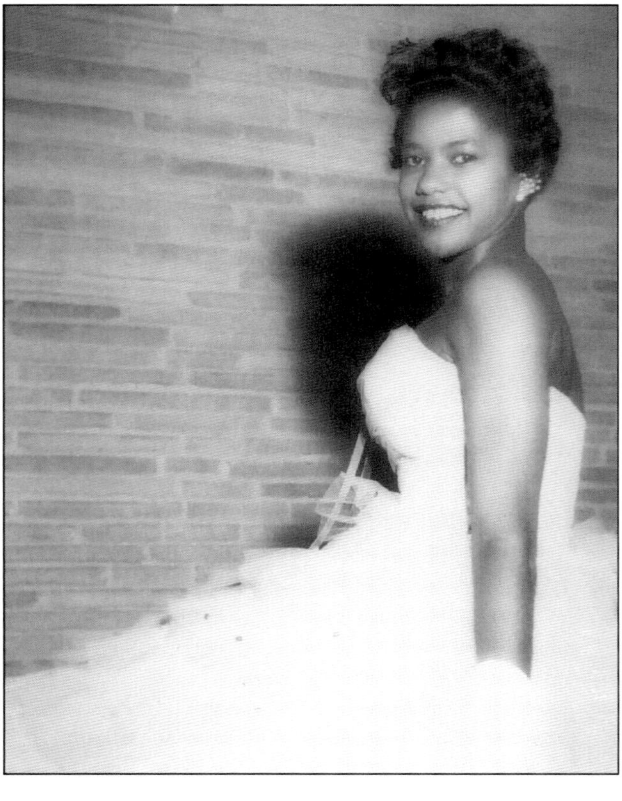

Jerri Singleton poses as Ms. Sophomore for 1958 at South Carolina State College. Singleton, a 1960 graduate of South Carolina State, is the wife of Richard Singleton. (Courtesy of Richard Singleton.)

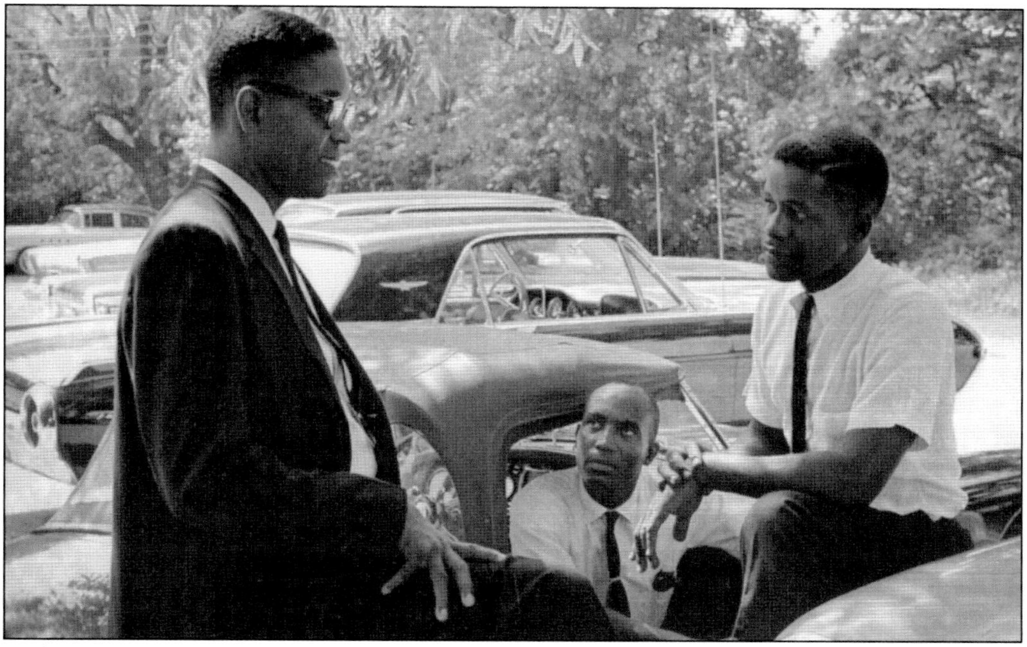

Zack Townsend (center) has been a practicing attorney in Orangeburg since 1963. His office was once located on the corner of Amelia and Middleton Streets, across from Bythewood Funeral Home. It is currently located on Amelia Street. In this early 1960s photograph, NAACP attorneys Matthew Perry (left, later US circuit court judge and US district judge) and Earl W. Coblyn discuss strategy in their defense of Claflin University and South Carolina State College students arrested during anti-segregation demonstrations in Orangeburg. (Courtesy of Cecil Williams.)

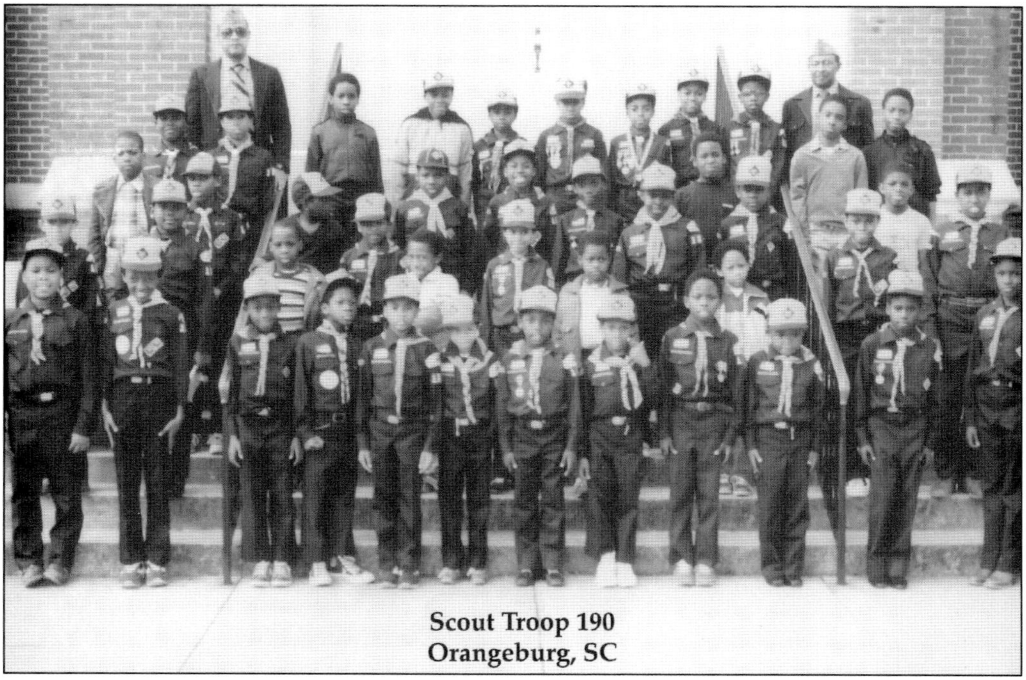

Trinity United Methodist Church troop leaders Sidney Young (back row, far right) and Charles Johnson (back row, far left) pose with Cub Scouts and Boy Scouts in 1976. (Courtesy of Sidney Young.)

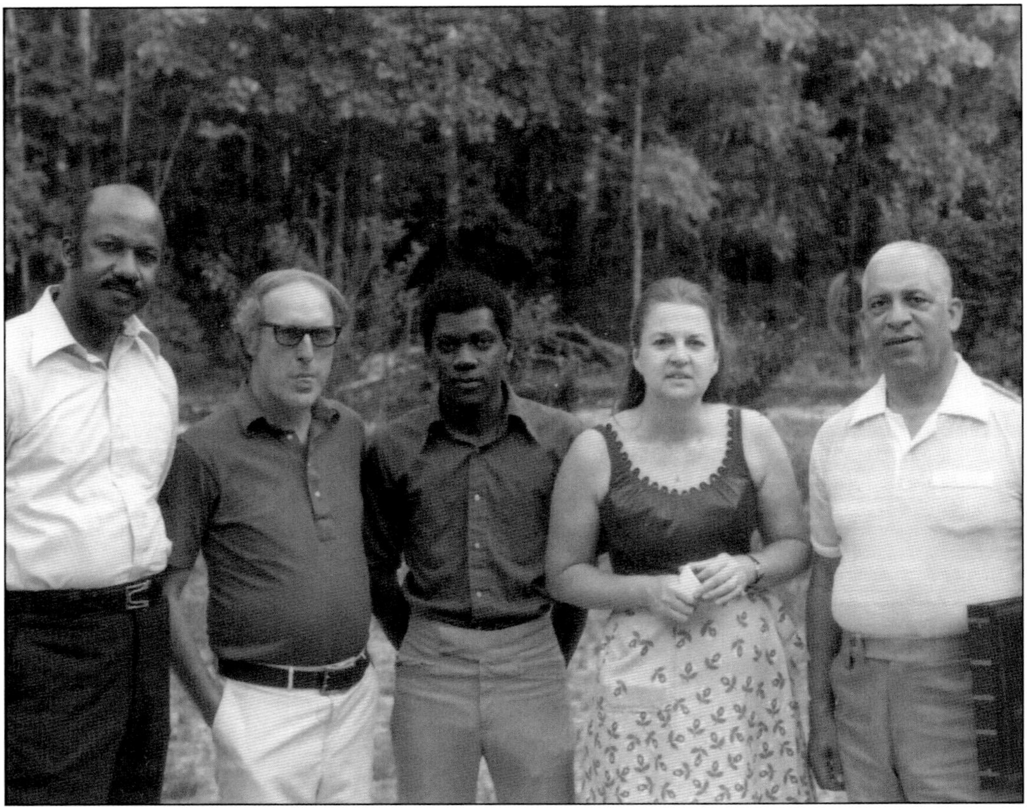

The Burrell E. Workman Jr. Memorial Scholarship was started in 1973 by George and Joy Barnes. In this 1980 photograph are, from left to right, Dr. James Arrington, George Barnes, scholarship recipient Sam Montgomery, Joy Barnes, and Dr. Lewie Roache. Montgomery attended South Carolina State College. The scholarship was started in honor of Joy Barnes's father, Burrell E. Workman Jr., and is awarded annually to an SC State student. (Courtesy of Joy Barnes.)

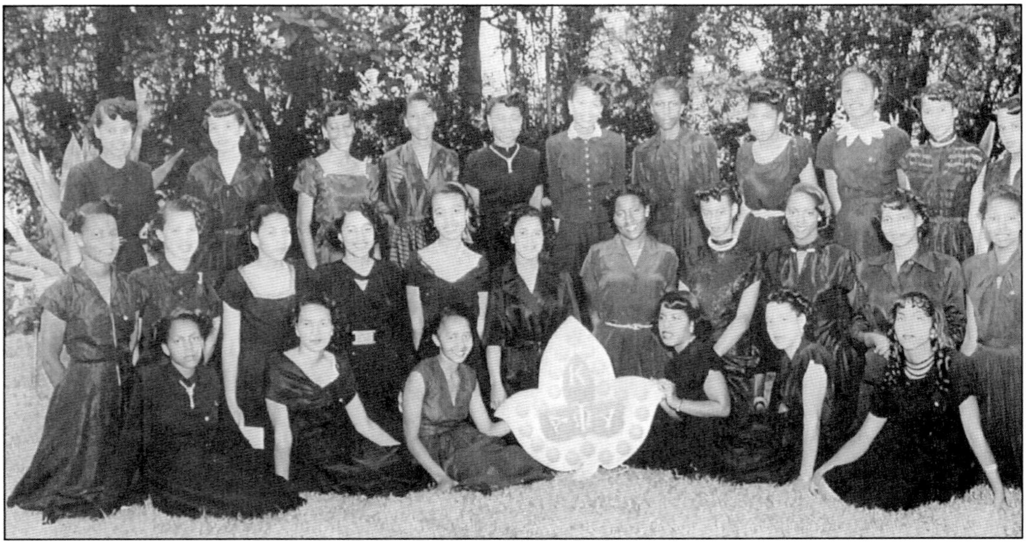

In this 1953 yearbook photograph, Alpha Kappa Alpha sorority members pose on the grounds of South Carolina State College. (Courtesy of South Carolina State University Library.)

Four

MILITARY LIFE

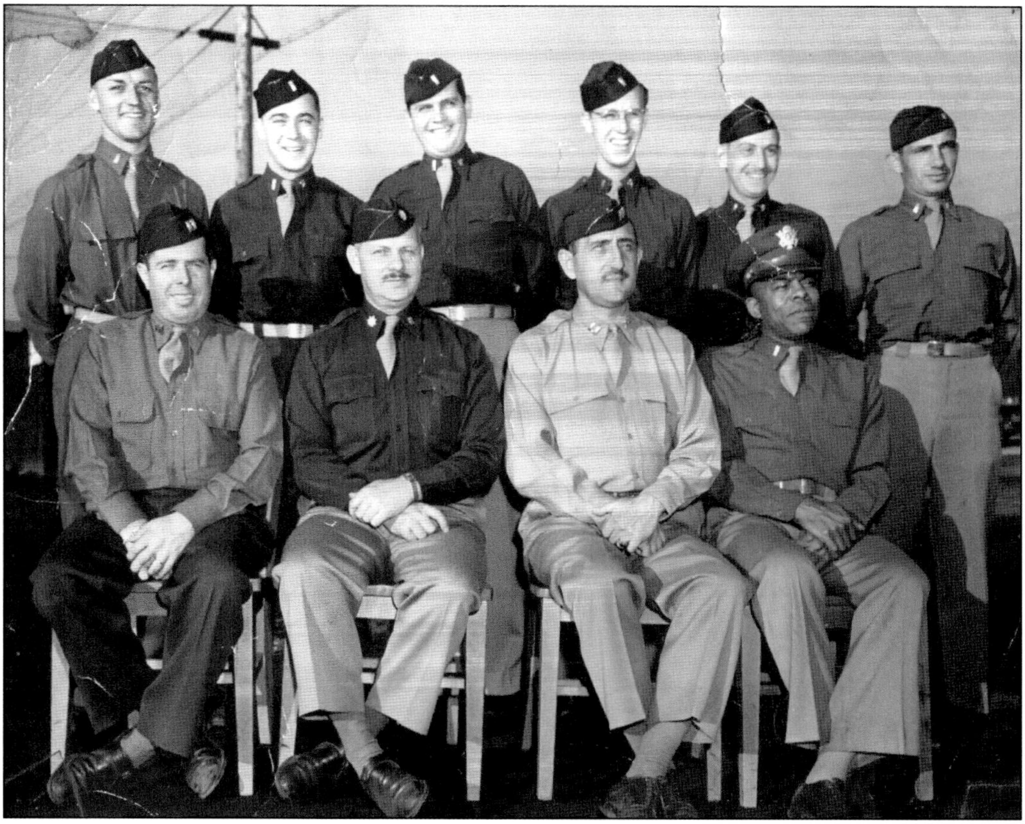

Joseph Deleon Bryan (1893–1986) served in the Quartermaster Corps in the US Army during World War I from June 30, 1918, to July 13, 1919, and again from 1940 to 1946, including World War II. He served as a chaplain and was promoted to major in 1946. Bryan (first row, far right) was a 1926 graduate of South Carolina State College, and received a master's degree, also from SC State, in 1951. He finished a chaplain course at Harvard University and was awarded a doctor of divinity degree at Wynwood, Pennsylvania. An active member of Mount Pisgah Baptist Church, Bryan served in many capacities, including as president of Seneca Junior College in Seneca, South Carolina, and as pastor of New Mount Zion Baptist Church in Orangeburg and Ebenezer Baptist Church in Manning. (Courtesy of Willie B. Bryan.)

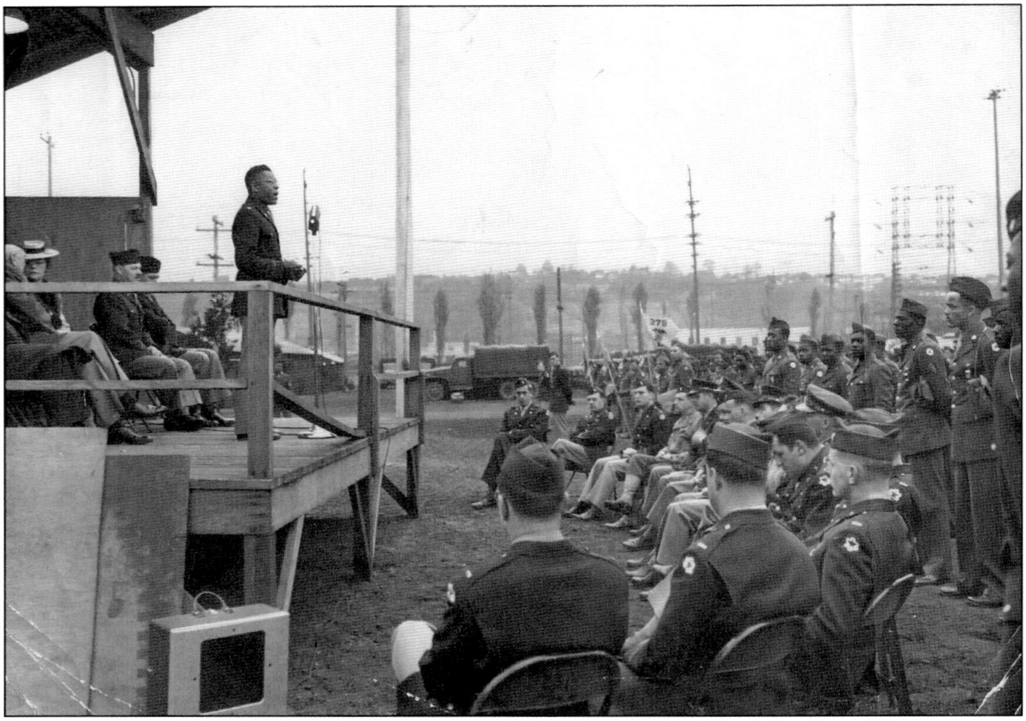

Maj. Joseph Deleon Bryan addresses a group of soldiers at Easter morning services in 1940. (Courtesy of Willie B. Bryan; photograph by Roger Dudley.)

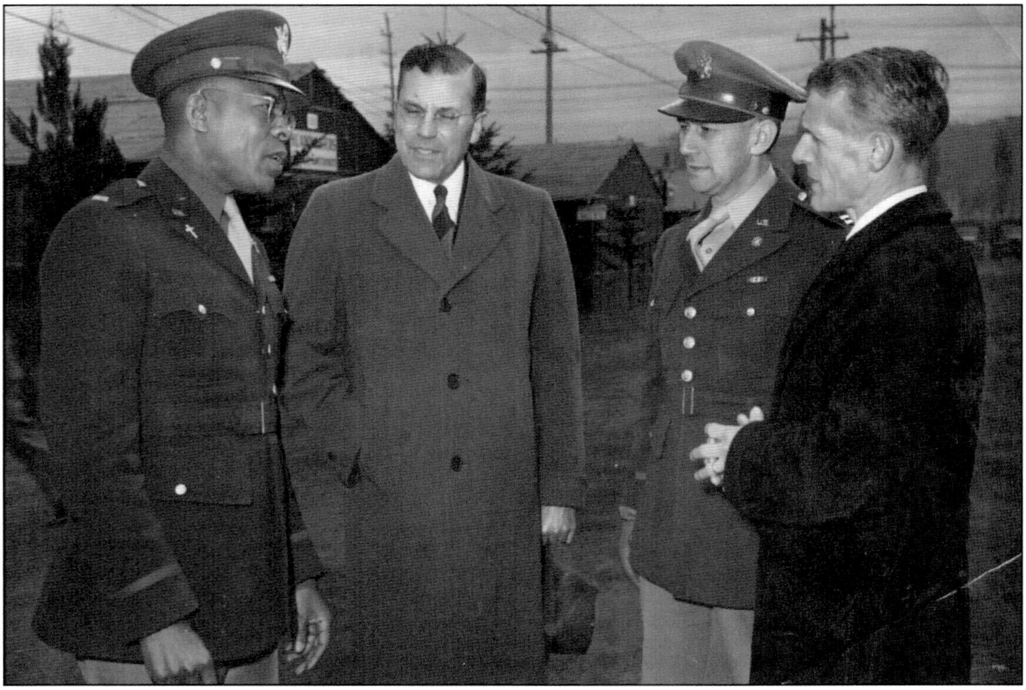

Joseph D. Bryan is shown being congratulated on his promotion to major in 1946 by other officers. Major Bryan also served as an Army chaplain. (Courtesy of Willie B. Bryan; photograph by Roger Dudley.)

Philip Middleton served in the US Army in World War II. Shown here in 1943, he was the brother of former representative Earl Middleton. (Courtesy of Joy Barnes.)

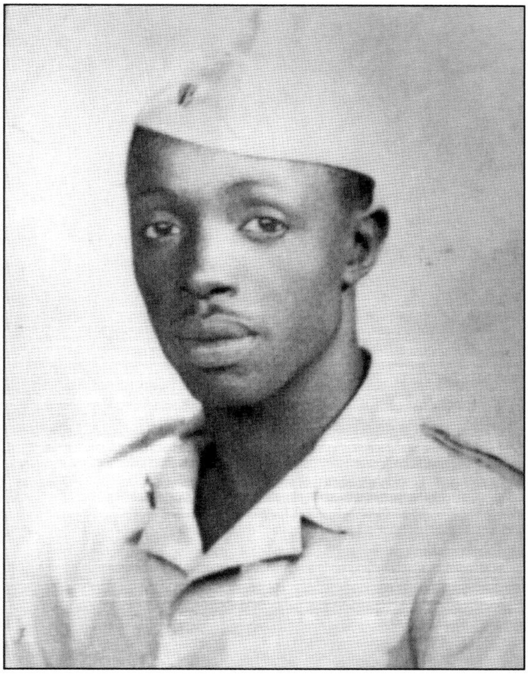

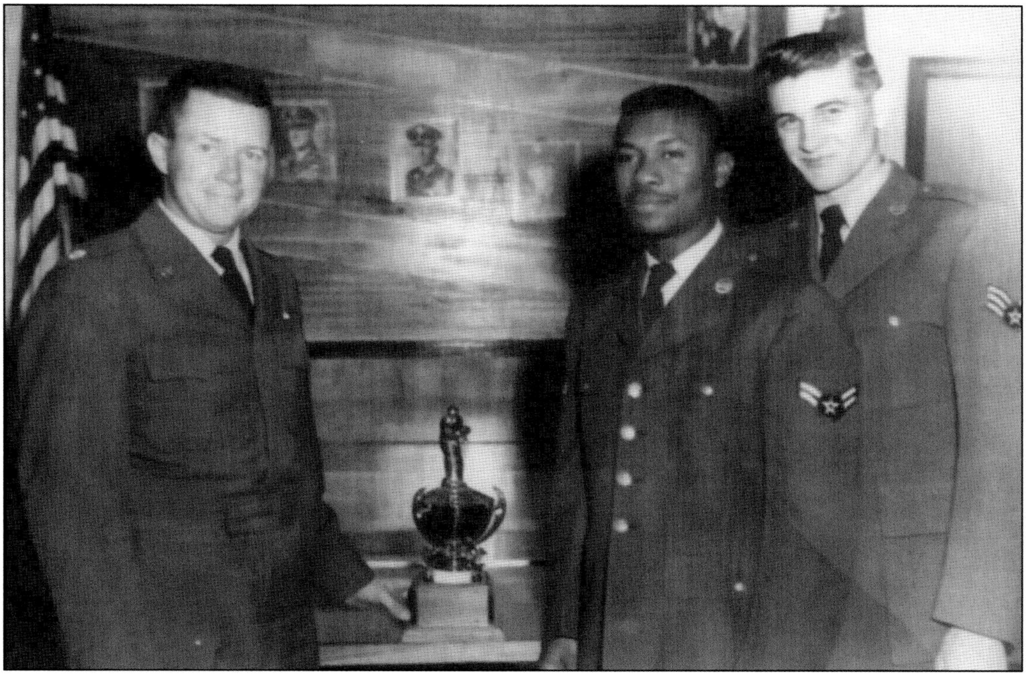

George "Mickey" Williams (center) was an air policeman in the US Air Force. He is shown with his award for being the ping pong champion in 1956. Williams was employed at Albemarle Corporation, a chemical company, for 40 years before retiring as a production analyst in 2000. Beginning in 1980 and in each subsequent year while he was employed at Albemarle, he organized a special community service project among his fellow employees, gathering funds from them to purchase gifts for seniors at nursing home facilities. The corporation now supplies Williams with a check. (Courtesy of George Williams.)

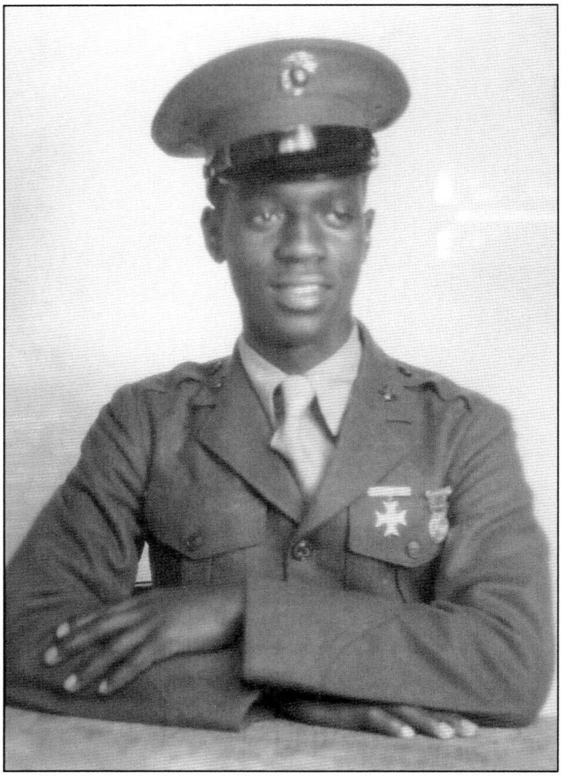

Charles Payne served in World War II from 1944 to 1946 as a Montford Point Marine. He was drafted before he completed high school. Payne recalls that, under Pres. Franklin D. Roosevelt, Negroes could enter the Marines. Approximately 20,000 African American recruits received training at Montford Point, Camp LeJune, in New River, North Carolina, during the war. (Courtesy of Charles Payne.)

Montford Point Marines Charles Payne (left), Lavel Lynch (center), and Edwin Harley pose at Camp Catlin, in Oahu, Hawaii, in 1945. In July 1948, Pres. Harry S. Truman issued Executive Order No. 9981, negating segregation. In September 1949, the Montford Point Marine Camp was deactivated, ending seven years of segregation. (Courtesy of Charles Payne.)

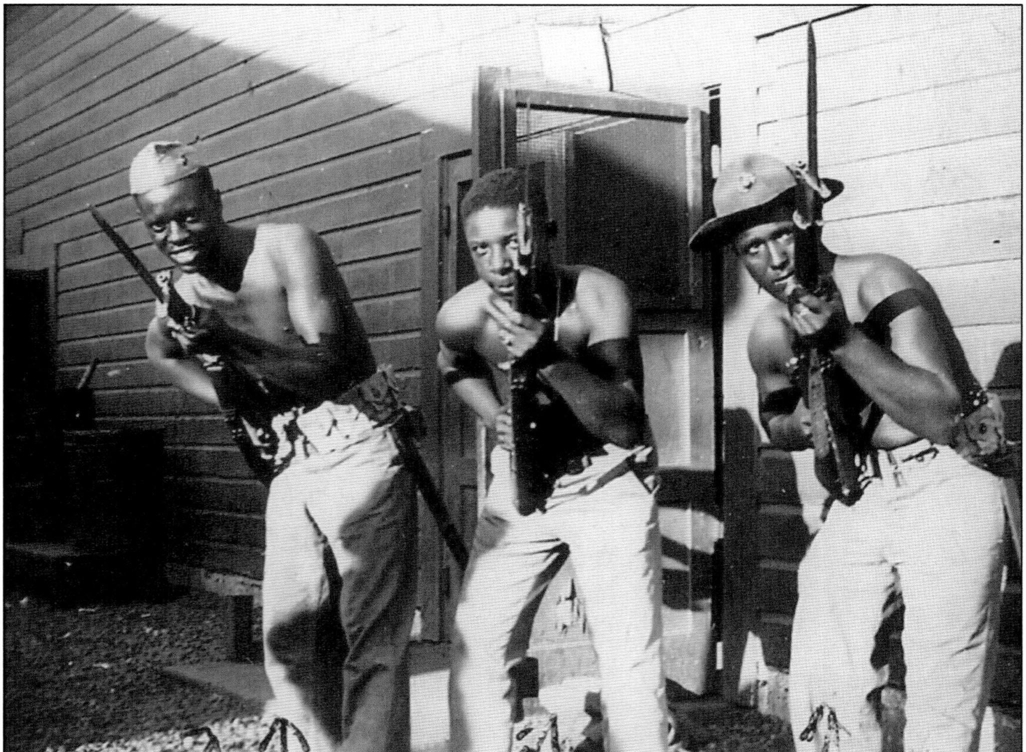

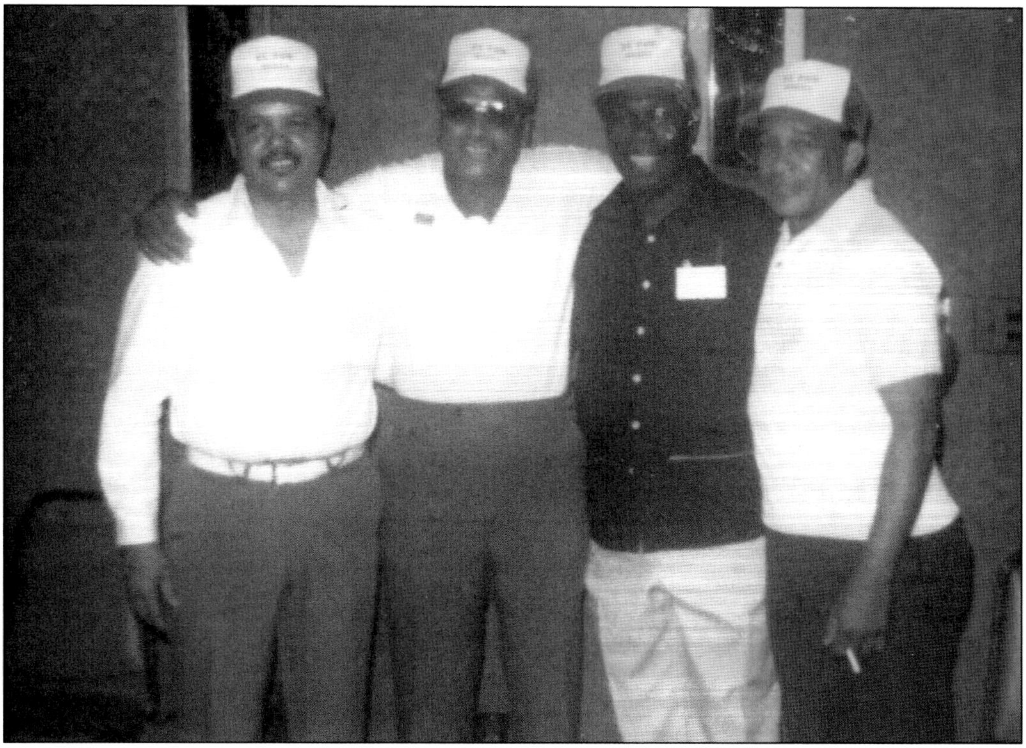

Albert Dixon (second from right) poses with other former prisoners of war from the Korean War at their reunion in the late 1980s. (Courtesy of Albert Dixon.)

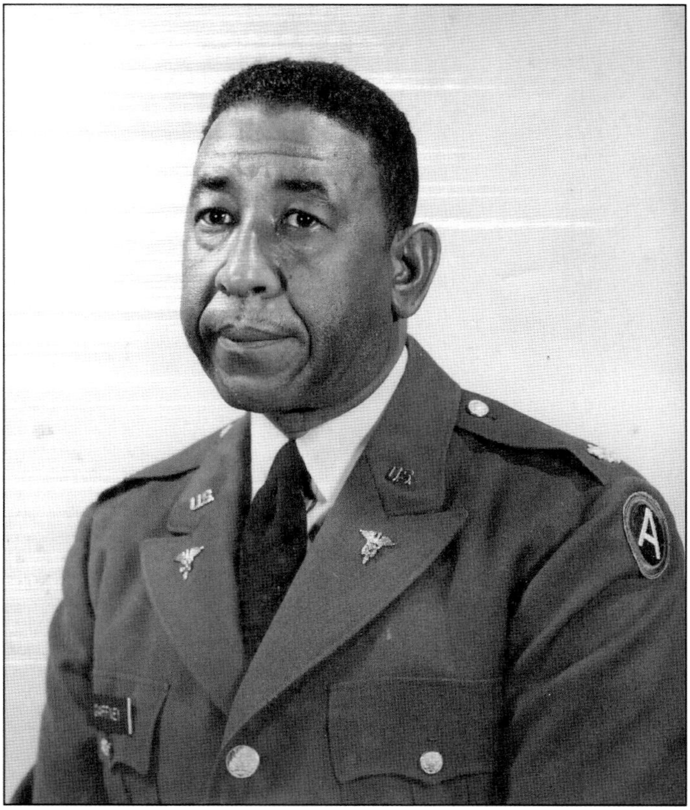

Retired major Raymond A. Gaffney Sr. served in the US Army from 1942 to 1963, during World War II and the Korean War. Upon retiring, he was employed at South Carolina State College for 21 years. Gaffney, who became the director of the student center at South Carolina State, is remembered by many students as a kind man who never let anyone go hungry. (Courtesy of Lillie Gaffney.)

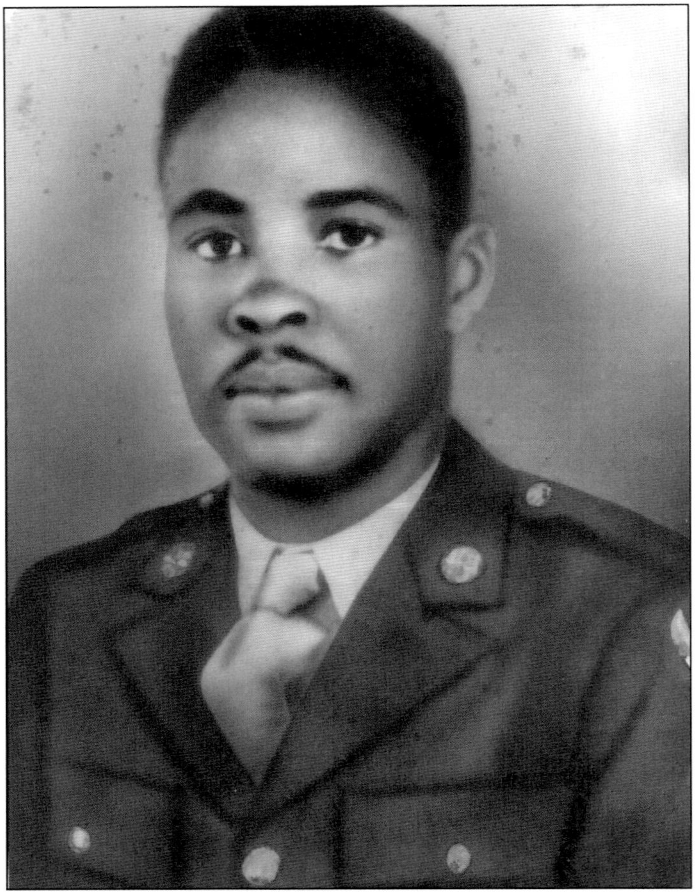

Broadus Jamerson Jr., of Orangeburg, is shown here in 1942. He served in the US Army during World War II and was killed in action in Italy in December 1943. He was originally reported missing in action. The news of his death was listed in the *Times and Democrat* newspaper in May 1944. (Courtesy of Broadus Jamerson III.)

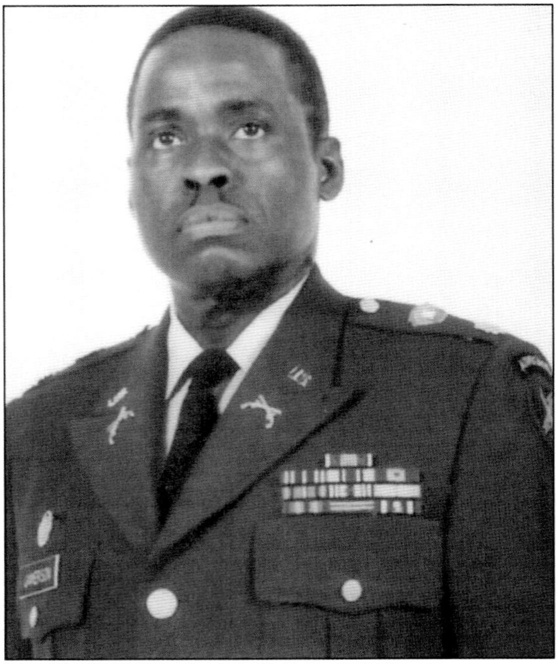

Broadus Jamerson III is a native of Orangeburg and a 1968 graduate of South Carolina State College. He earned two master's degrees, in vocational rehabilitation counseling and counseling education, from SC State College in 1977 and 1978, respectively. He is a retired lieutenant colonel, US Army Reserve. From 1996 until his retirement in 2010, Jamerson was director of the South Carolina State Employees Association. He is a recipient of the Order of the Palmetto, South Carolina's highest civilian honor. He is the son of Broadus Jamerson Jr. and Lillie Jamerson Limehouse. Jamerson III did not have the chance to know his father, who was killed during World War II. He is a member of Mount Pisgah Baptist Church. (Courtesy of Broadus Jamerson III.)

Albert Dixon, shown here in 1941, was a retired sergeant first class who served in three wars (World War II, Korea, and Vietnam). Dixon entered the US Army on September 8, 1941, when he was only 14, exaggerating his age to get in. Exactly three months after he entered the service, the United States entered World War II. Dixon was assigned to the 93rd Infantry Division, which was deployed to the southwest Pacific area. During the Korean War, he and others were captured by the enemy and held for three years, until the end of the war. Dixon returned home after the conflict, but reenlisted during the Vietnam War. Dixon served for 32 years in the military before retiring. (Courtesy of Albert Dixon.)

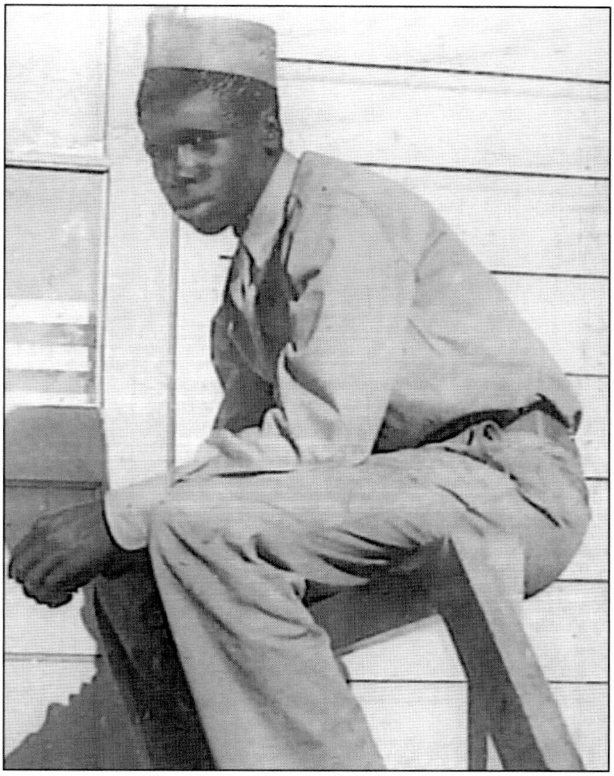

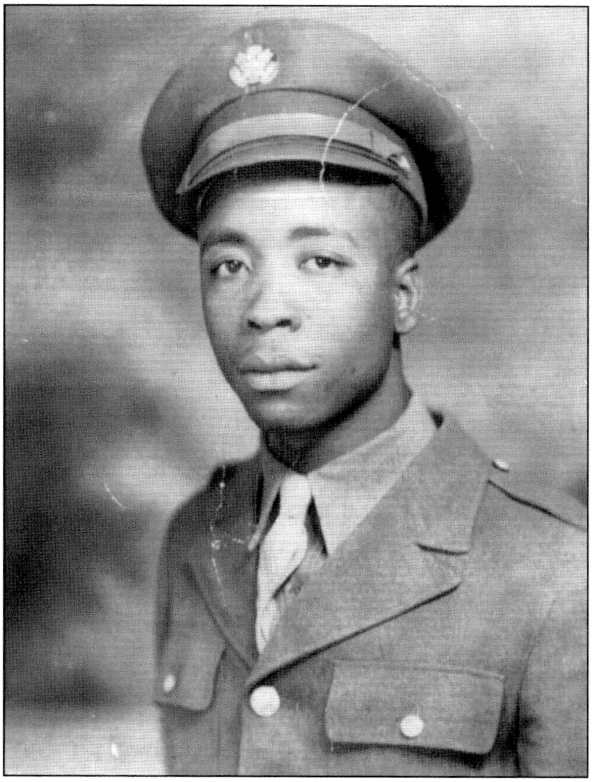

Henry Lee Avinger Sr. (1920–1975), of Vance, served in the US Army from 1944 to 1947. He was a farmer, well known in his community for giving away fresh vegetables to neighbors and people in the community. (Courtesy of Judy Wright.)

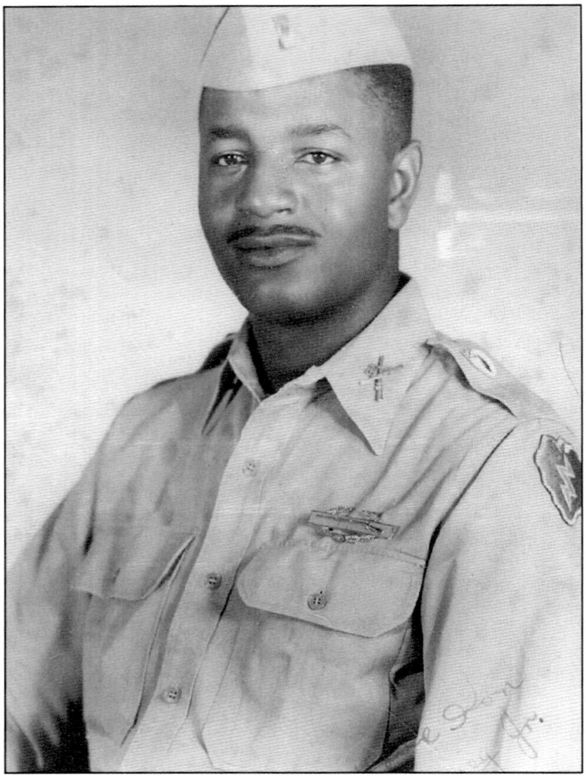

Harvey Durant Jr. of Orangeburg is an educator, licensed master plumber, and a Korean War veteran. He attended the elementary school at Claflin College through fourth grade until the school was discontinued. He attended Dunton Memorial Elementary and graduated from Wilkinson High School, on Goff Avenue, in 1947. The graduation program was held at Mount Pisgah Baptist Church, on Green Street in Orangeburg. He graduated from South Carolina State College in 1951 and received his masters degree in 1957. The class of 1951 was the first four-year graduation class of ROTC at South Carolina State, where he was commissioned as a second lieutenant. He is a member of Mount Pisgah Baptist Church. (Courtesy of Harvey Durant Jr.)

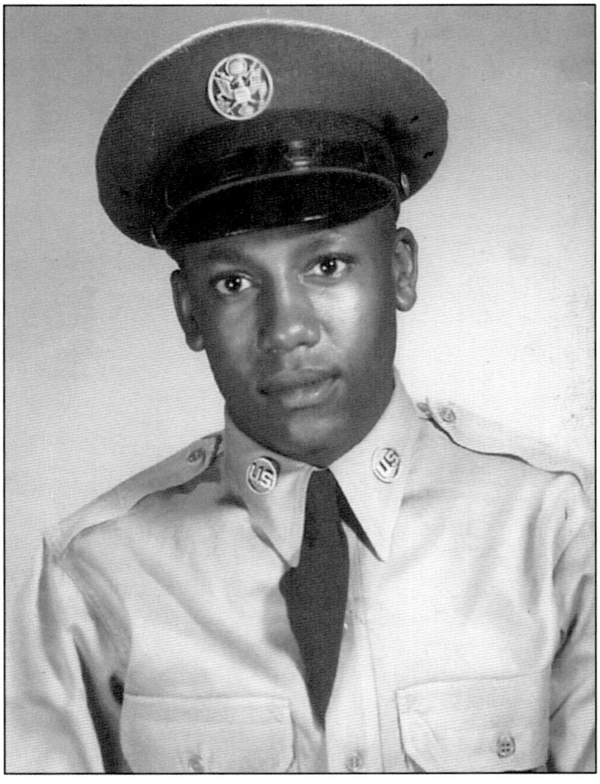

Elijah Richardson, of Orangeburg, was a community leader and a veteran. He served in the US Air Force for four years, completing school during that time. He started work at the age of eight to help his mother support the family. He was a security officer and organizer of security at the Daniel Hale Co-op in New York. When he came to Orangeburg, he was very active in the community. He helped to organize a group of retired men, called the street committee. Richardson was employed as a security officer at Claflin University and was a Greenwood Mills supervisor. He was a member of Mount Pisgah Baptist Church and served as its first security officer. (Courtesy of Dorothy Richardson.)

Clifton Reid served in the US Army during World War II, from 1944 to 1946. After completing his tour of service in the Army, one of his pastimes was to perform as a member of the Gospel Holy Lights quartet. (Courtesy of Helen Reid.)

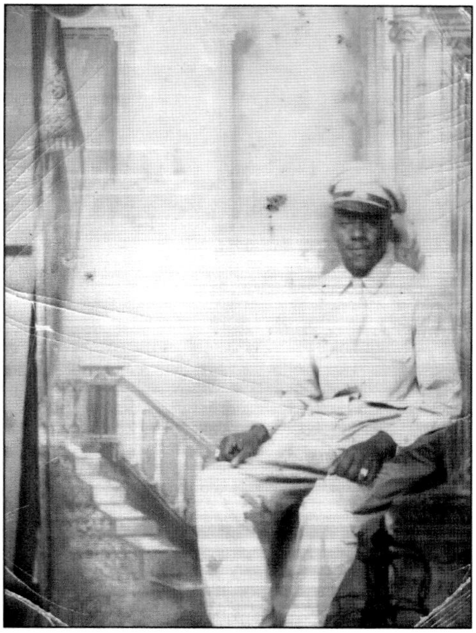

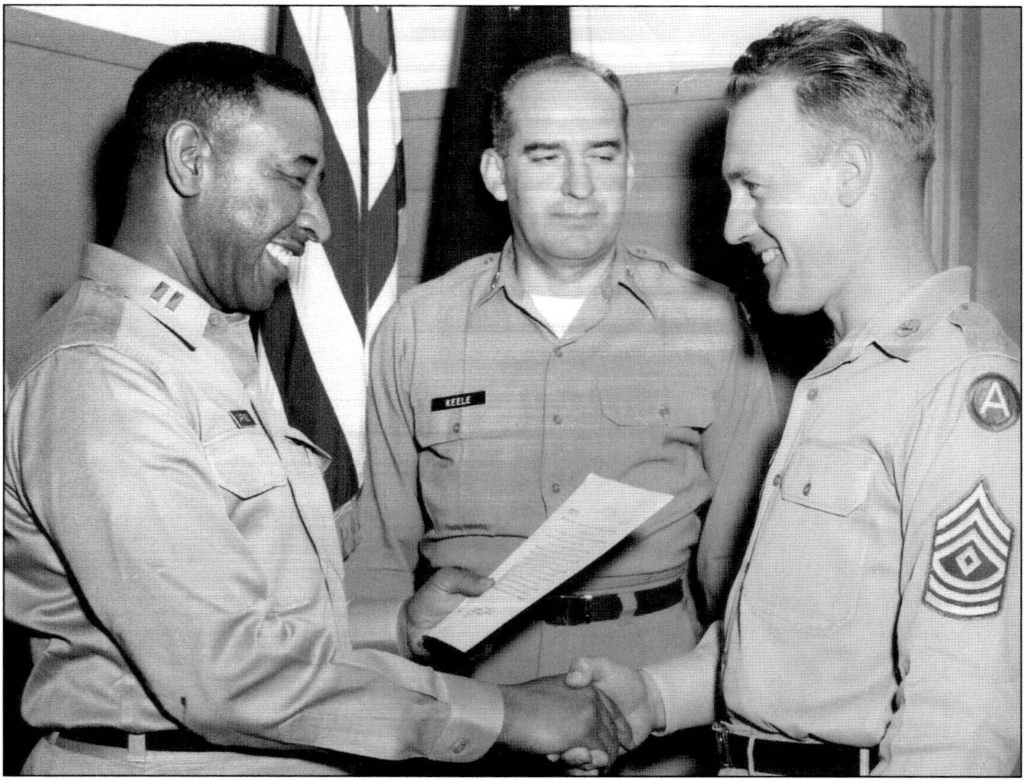

In 1960, Raymond Gaffney Sr. (left) is shown as a captain and commanding officer of the 2nd Surgical Hospital, as he presents E-8 promotion orders to M.Sgt. James Wilson (right), first sergeant, Second Surgical, as Lt. Col. John C. Keele Jr., 55th Medical Group executive officer, looks on. Gaffney was first assigned to the artillery unit and then became a medical assistant. (Courtesy of Lillie Gaffney; Army photograph by George Weeks.)

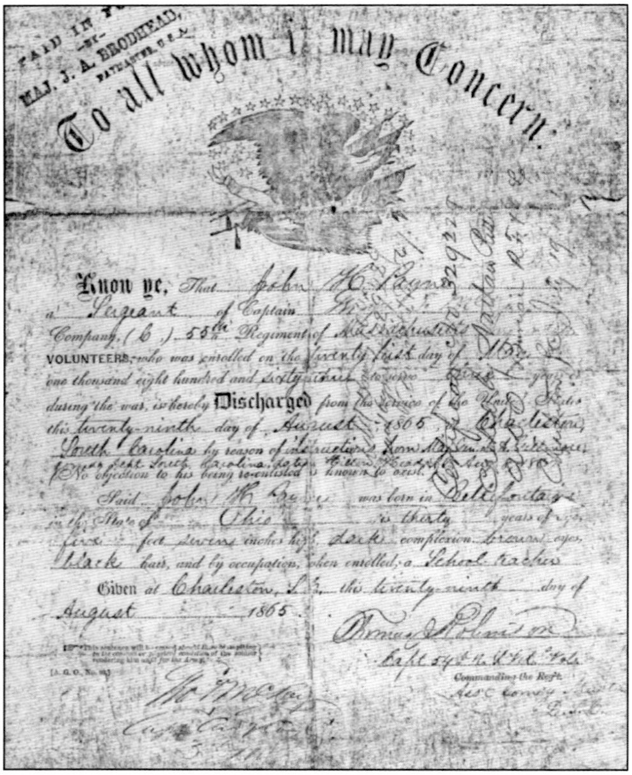

PAID IN F...
—BY—
MAJ. J. A. BRODHEAD,
PAYMASTER, U.S.A.

To all whom it may Concern:

Know ye, That John H. Payne a Sergeant of Captain [illegible] Company, (C) 55th Regiment of Massachusetts VOLUNTEERS, who was enrolled on the twenty first day of [illegible] one thousand eight hundred and sixty three to serve [illegible] years during the war, is hereby Discharged from the service of the United States this twenty-ninth day of August 1865 at Charleston, South Carolina by reason of [illegible]

(No objection to his being re-enlisted is known to exist.)

Said John H. Payne was born in Bellefontaine in the State of Ohio is thirty years of age, five feet seven inches high, dark complexion, brown eyes, black hair, and by occupation, when enrolled, a School teacher

Given at Charleston, S.C. this twenty-ninth day of August 1865.

Thomas Robinson
Capt 54th M. V. Vols
Commanding the Regt.

The Civil War discharge papers of Charles Payne's great great grandfather, John Payne, are shown here. The order discharging the elder Payne's Company C, 55th Regiment of Massachusetts was signed in Charleston, South Carolina, by Thomas Robinson in August 1865. The paper states that Payne's occupation was schoolteacher. (Courtesy of Charles Payne.)

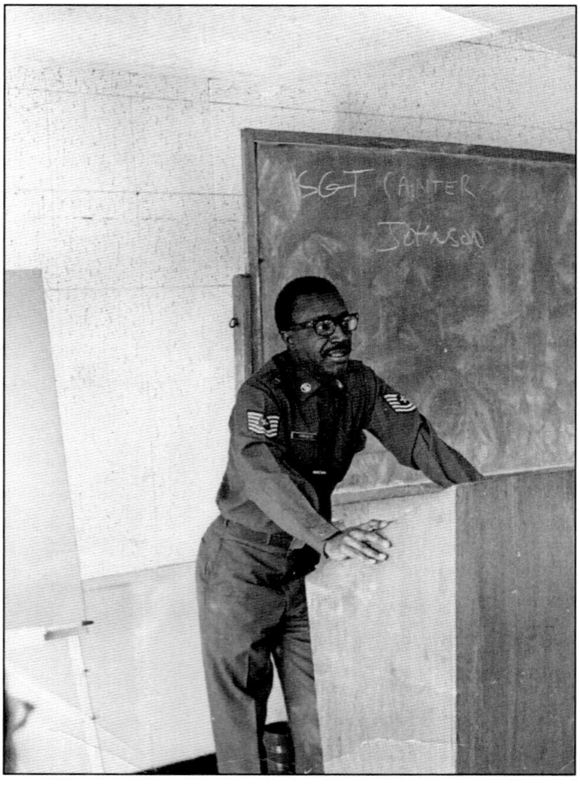

Leonard Irvin Johnson is shown teaching a class in the Air Force during the late 1950s. He moved away from Orangeburg for better opportunities after he was discharged from the service. He is the brother of Catherine Phillips. (Courtesy of Catherine Phillips.)

Ladson and Ethel Salley, parents of Booker T. Salley, are shown receiving a US flag in 1952. Booker T. Salley was killed in action in the Korean War in 1950 at the age of 22. Salley was posthumously awarded the Purple Heart. His remains were recovered and finally sent home to Colleton County for funeral and burial services in 1952. Booker T. was the brother of Evangeline Salley Hill, a 1944 graduate of Claflin University. (Courtesy of Evangeline Hill.)

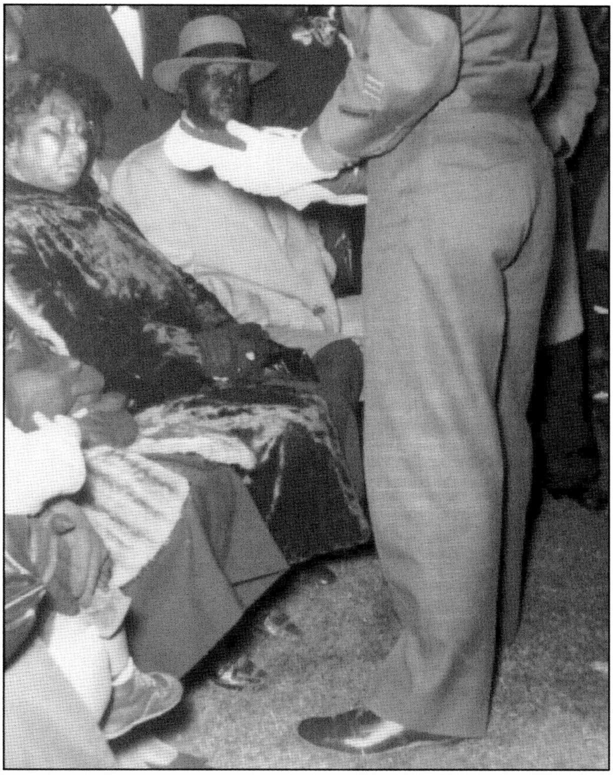

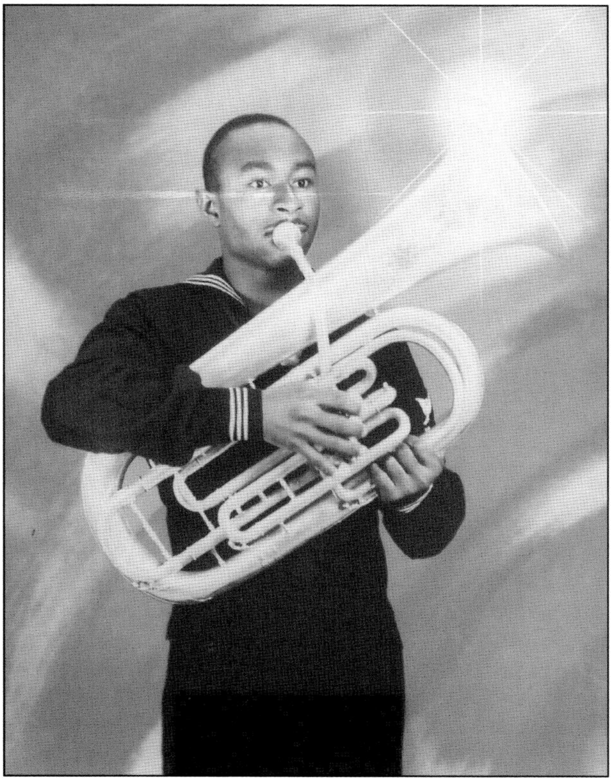

Sidney Young is a veteran, retired educator, and volunteer. He is shown with his baritone horn in 1942. During his military tenure, from 1942 to 1945, he served in the Navy band as a musician third class. He taught music and was bandmaster at Claflin University for over 30 years. Young was known for his antics as he walked beside the band as it participated in parades. After retiring from Claflin University, he could be seen all over town participating in activities with his Boy Scout Troop 190. (Courtesy of Sidney Young.)

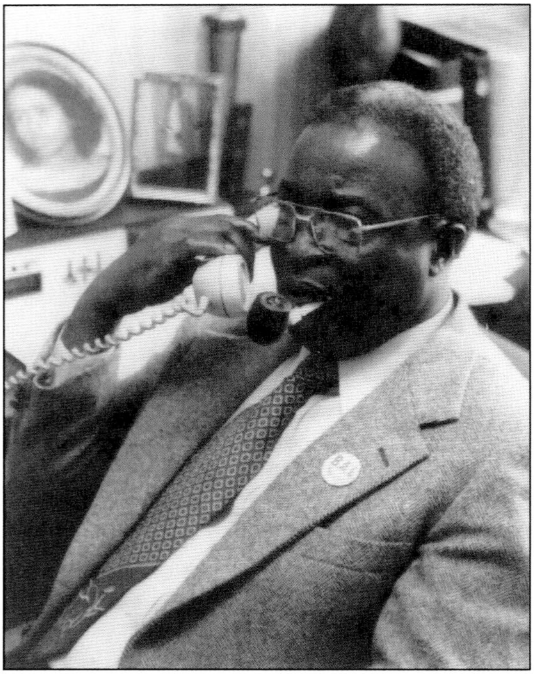

Earl Middleton (1919–2007) was a legislator, businessman, author, and veteran of World War II. He trained in 1942 as one of the famed Tuskegee Airmen, and served as an infantry soldier. After returning to Orangeburg, he served in the South Carolina legislature for 10 years and owned a real estate and insurance business now operated by his son, Kenneth Middleton. A graduate of Claflin College, Middleton was the author of *Knowing Who I Am*, published in 2008. His father was a carpenter and his mother was a 1903 graduate of South Carolina State College. His grandfather was Abram Middleton. (Courtesy of Joy Barnes.)

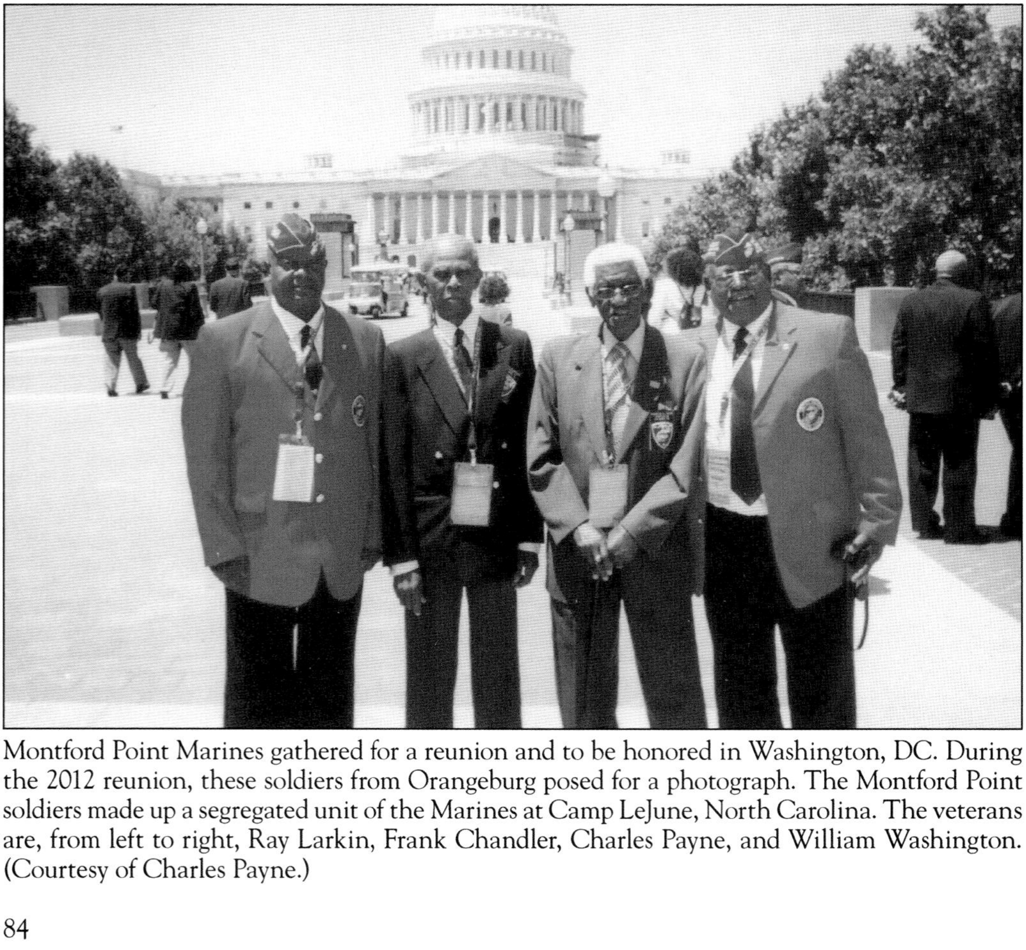

Montford Point Marines gathered for a reunion and to be honored in Washington, DC. During the 2012 reunion, these soldiers from Orangeburg posed for a photograph. The Montford Point soldiers made up a segregated unit of the Marines at Camp LeJune, North Carolina. The veterans are, from left to right, Ray Larkin, Frank Chandler, Charles Payne, and William Washington. (Courtesy of Charles Payne.)

Five

People, Places, and Events

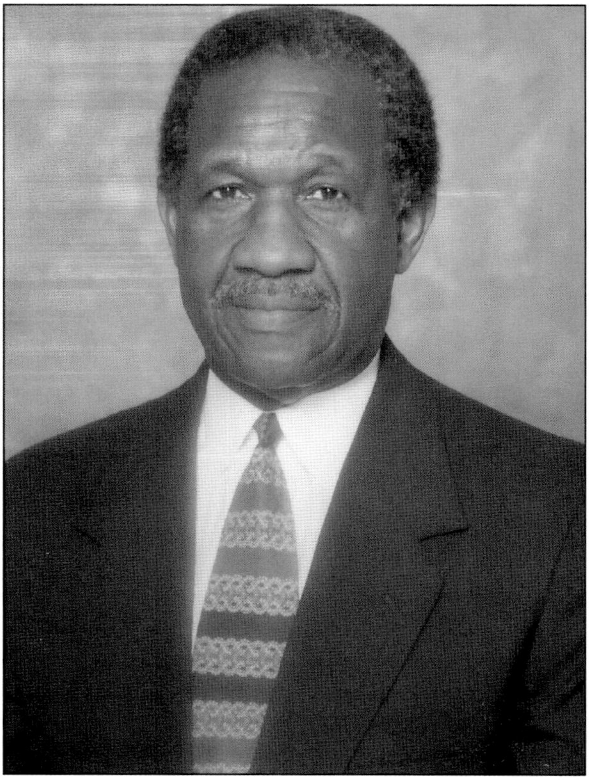

John W. Matthews Jr. (1940–) of Bowman is a businessman, retired educator, legislator, and community leader. A graduate of South Carolina State College, he has served as senator of District 39 (Bamberg, Colleton, Dorchester, Hampton, and Orangeburg Counties) from 1985 to the present. Matthews served in the House of Representatives from 1975 to 1984 and chaired the South Carolina Legislative Black Caucus and Orangeburg County Legislative Delegation. He has received many awards, including South Carolina Primary Health Care Legislator of the Year, induction into the South Carolina Black Hall of Fame, Orangeburg Democrat of the Year, and Minority Business Advocate of the Year. (Courtesy of John W. Matthews Jr.)

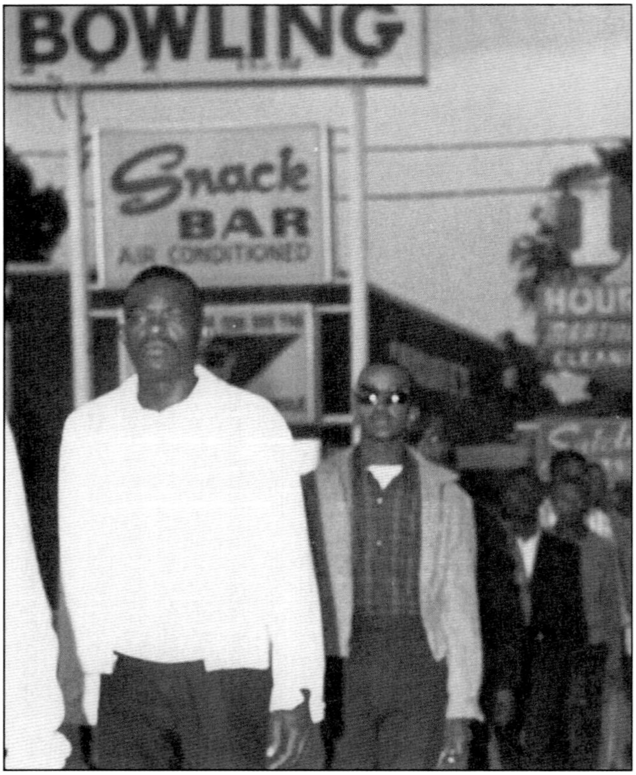

Students from Claflin College, South Carolina State College, and Wilkinson High School march past the All-Star Bowling Alley in a demonstration against the segregated facility in 1968. One of many incidents during this era was the 1968 Orangeburg Massacre, which resulted in two college students, Samuel Hammond Jr. and Henry E. Smith, and one high school student, Delano Middleton, being killed on the front lawn of South Carolina State University. (Courtesy of Cecil Williams.)

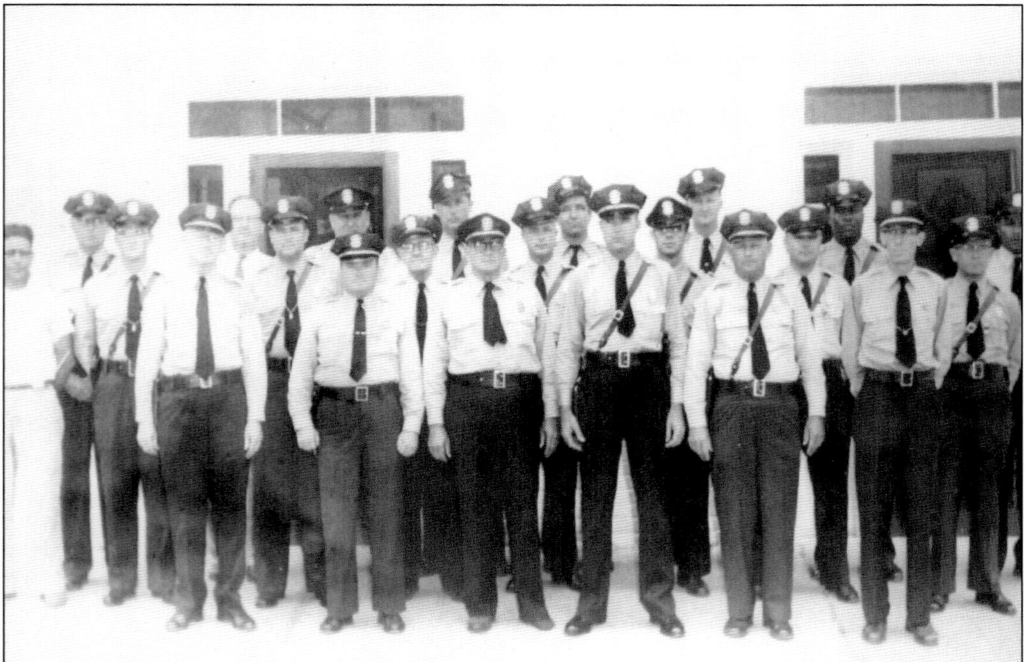

The Orangeburg City Police Department poses for a photograph in the late 1950s. Marion Harrison (back row, second from left) and Joseph Hodges (back row, last on right) were the only blacks employed as policemen at that time. (Courtesy of the City of Orangeburg.)

Dr. Joseph Rice was the first African American superintendent of Orangeburg County School District No. 2 in Bowman. Before consolidation of the schools in 1970, there were eight districts that merged into three. In 1970, Dr. Mildred Rice became one of the first African American teachers to participate in the integration of Orangeburg High School. In 1991, she became the first African American female hired as director of the Calhoun-Orangeburg Vocational Education Center after being coordinator of student services in 1980. (Courtesy of Mr. and Mrs. Joseph Rice Jr.)

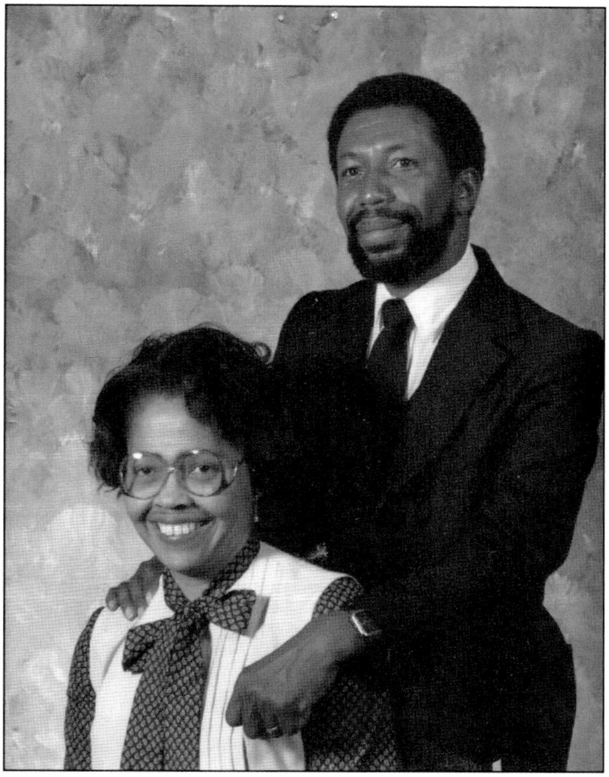

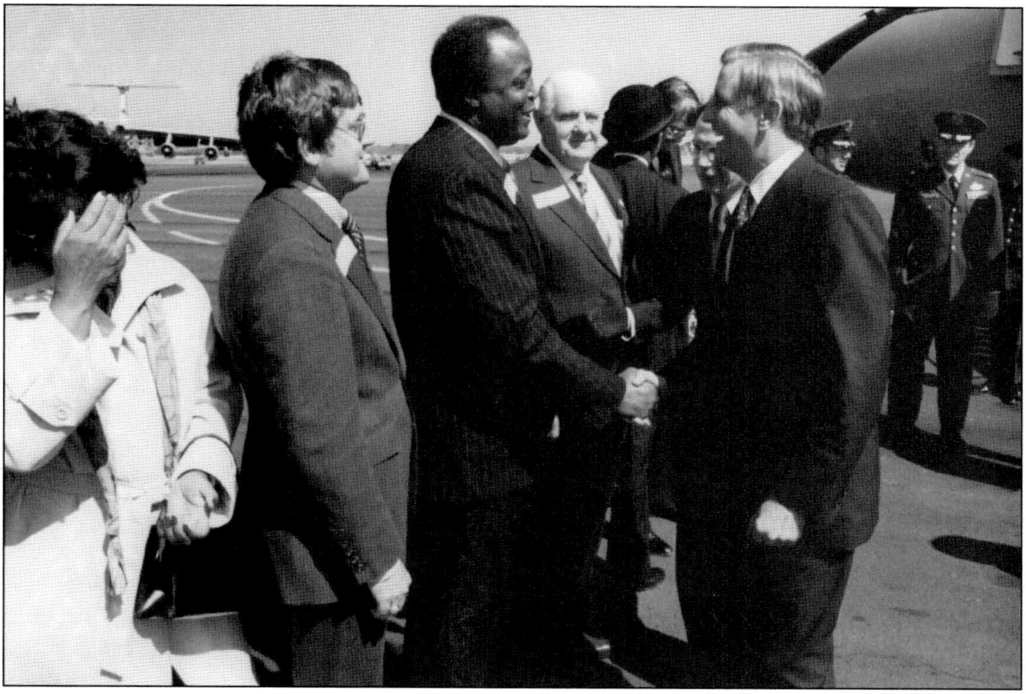

State representative Earl Middleton of Orangeburg welcomes Vice Pres. Walter Mondale to South Carolina at the Charleston Air Force Base in March 1980. Mondale was visiting states while on the campaign trail. (Courtesy of Joy Barnes.)

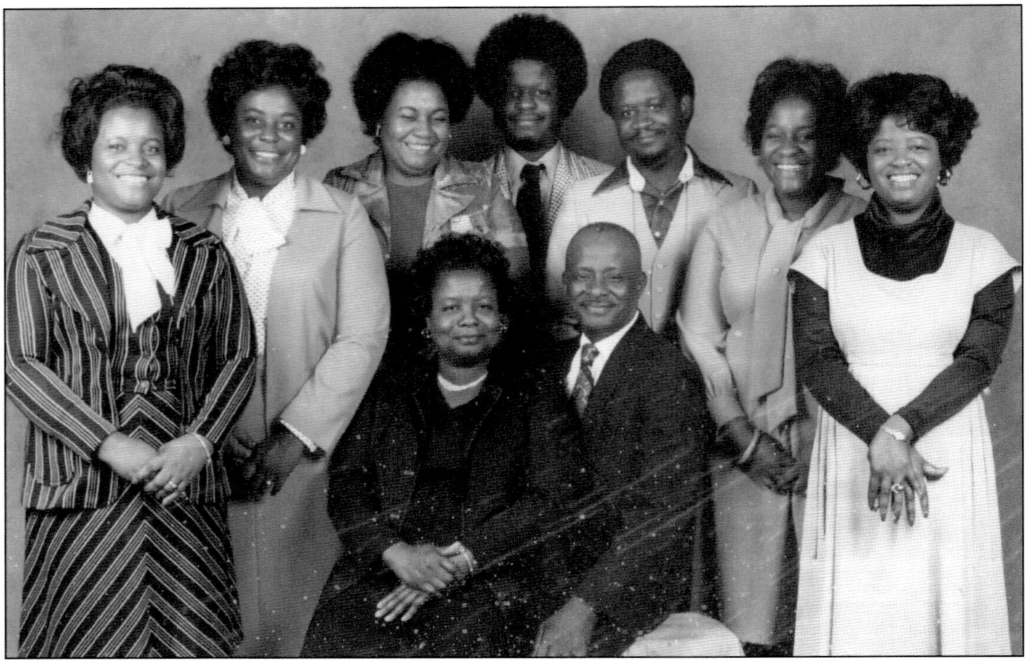

The Simpson family poses for a family photograph in 1978. Ruth and John Simpson (front, seated) were sharecroppers in the early 1950s. Ruth convinced her husband to move from the farm in order to make a better life for their seven children (shown standing from left to right): Ruth, Beatrice, Frances, Frank, Johnny, Catherine, and Ellen. They both found employment at various jobs in Orangeburg. Sometimes, they both worked two jobs to make ends meet. Ruth always stressed the importance of education in her household. All seven children finished college, some completed master's degrees, and one obtained a law degree. (Courtesy of Johnny Simpson.)

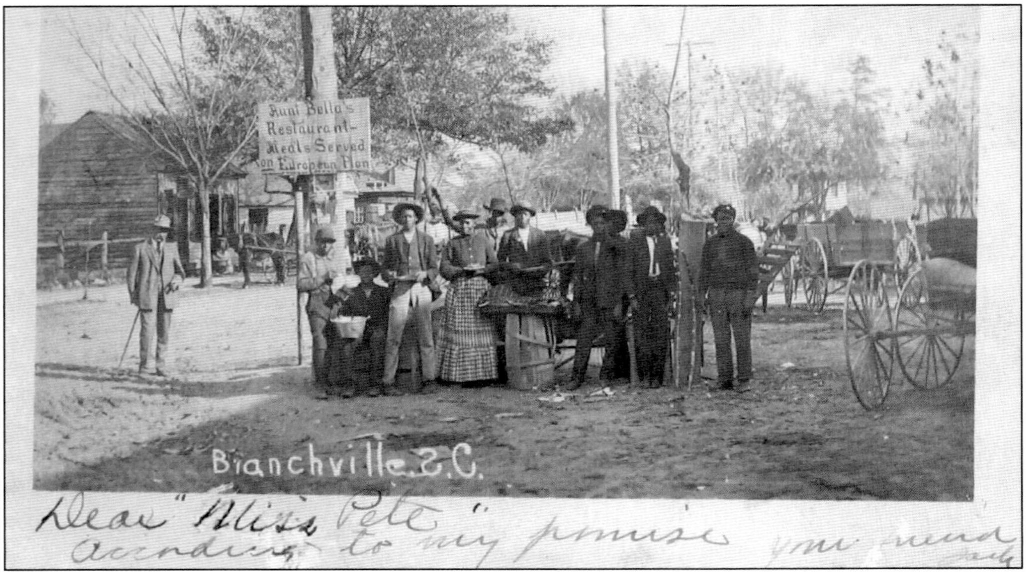

African Americans pose for a picture in Branchville in 1907. Branchville is located at the extreme southeastern tip of Orangeburg County. The town is known for having the oldest railroad depot in the nation. Every year, the town hosts the Raylrode Daze Festivul during the last weekend in September. (Courtesy of South Caroliniana Library, University of South Carolina, Columbia.)

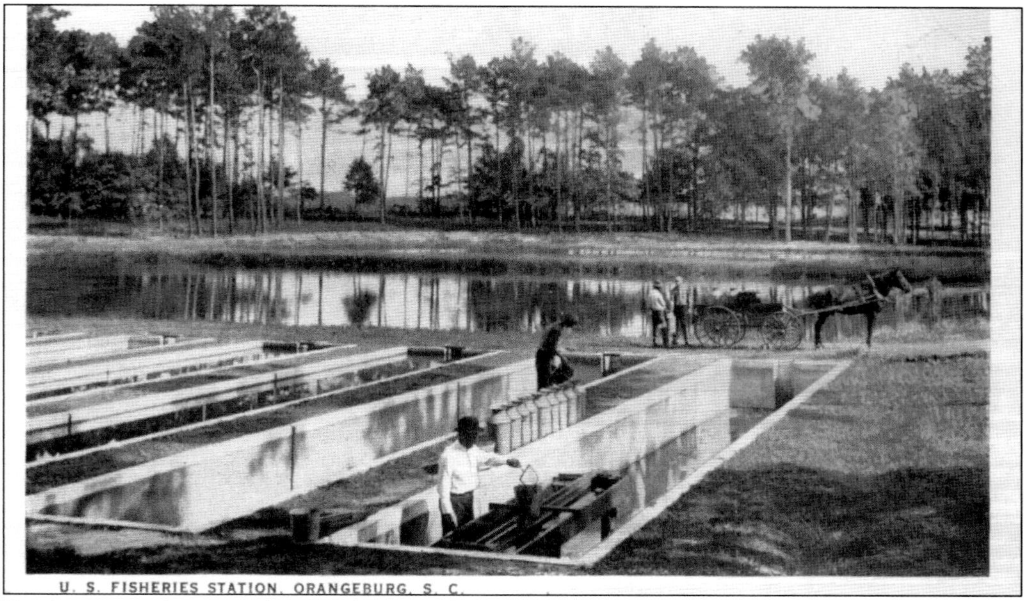

Employees are shown working at the US Fishery in the early 1900s. (Courtesy of South Caroliniana Library, University of South Carolina, Columbia.)

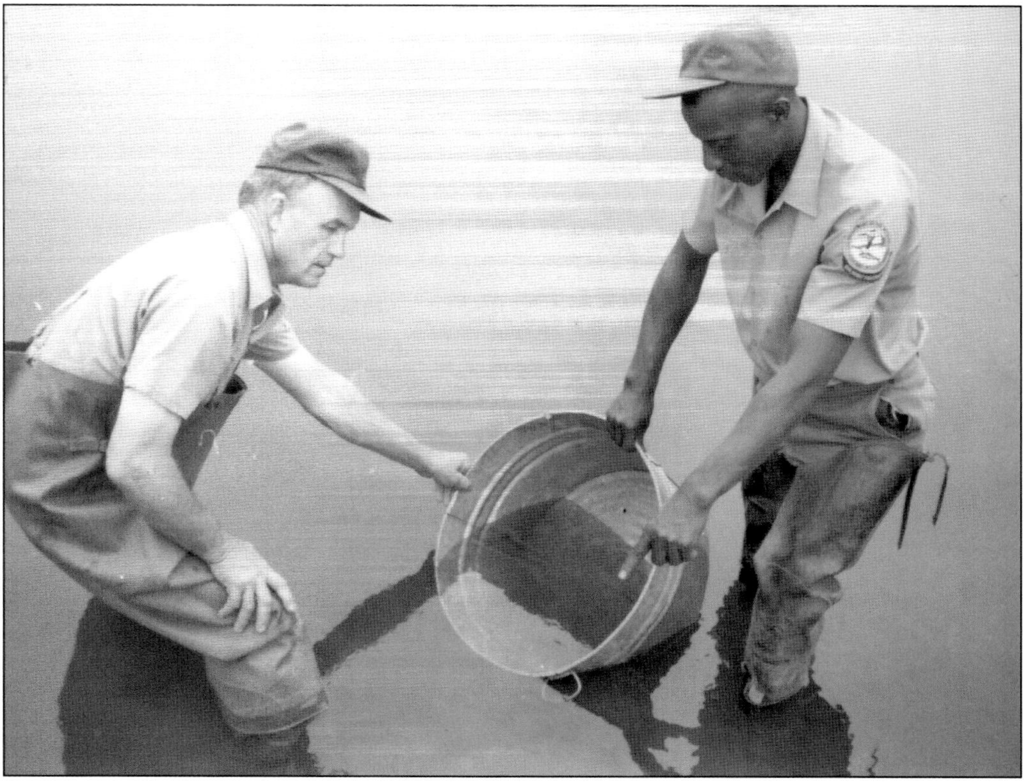

Linwood Carter (left) and Roy Felder stock a pond with largemouth bass at the Orangeburg National Fish Hatchery in 1971. The hatchery continues to produce a number of species, including striped bass, bluegill sunfish, lake sturgeon, and redbreast sunfish. These fish are used to stock streams throughout the Southeast. (Courtesy of Orangeburg National Fish Hatchery.)

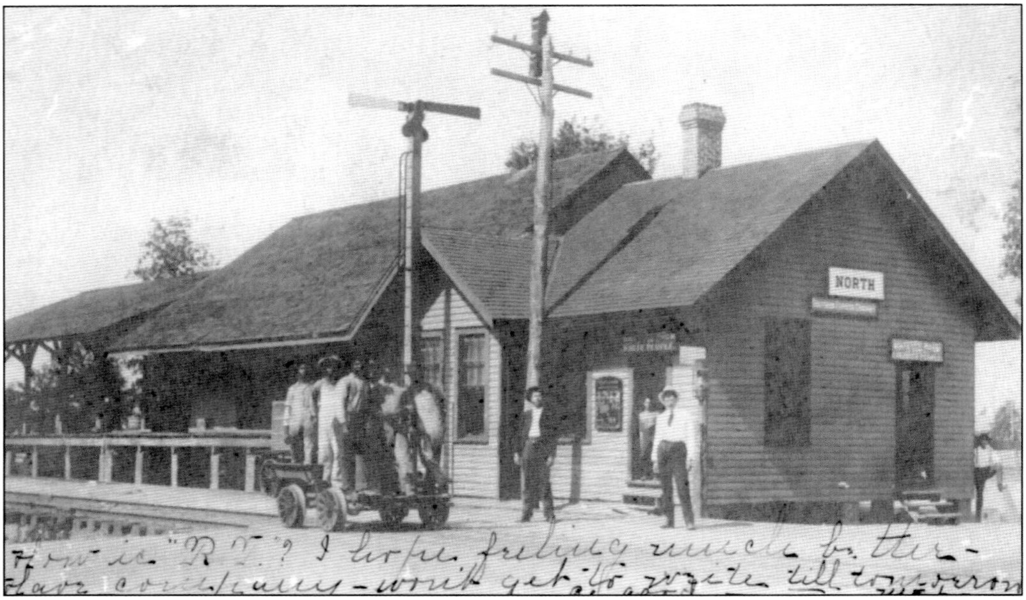

The town of North's first depot and cotton platform was built in 1905; this photograph was taken two years later. The town of North is home to North Air Base, an auxiliary field for Charleston Air Force Base, used in training C-141 pilots. (Courtesy of South Caroliniana Library, University of South Carolina, Columbia.)

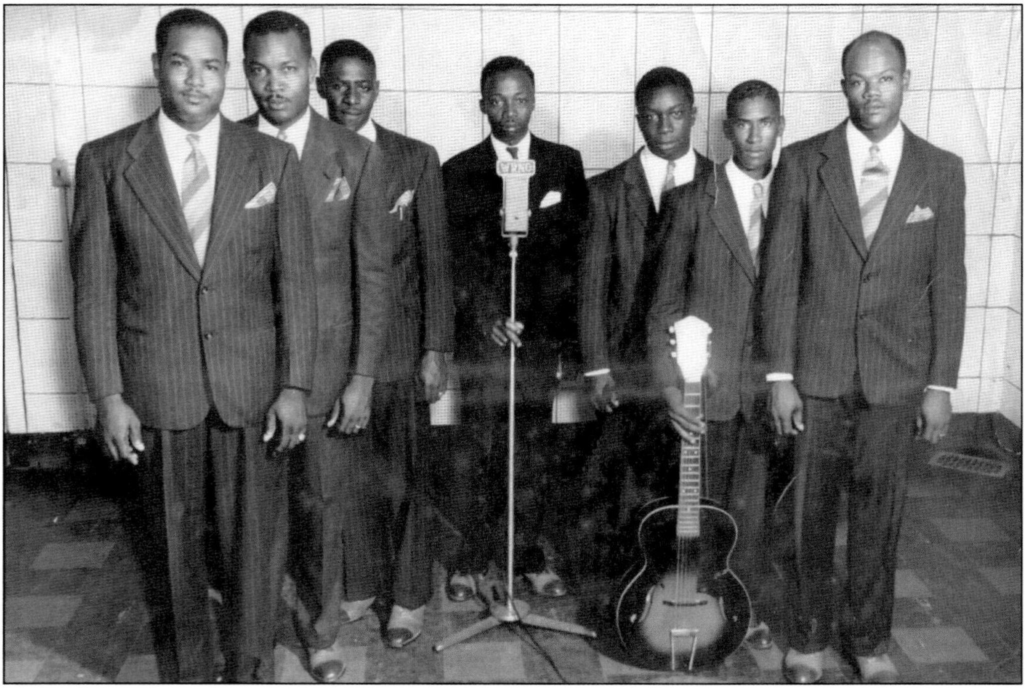

The Gospel Holy Lights, a local gospel group in Orangeburg, was known throughout Orangeburg County. In 1951, the group posed for a photograph at Sharp Studio on College Avenue in Orangeburg. They were the first African American gospel group to sing on WTND Radio on Five Chop Road. Pictured from left to right are John H. Johnson, Elijah Cobbs, Clifton Reid, Willie Spigner, Sammie Seawright, John Fersner, and James Johnson. (Courtesy of Helen Reid.)

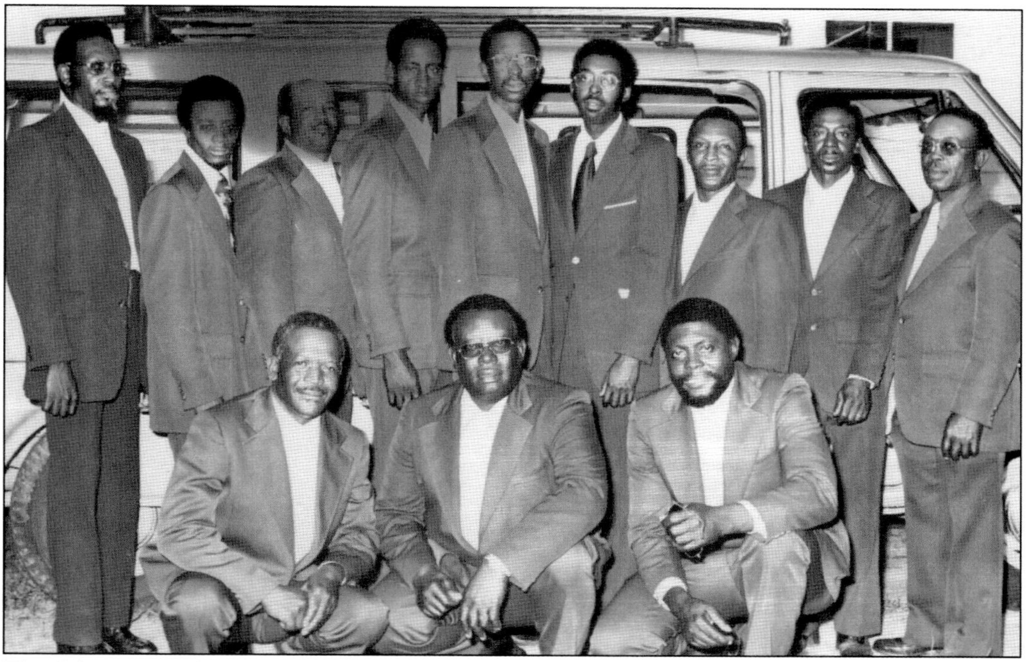

The Silver Stars Quintet of Holly Hill was started in 1936 by Robert White, who was also the group's first manager. Ernest Brown became the manager after White; then, after Brown became sick, Nehemiah Smalls became the group's manager. Over the years, the group has undergone many personnel changes, but the Silver Stars continue to sing and spread the word of God through songs. (Courtesy of Nehemiah Smalls.)

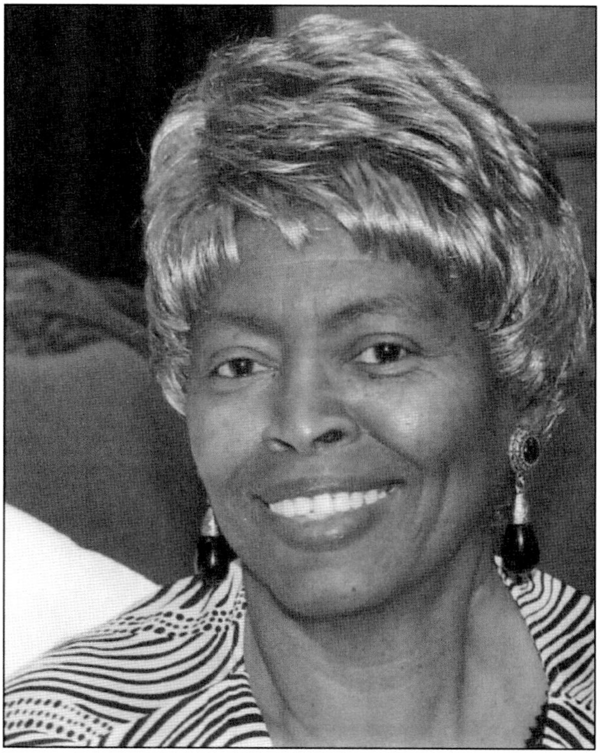

Barbara Clark is a retired educator, professional counselor, and a presenter, poet, and author. She received her bachelor's degree from MSU/Baltimore, a master's degree from South Carolina State University, and a specialist degree from South Carolina State University and the University of South Carolina. She has authored 12 books and coauthored the *KIDS in Character* book for elementary children with Frank Martin. (Courtesy of Barbara Clark.)

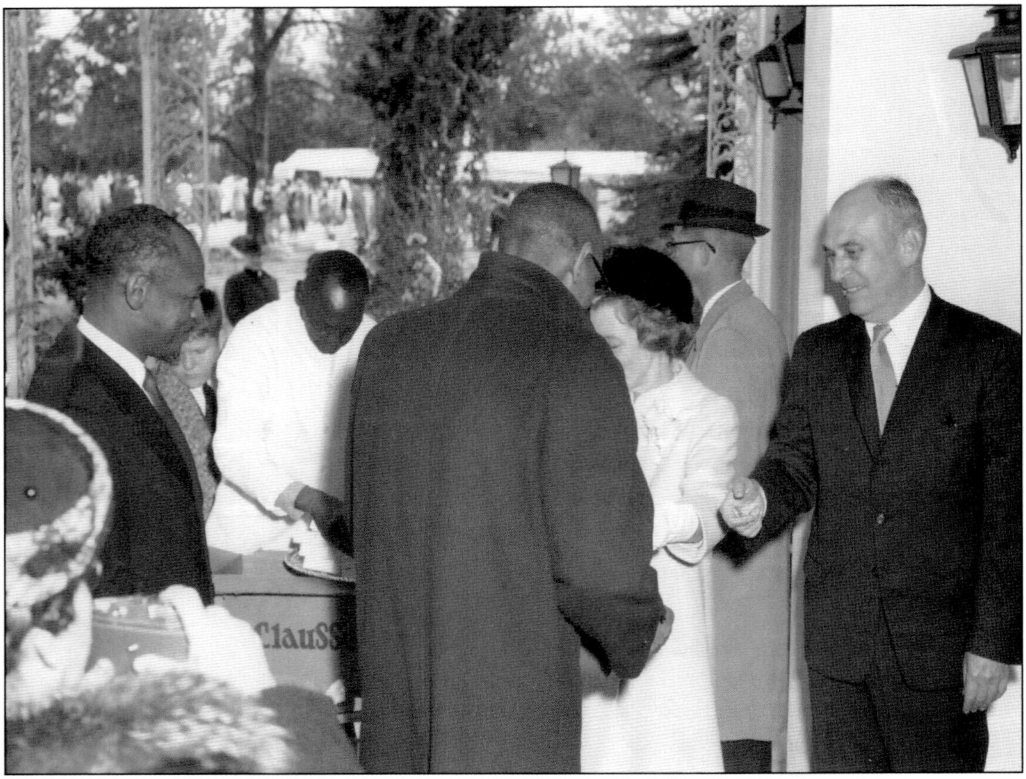

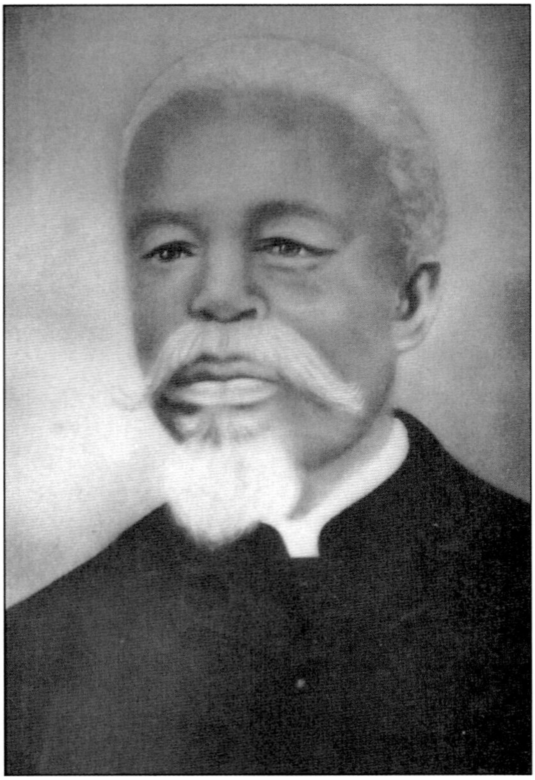

Rev. J. Herbert Nelson (center), I. Dequincy Newman (left), and others attend Gov. Donald Russell's inauguration at the capitol. This day, January 3, 1963, was a historic one for African Americans in Columbia. Governor Russell prepares to shake Reverend Nelson's hand at the inaugural affair. (Courtesy of Jonalee Nelson.)

Abram Middleton (1847–1901) was a Methodist minister, skilled carpenter, and mechanic. He is credited with building 28 churches during his career. The first trustee board of Claflin College consisted of four whites and four blacks. These blacks were Samuel Weston, Abram Middleton, J.A. Sasportas, and Thomas I. Phillips. Middleton attended private schools in Charleston, South Carolina, and the Baker Bible Institute, entering the first class of enrollment. He was the grandfather of legislator Earl Middleton. (Courtesy of Kenneth Middleton.)

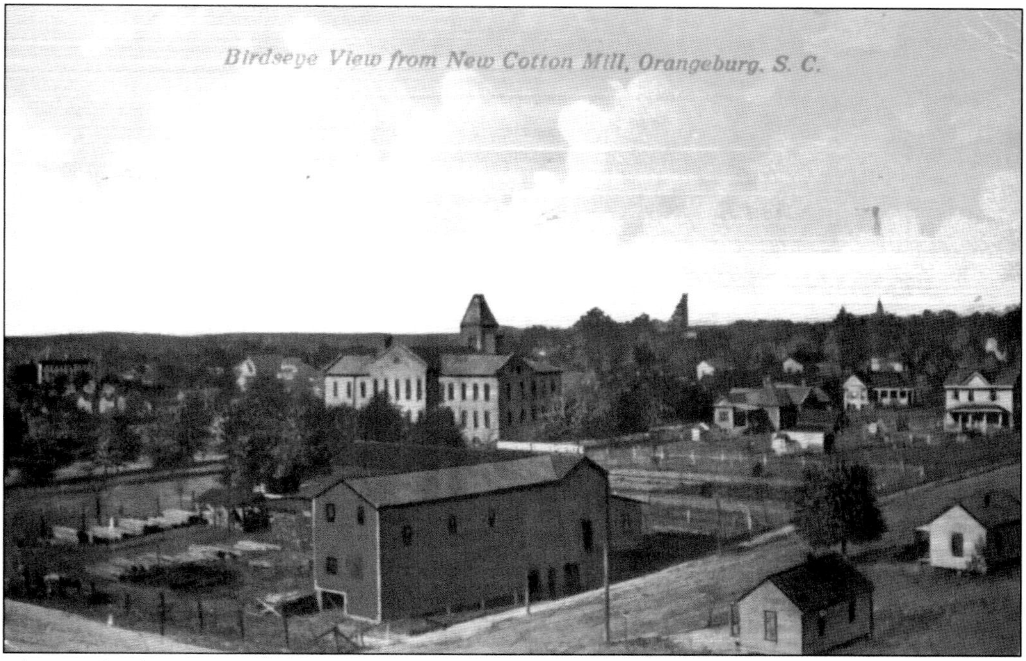

This is a bird's-eye view of the New Cotton Mill in Orangeburg. The postcard is inscribed with the year 1916. Cotton was king during the early and mid-1900s. (Courtesy of South Caroliniana Library, University of South Carolina, Columbia.)

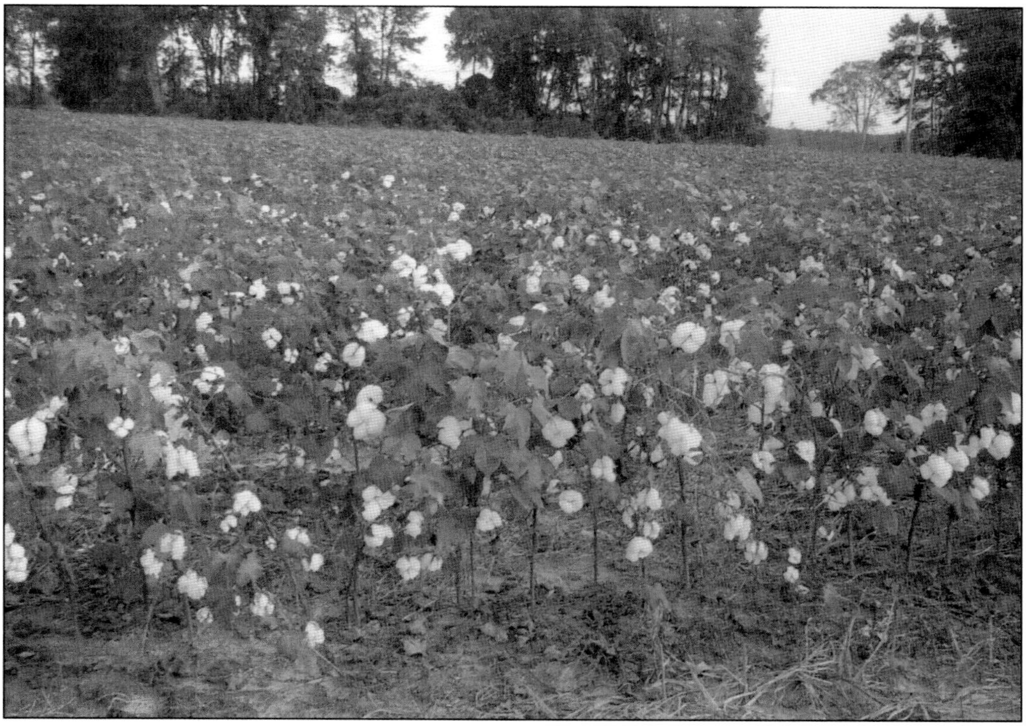

A field of cotton such as this was a familiar site to those traveling through the South during the 1900s. One of the biggest news events each year was the ginning of the first bale of cotton for the season in Orangeburg County. (Courtesy of Lauritza Hill.)

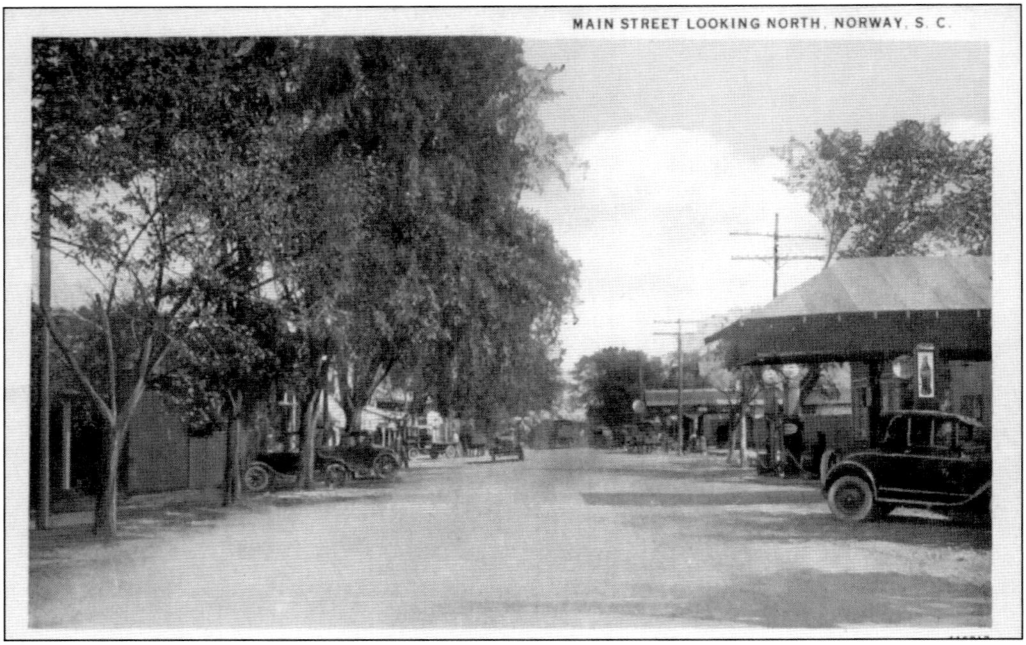

This postcard shows Main Street in Norway, a rural town on the western edge of Orangeburg County. According to town history, Norway was founded in 1891 and almost lost its name when the similarity between North and Norway nearly caused a train wreck. Railroaders began calling the small town Waynor in order to avoid chaos. (Courtesy of South Caroliniana Library, University of South Carolina, Columbia.)

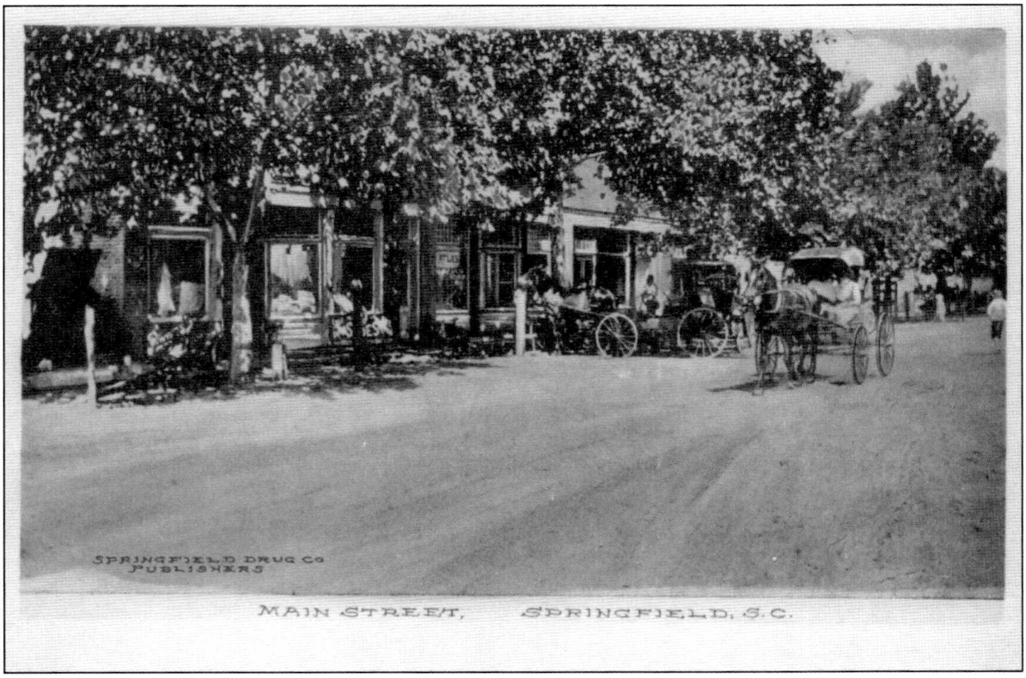

Main Street in Springfield, a rural town in Orangeburg County, is shown in this postcard. The Governor's Frog Jump and large flea markets are major attractions in this town. (Courtesy of South Caroliniana Library, University of South Carolina, Columbia.)

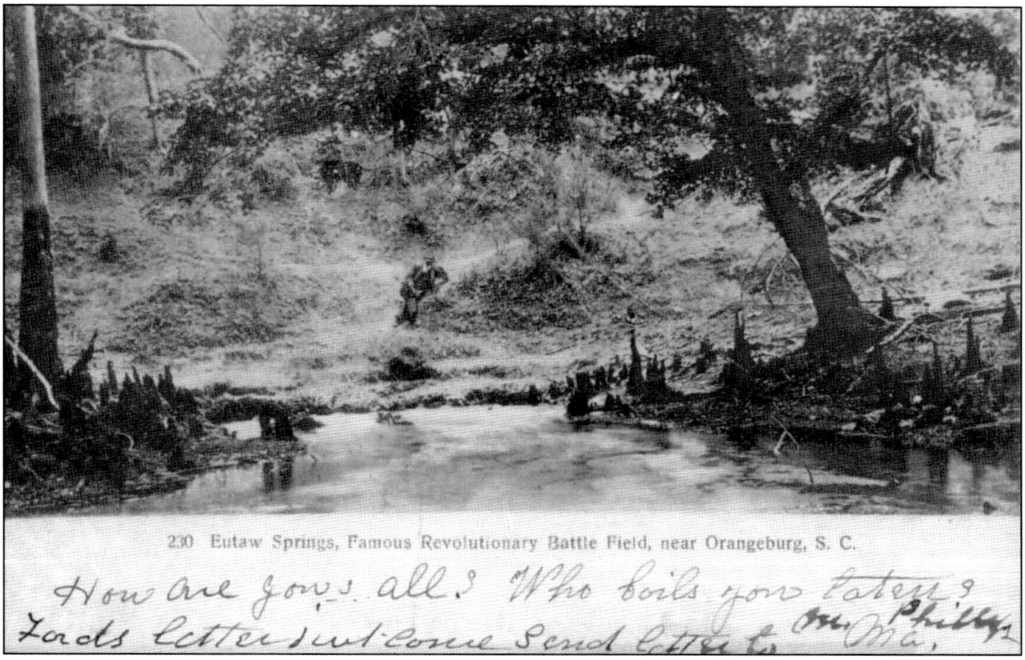

Eutaw Springs was the site of a Revolutionary War battle near Orangeburg. Eutaw Springs is located near the town of Eutawville. This postcard is postmarked 1907. (Courtesy of South Caroliniana Library, University of South Carolina, Columbia.)

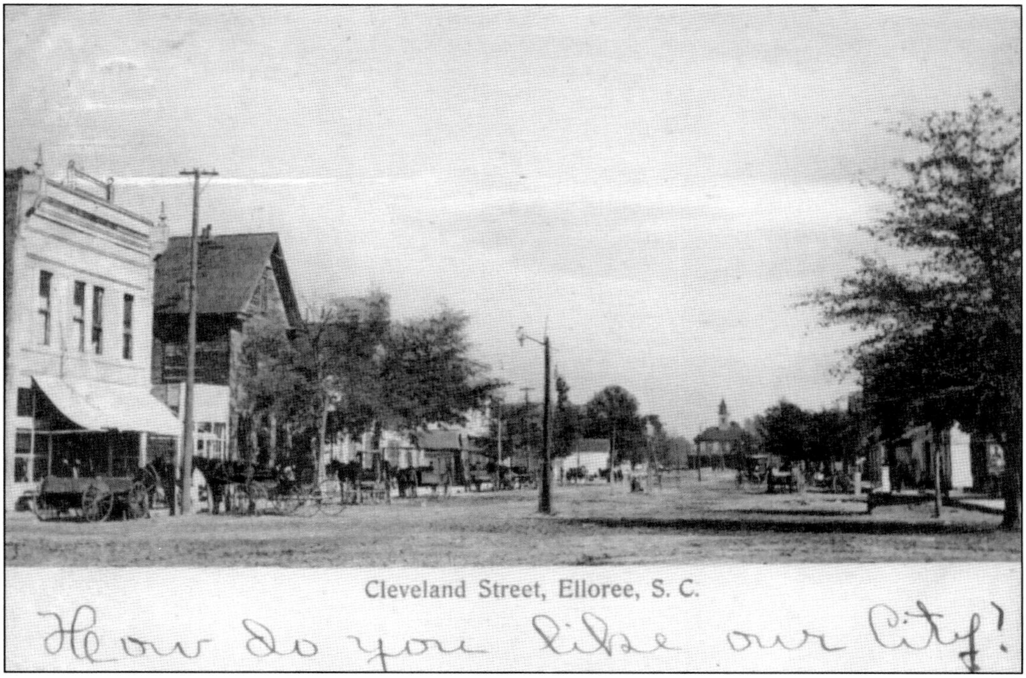

Cleveland Street in Elloree is shown in this postcard, postmarked in 1908. Elloree's major attraction is the famous Elloree Trials, attended by horse lovers every March. (Courtesy of South Caroliniana Library, University of South Carolina, Columbia.)

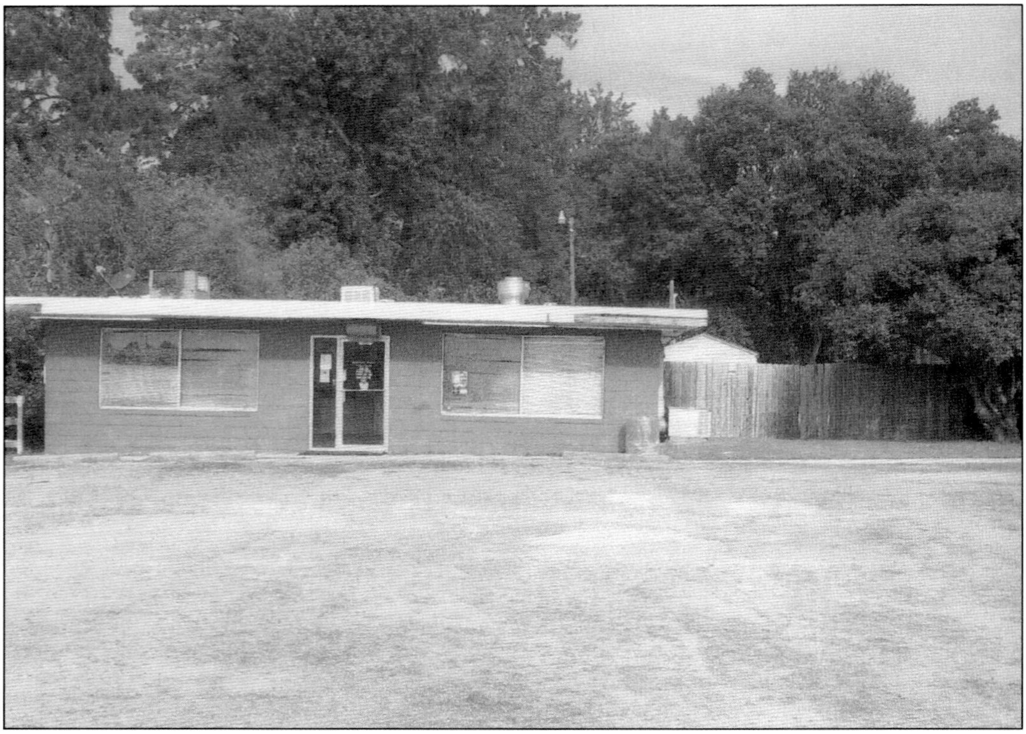

This is a photograph of the Brown Derby restaurant in Orangeburg as it stands now. It was opened in 1954 by Emma and Adam Brown. Always a familiar site in the community, this popular restaurant is still known for its soul food menu and barbecue dinners. (Courtesy of Lauritza Hill.)

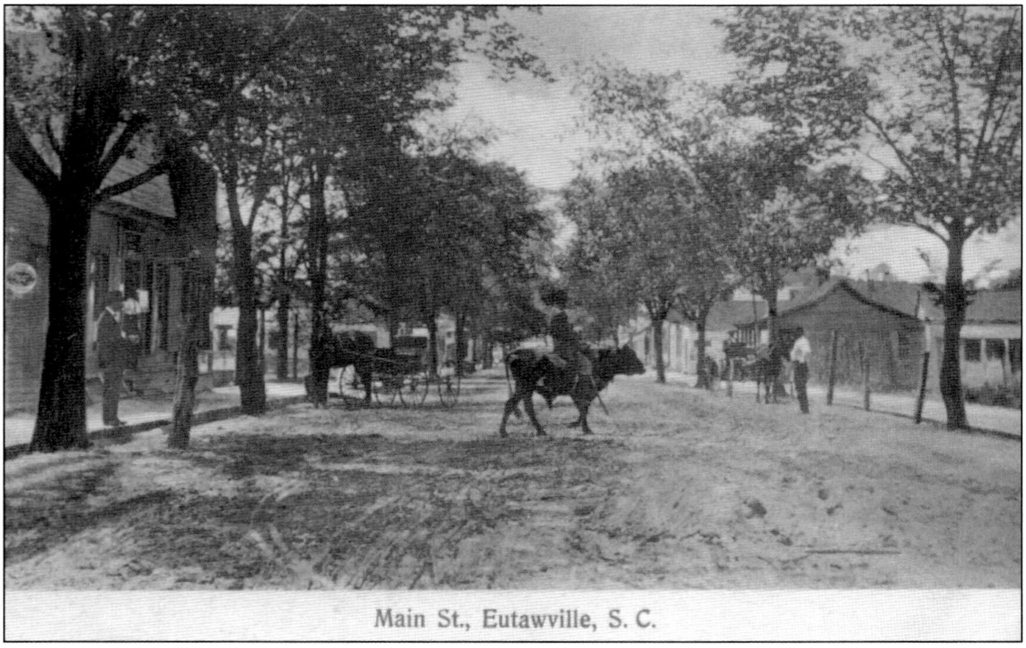

This is a view of Main Street in Eutawville, a rural town in Orangeburg County. The battle of Eutaw Springs, on September 8, 1781, was the last major Revolutionary War battle in South Carolina. (Courtesy of South Caroliniana Library, University of South Carolina, Columbia.)

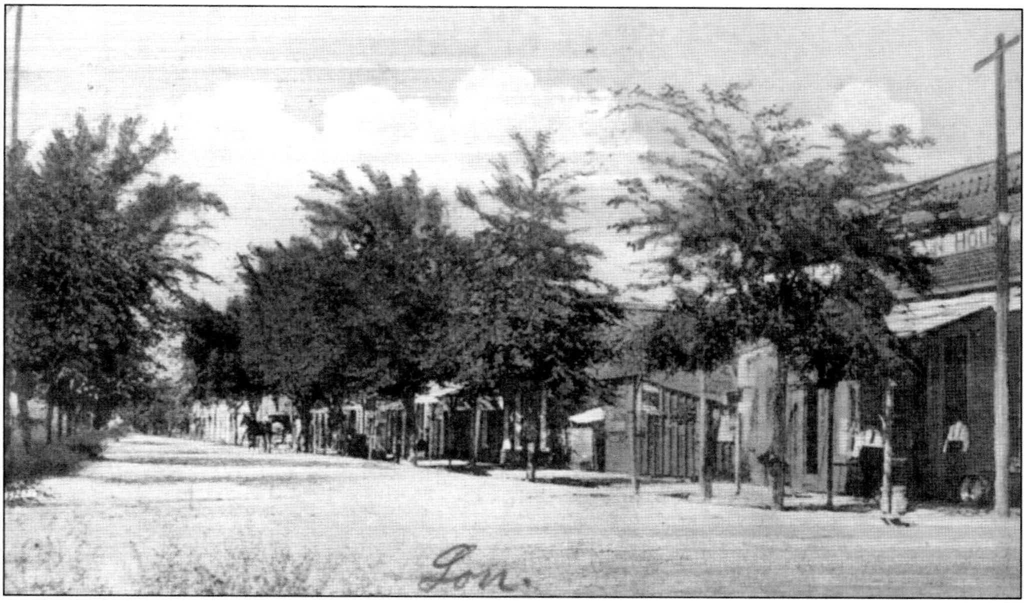

This postcard shows Main Street in North. According to local history, the town was incorporated in 1892. Like many towns established during the 1800s, it was named for its first mayor, John F. North. Residents are never at a loss for conversation. They only have to say that they are from North, South Carolina, and wait for a response. (Courtesy of South Caroliniana Library, University of South Carolina, Columbia.)

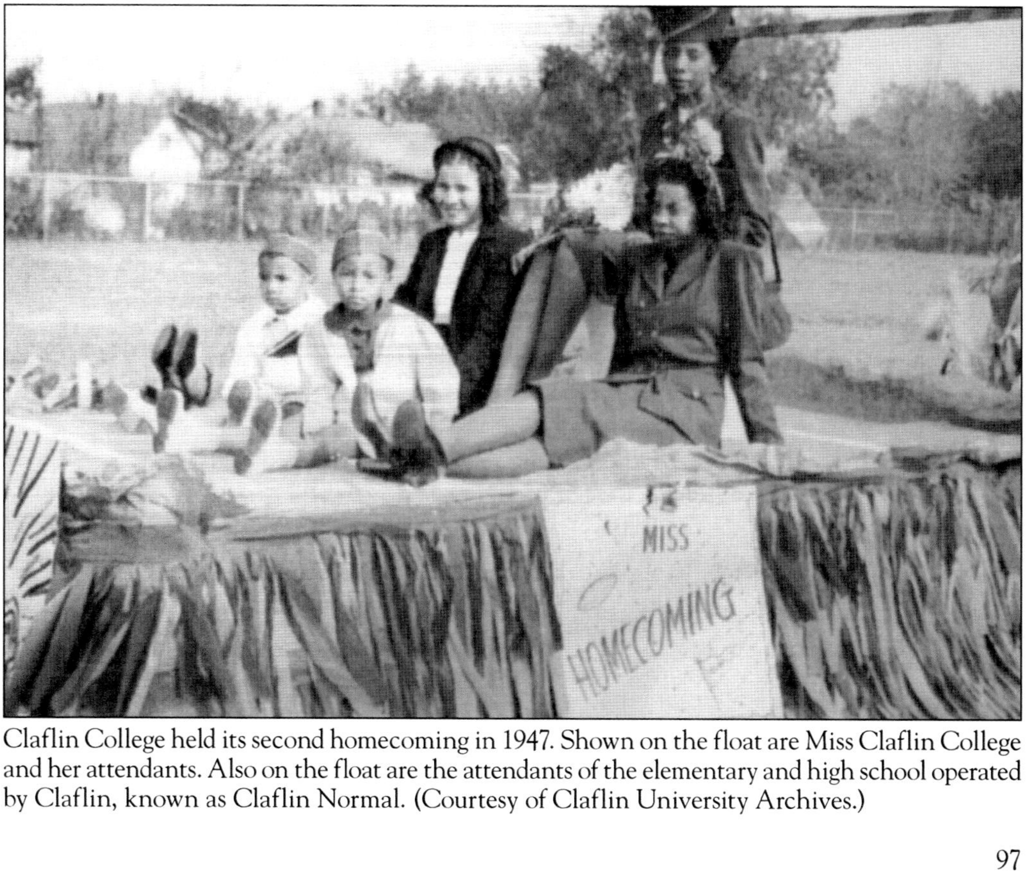

Claflin College held its second homecoming in 1947. Shown on the float are Miss Claflin College and her attendants. Also on the float are the attendants of the elementary and high school operated by Claflin, known as Claflin Normal. (Courtesy of Claflin University Archives.)

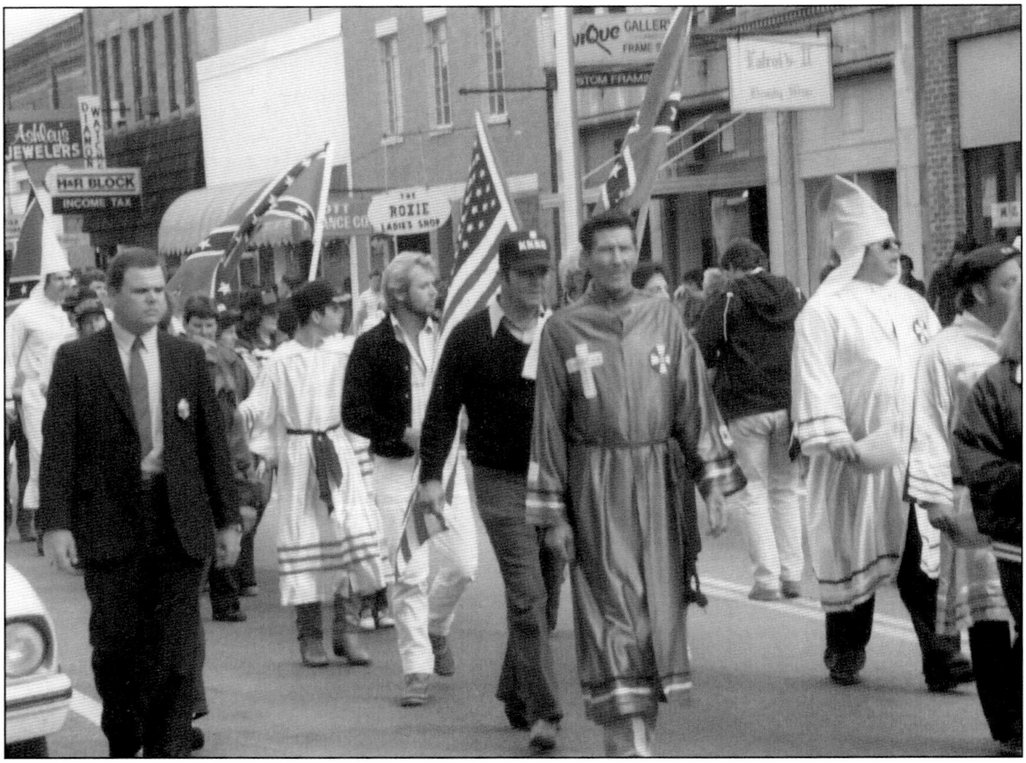

The Ku Klux Klan was still in existence and marched through downtown Orangeburg with their Confederate flags as late as the 1980s. The only African Americans in attendance were a few curious bystanders. (Courtesy of Carl Kennerly.)

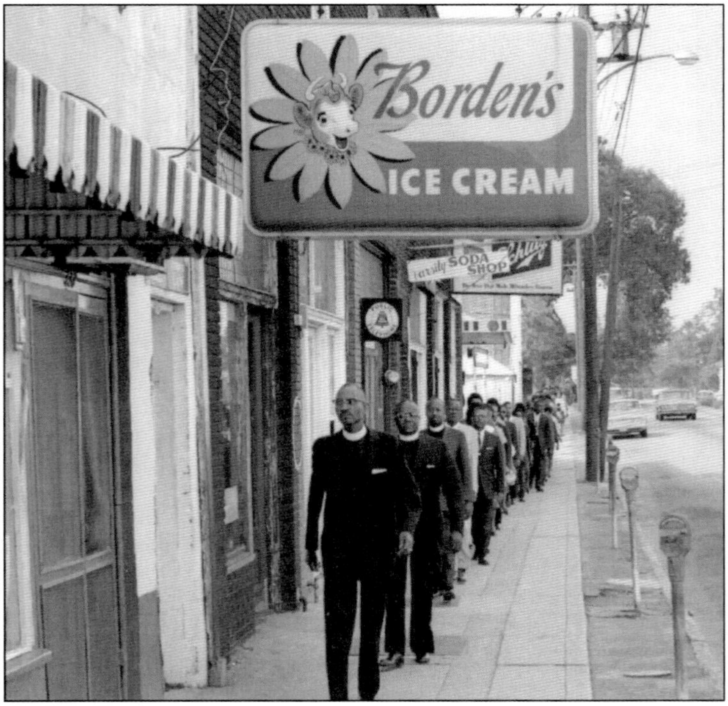

Rev. J. Herbert Nelson led a massive nonviolent demonstration in Orangeburg in 1963. Ministers and community members vividly displayed their dissatisfaction with the social inequities of segregation. Shown marching are, from front to back, Reverend Nelson, Rev. J.W. Curry, Rev. Chappelle Davis, an unidentified protester, Elease Thomas, Dr. Charles H. Thomas, and a multitude of others—students and ordinary working people in the community. (Courtesy of Cecil Williams.)

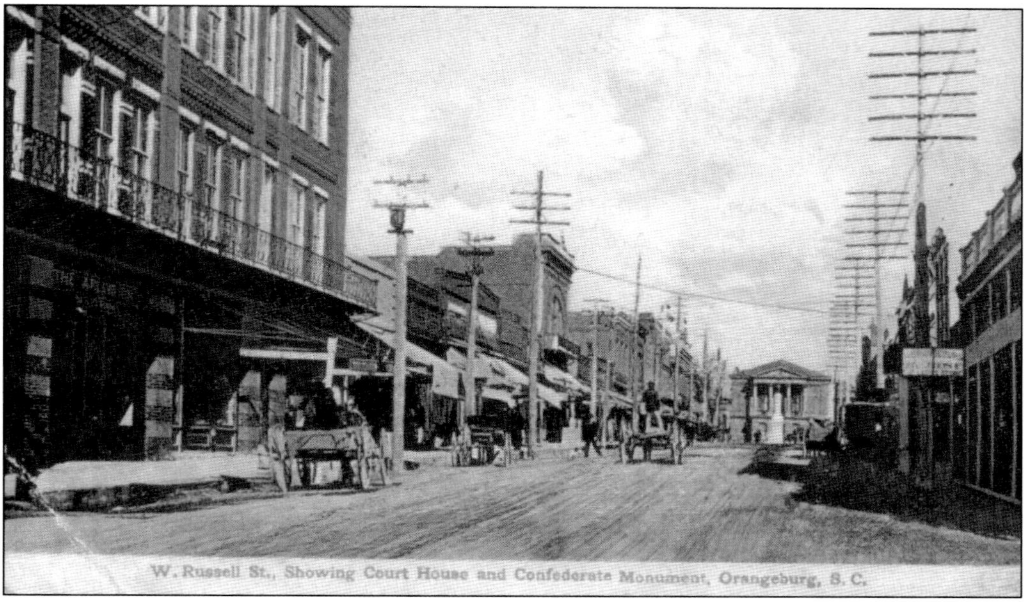

This postcard from the early 1900s shows West Russell Street in Orangeburg, including the Confederate monument. The city of Orangeburg serves as the county seat. In 1704, an Indian trader named George Sterling was said to be the first to come to the area, which became known as the Orangeburg District. (Courtesy of South Caroliniana Library, University of South Carolina, Columbia.)

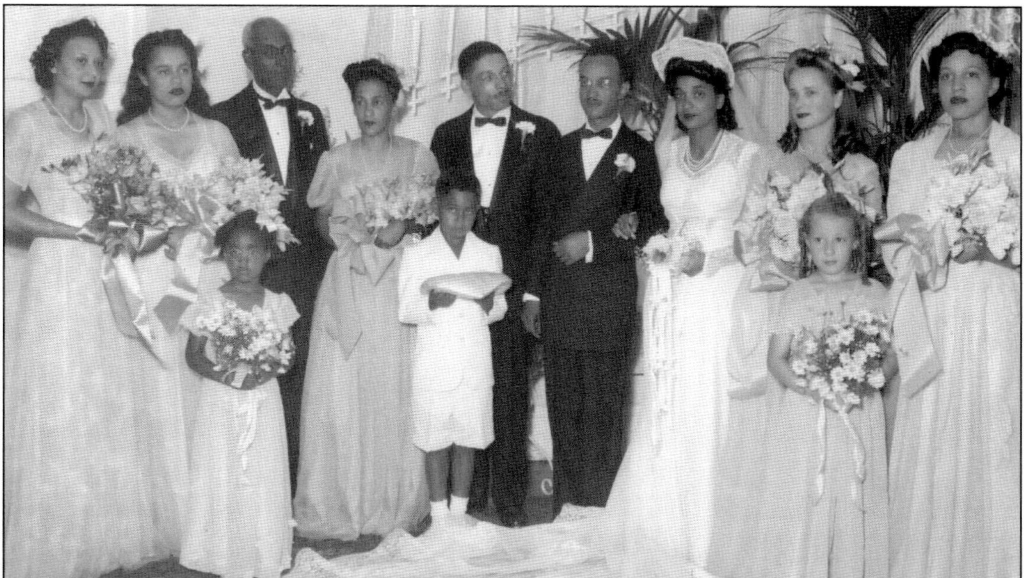

Shown here is the wedding of Reginald R. Thomasson and Carmen H. Sulton in 1945. The bride's dress and headpiece were designed and made by Annie Bell Williams, a sewing instructor at South Carolina State College. In 1966, Williams Hall, a dormitory for women at the college, was named in her honor. Pictured here are, from left to right, (first row) Valeda Thomasson, Hume Sulton Jr., and Angie Sheffield; (second row) Helen L. Daniels, Doris L. Best, John J. Sulton Jr., Isabel Evans, Carl Thomasson, Reginald Thomasson (groom), Carmen Sulton (bride), Marian Clarkson, and Kathleen Sulton. (Courtesy of Carmen Sulton Thomasson.)

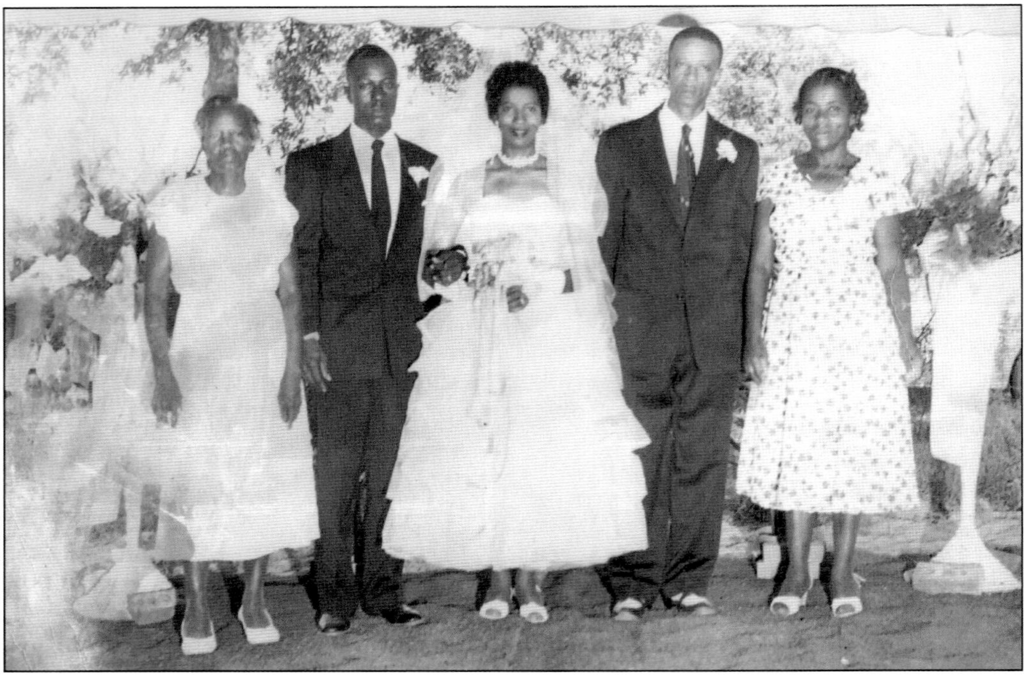

The wedding party of Ruth and Julius Harrison poses for a photograph in 1955. Shown from left to right are mother of the groom Angie Harrison, the groom, the bride, father of the bride Ellison Bradley, and mother of the bride Margaret Bradley. (Courtesy of Ruth Harrison.)

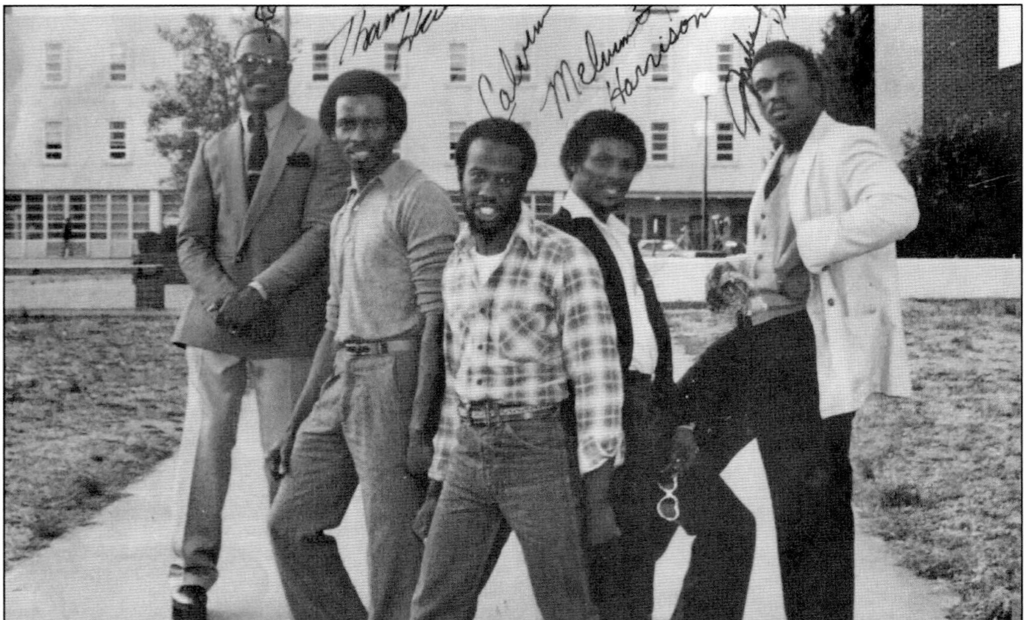

Small bands were popular among the colleges. This photograph shows the members of the band Freestyle Production standing in front of a building at South Carolina State College in the early 1970s. The members are, from left to right, Edward Johnson, Thomas Hunter, Calvin Boatwright, Melvin Harrison, and Jackie "Dink" Robinson. Other popular bands included the Showtakers, the Vibrations, the Soul Agents, and many more. (Courtesy of Jackie Robinson.)

Six

Pioneers and Trailblazers

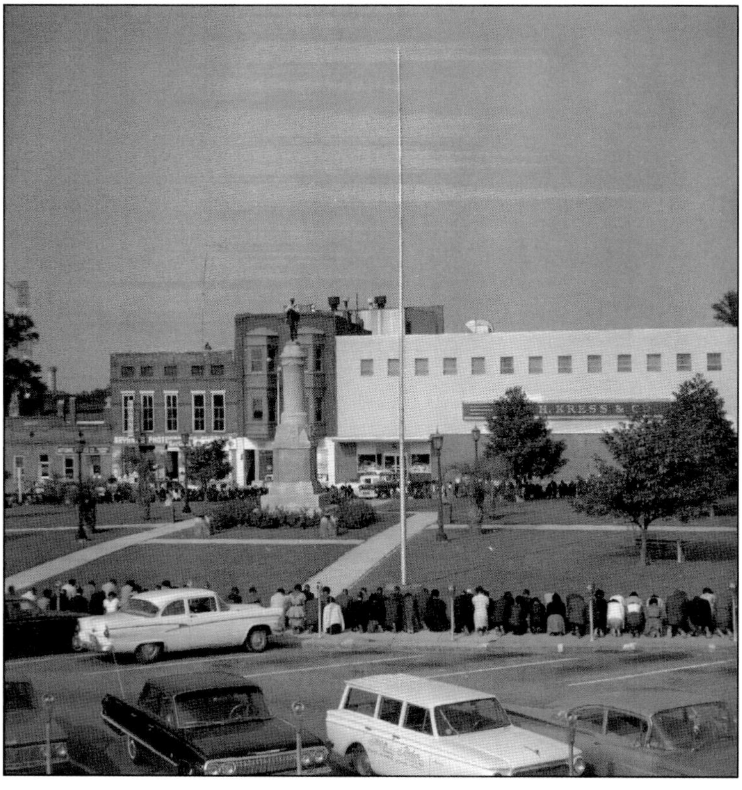

College students, church members, and others in the community rally around the town square to pray and to protest against segregation in 1963. The huge crowd of marchers in attendance indicates the tremendous support and commitment of the community for this cause. (Courtesy of Cecil Williams.)

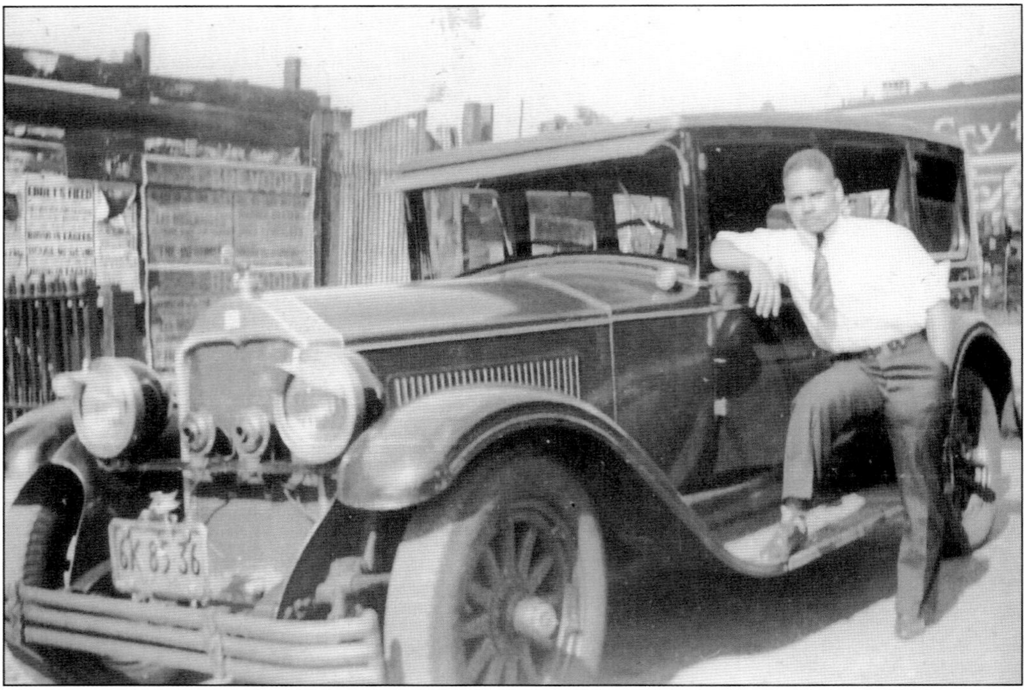

Brad Gaffney, cousin of Raymond Gaffney Sr., poses by his car in the early 1940s. He was a native of Orangeburg who went to New York for better opportunities. He moved back to Orangeburg for many years before returning to New York. (Courtesy of Lillie Gaffney.)

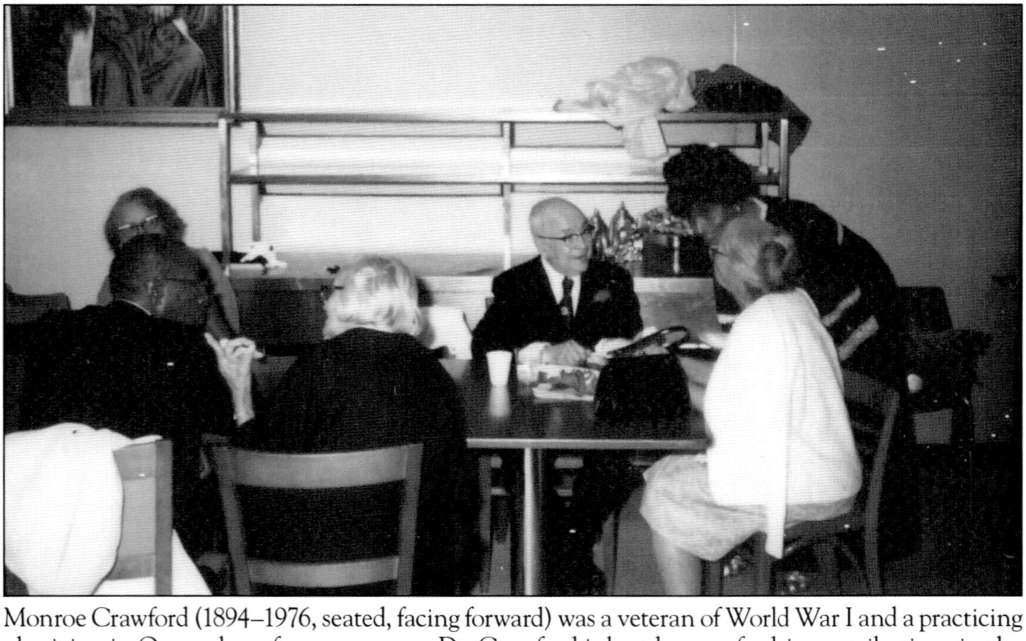

Monroe Crawford (1894–1976, seated, facing forward) was a veteran of World War I and a practicing physician in Orangeburg for many years. Dr. Crawford is best known for his contributions in the field of medicine. In 1927, he was recognized for diagnosing the first known case of Tularemia (rabbit fever) in South Carolina. In 1934, he received recognition for his special treatment of Malaria in Orangeburg County. His son Ernest was a surgeon in Houston and his other son George was an attorney in Orangeburg. (Courtesy of Shirley James.)

Dr. Spencer C. Disher was a practicing physician for over 50 years. He became an employee of the hospital in Orangeburg in 1970, and was the first African American chief of staff of the Regional Medical Center in 1988. He received his bachelor of science degree from South Carolina State College and his medical degree from Meharry Medical College in Nashville. (Courtesy of the Regional Medical Center.)

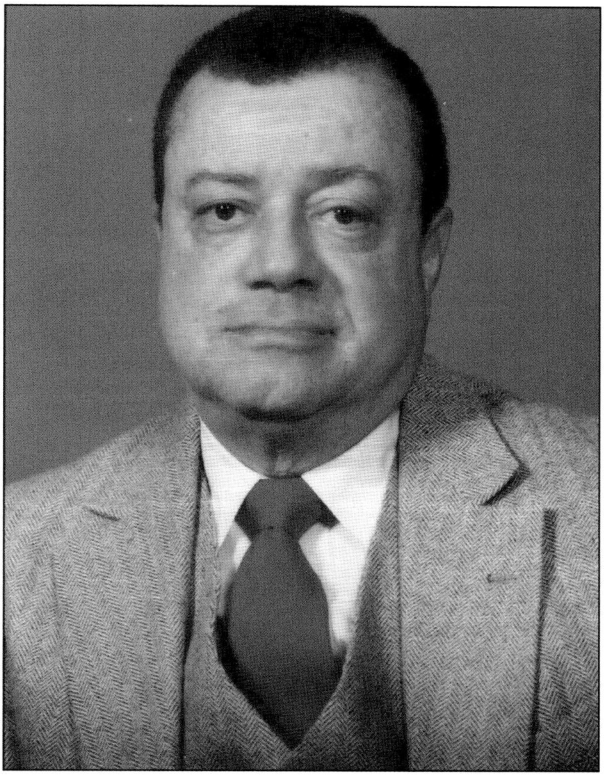

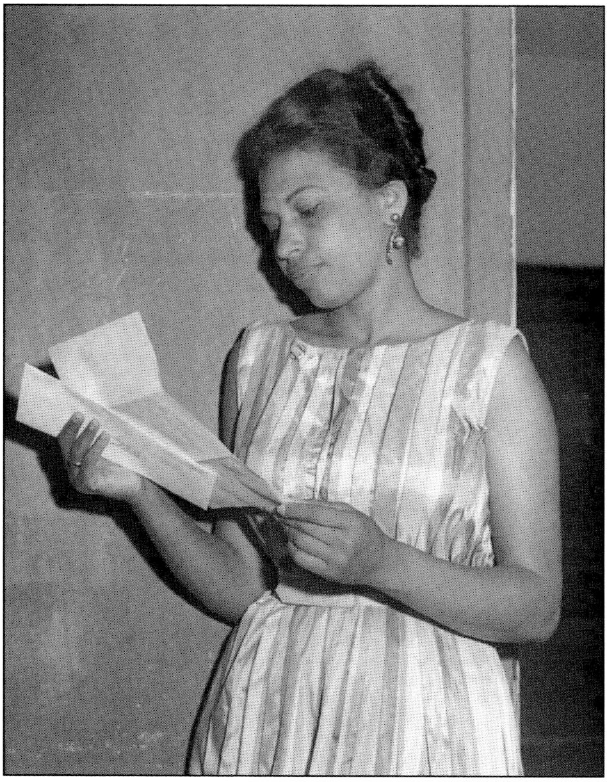

Gloria Rackley Blackwell, shown here around 1960, was an educator and civil rights activist. She is reading a letter stating that she was fired from a teaching position in the Orangeburg public school system because she refused to renounce her membership in the National Association for the Advancement of Colored People (NAACP). (Courtesy of Cecil Williams.)

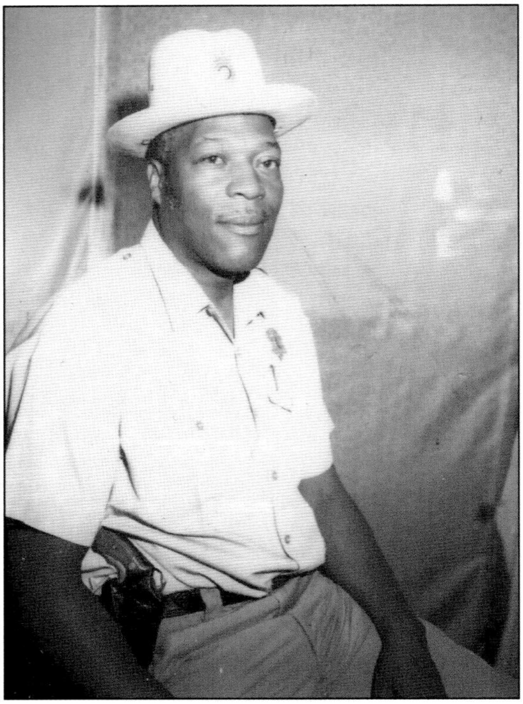

Marion Harrison, a World War II veteran, was one of the first African Americans hired by the Orangeburg Police Department and the first African American deputy sheriff hired by Orangeburg County, where he served for over 30 years. He was a 1952 graduate of the Colored Normal, Industrial, Agricultural, and Mechanical College, now South Carolina State University. (Courtesy of Edna Harrison.)

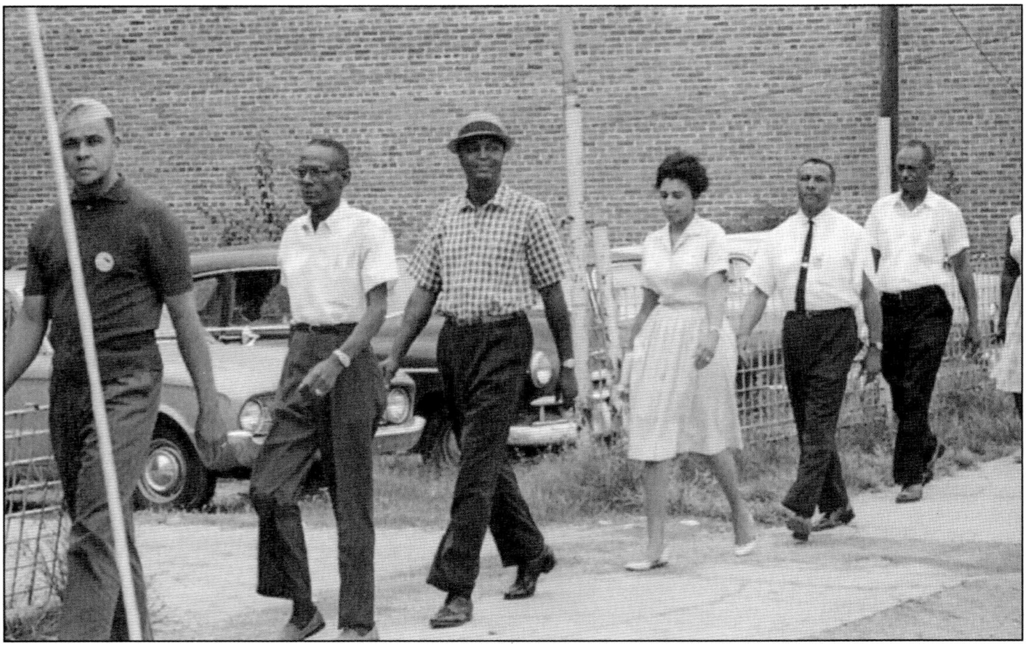

James Sulton (1923–2008) was a businessman, community leader, and a veteran of the US Army. He completed the high school program at Claflin University and continued his education at Morehouse College in Atlanta. He (far left) and a large group of citizens concerned about the inequalities of the segregationist system are shown in 1960 marching to the mayor's office to reiterate aims and objectives of the Orangeburg Movement. Others identified include, from left to right, John Brunson, Earl Middleton, Gloria Rackley Blackwell, Dr. Charles Thomas, Rev. I. DeQuincey Newman, and Katie Smith. (Courtesy of Cecil Williams.)

Benjamin Spells is a retired educator and magistrate of Holly Hill, South Carolina. He was principal of Roberts High School, now called Holly Hill–Roberts High School, from 1955 to 1981, and served as the local magistrate in Holly Hill for many years before retiring. There was tremendous progress in the growth of the school under his leadership. A new stadium was built and named in his honor. James Roberts was the previous principal of the school (1929–1955), which was then called Holly Hill Rosenwald Colored. (Courtesy of Benjamin Spells.)

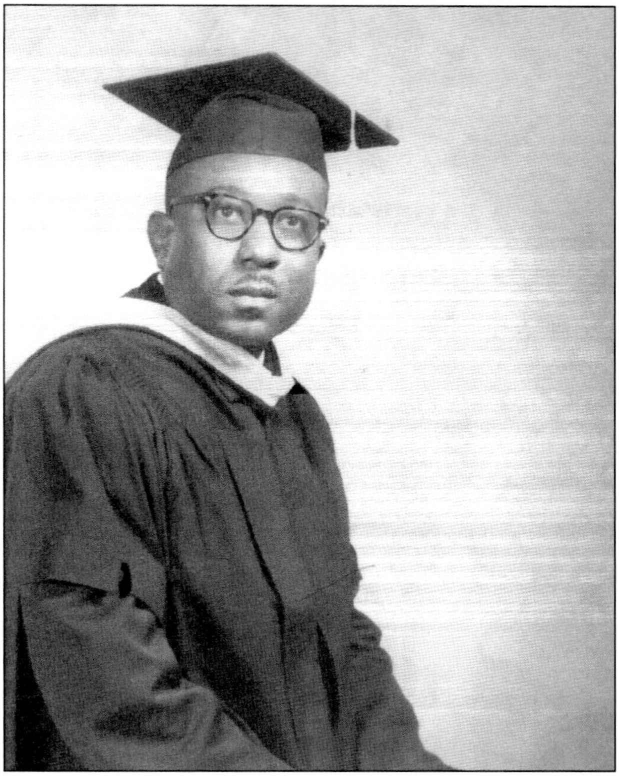

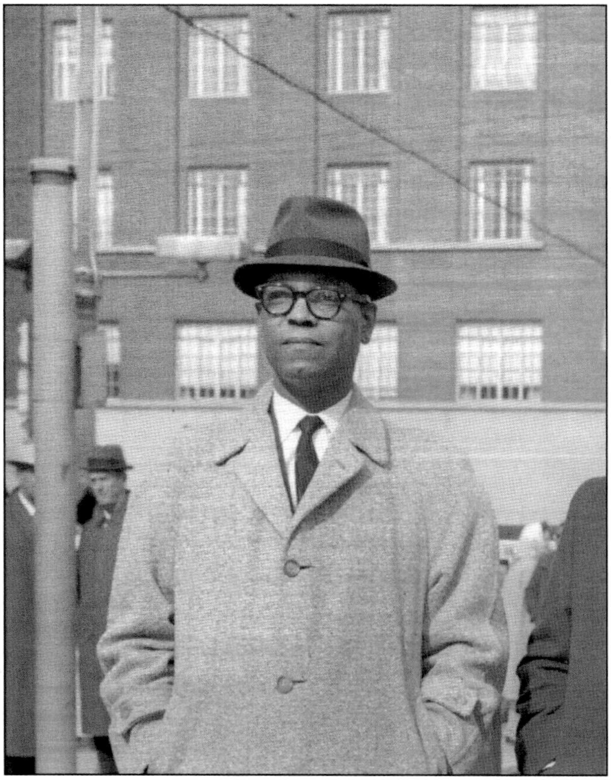

Matthew J. Perry Jr. (1921–2011) was a World War II veteran, lawyer, and civil rights pioneer. In 1976, he became South Carolina's first African American United States District Court judge. Perry became the first African American federal district judge when he was appointed by Pres. Jimmy Carter in 1979 to the United States District Court for the District of South Carolina. A 1951 graduate of South Carolina State College, Perry became a federal judge in 1976 with the support of Sen. Strom Thurmond. In 1961, Perry became chief counsel of the South Carolina state conference of the NAACP, a position he held for 20 years. (Courtesy of Cecil Williams.)

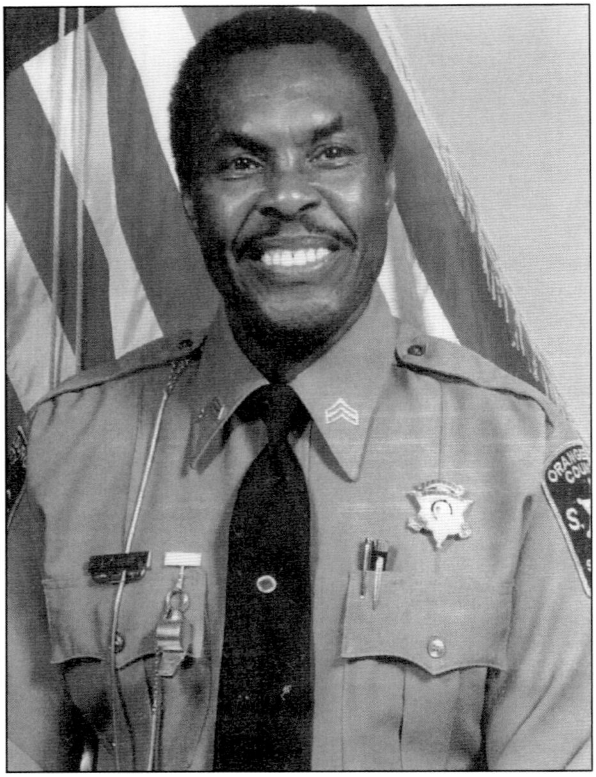

James Elmore (1931–2002) was self-employed as a master licensed plumber for more than 50 years and an honored reserve officer of the Orangeburg County sheriff's office. He was a graduate of the South Carolina Police Academy and received an honorary doctorate of humane letters from Claflin University. A member of the board of visitors, he was inducted into the Claflin Hall of Fame in 1997. The chapel on the Claflin campus is named in his honor. (Courtesy of Dorothy Elmore.)

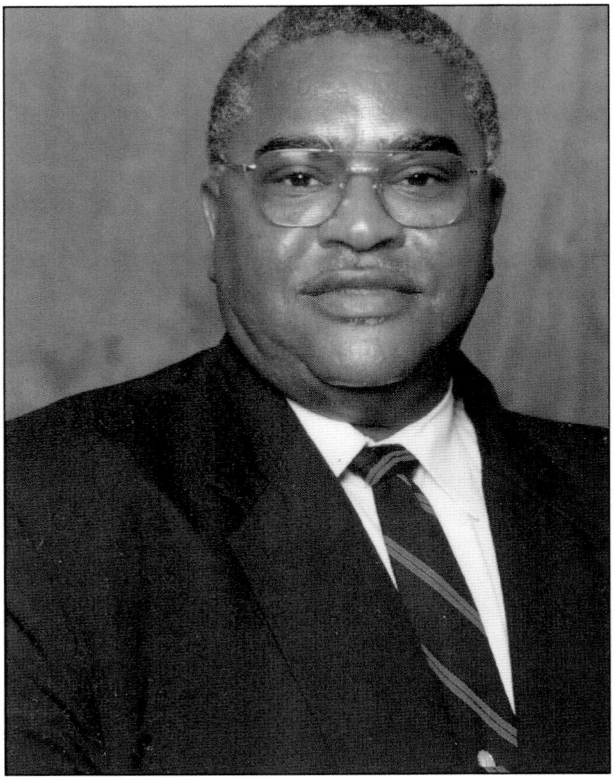

James "Poppa" Johnson was a lieutenant with the Orangeburg Department of Public Safety prior to his election as the first African American sheriff in Orangeburg County since Reconstruction. Edward Cain was the first African American sheriff, serving from 1872 to 1877. Johnson served as sheriff from 1997 to 2000. He also volunteered many hours with the Orangeburg Track Club. Under his leadership, several of the club's members won gold medals in the Junior Olympics. (Courtesy of James Johnson.)

Richard Singleton is a 1958 graduate of South Carolina State College and a retired Army colonel. He was employed as the first African American public safety director in the city of Orangeburg in 1992. Singleton obtained a master's degree in public administration from the University of Missouri. He entered the US Army as a second lieutenant in 1958, and received many awards and decorations. After serving 30 years in the military, he retired in 1988. Before coming to Orangeburg, he was employed as a warden in one of the toughest prisons in Maryland, becoming known as the "Fix-it Man" in the correctional industry. (Courtesy of Richard Singleton.)

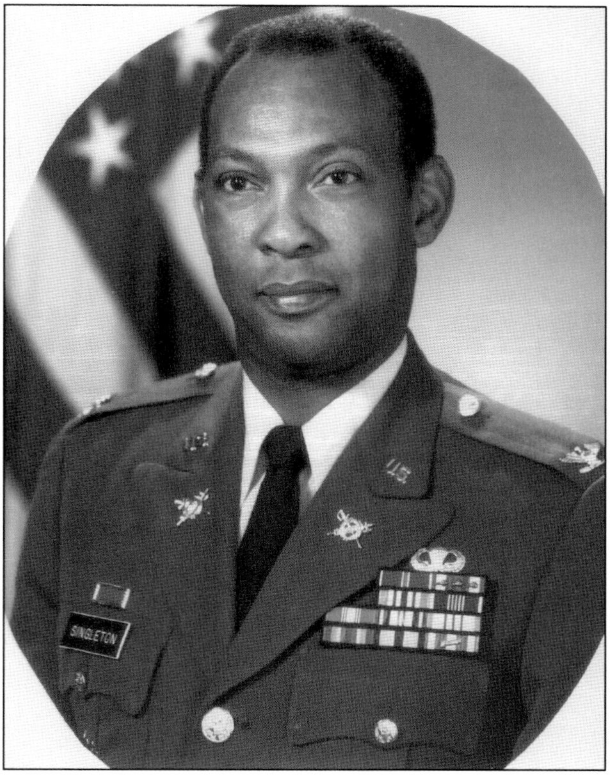

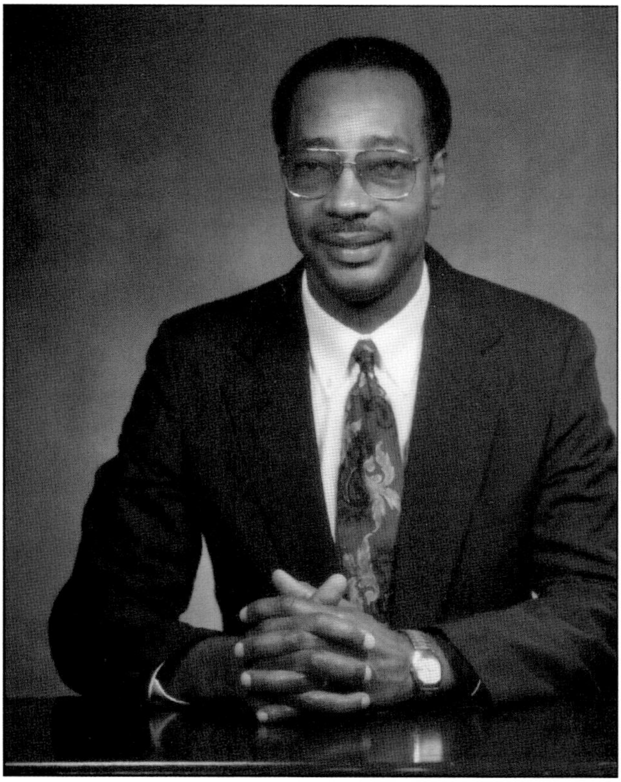

Dr. David Longshore Jr. was an assistant professor and principal before becoming the first African American superintendent of Orangeburg School District No. 3 in 1988. He earned bachelor's and master's degrees from South Carolina State University in 1970 and 1973, respectively. He also earned a master's degree in mathematics and a Ph.D. in secondary mathematics education from the University of South Carolina in 1975 and 1983, respectively. Dr. Longshore, a veteran, has received many awards, including an Army Good Conduct Medal in 1972, a Principal Incentive Award in 1988, Superintendent of the Year in 1996, and the William B. Harley Lifetime Achievement Award in 2006. (Courtesy of David Longshore.)

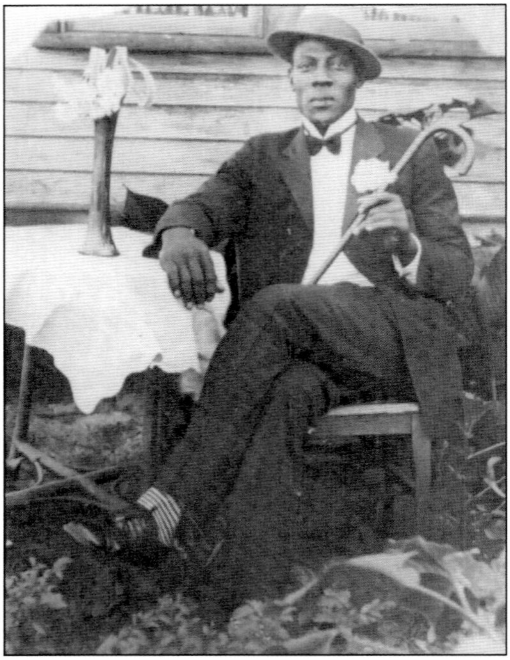

James Salley Sr. (1906–1993), a World War II veteran and farmer, retired from Douglas Jennings Construction Company. He was educated in the Orangeburg County Public Schools and received his vocational training at South Carolina Agricultural and Mechanical College. He served as a military policeman in the US Army and enjoyed farming to provide fresh vegetables for his family, friends, and neighbors. He also sang with many quartet groups while living in the Jackson and New Ellenton areas in Aiken County. (Courtesy of Eartha Stephens.)

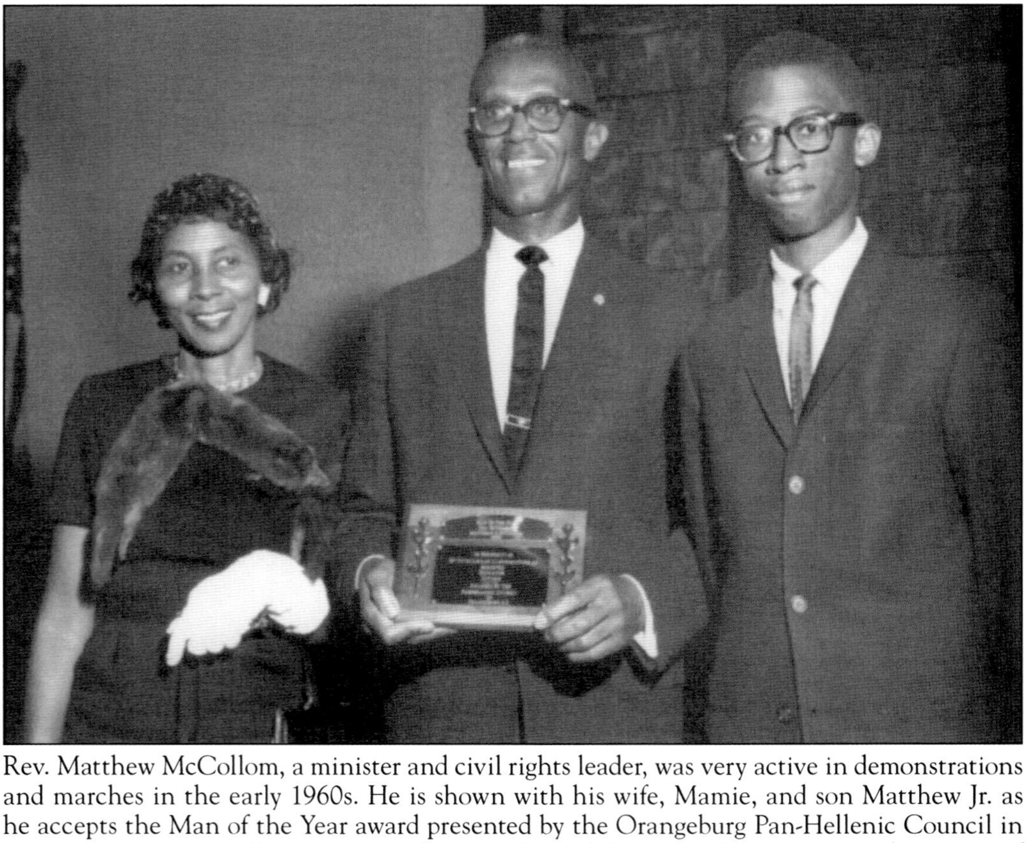

Rev. Matthew McCollom, a minister and civil rights leader, was very active in demonstrations and marches in the early 1960s. He is shown with his wife, Mamie, and son Matthew Jr. as he accepts the Man of the Year award presented by the Orangeburg Pan-Hellenic Council in 1992. Reverend McCollom also served as president of the Orangeburg NAACP. (Courtesy of Cecil Williams.)

Ralph B. Everett, a native of Orangeburg, is the president and CEO of the Washington, DC–based Joint Center for Political and Economic Studies, the nation's leading African American think tank. In 1989, Everett became the first African American partner at Paul, Hastings, Janofsky & Walker LLP, a leading international law firm with more than 1,200 attorneys and offices throughout Europe, Asia, and the United States. He is the son of Rev. F.G.S. Everett, who was a councilman and pastor of Mount Pisgah Baptist Church. (Courtesy of Ralph Everett.)

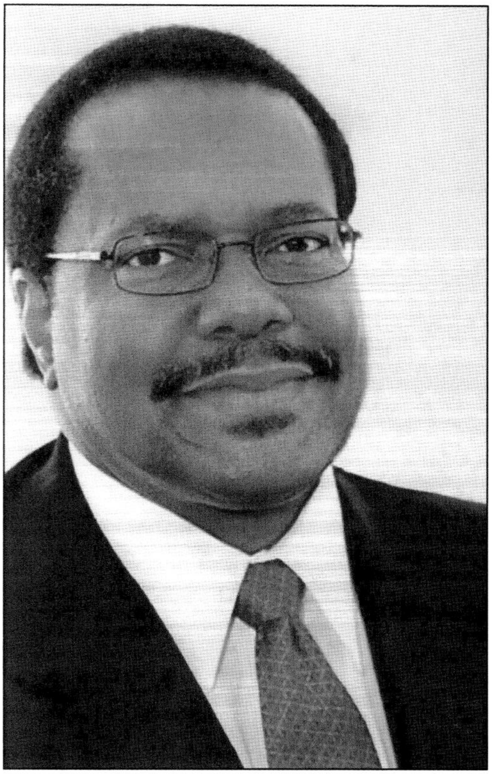

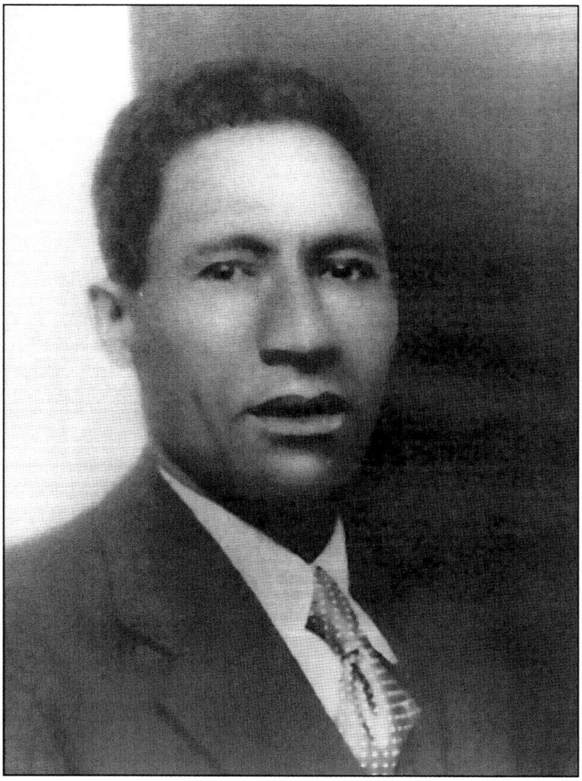

Harry K. Dowdy Sr., of North, was an educator and community leader. Dowdy, known affectionately as "Professor" and by his initials "H.K.," completed high school and junior college at Voorhees College in Denmark, South Carolina. He also attended South Carolina State College. For 40 years, Dowdy was the principal of North Industrial Institute, later named Dover Elementary School in North. In this capacity, he contributed to the professional success of thousands of students and touched hundreds of lives in the North community. From the 1930s through the 1970s, he played a major role in the educational and civic life of North and the surrounding areas. He brought innovations to the farmers, often inoculating area hogs against cholera and introducing other new agricultural ideas. The Dover Elementary School gymnasium was named in his honor. (Courtesy of Harry K. Dowdy Jr.)

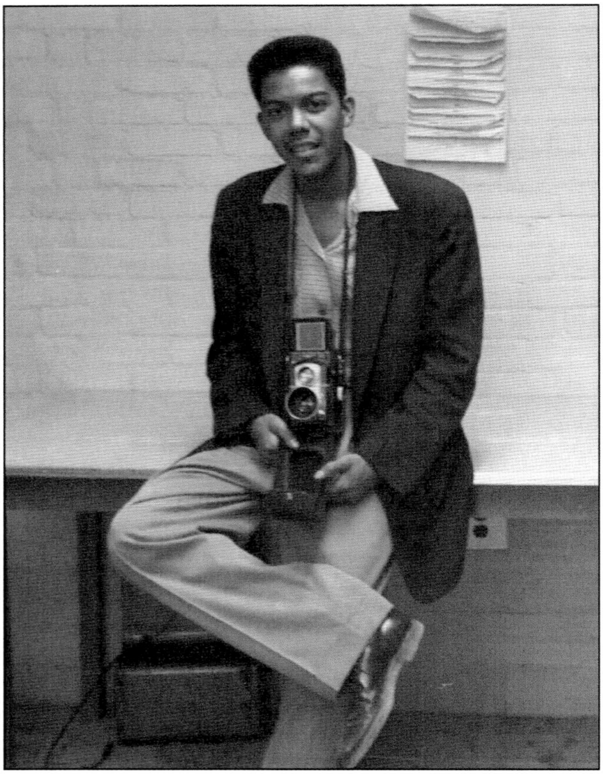

Cecil Williams is an award-winning photographer, artist, businessman, publisher, and author. He is a native of Orangeburg and a 1960 graduate of Claflin University. He has been taking documentary photographs since he was nine years old; by the time he was a teenager, he had sold photographs to *Jet* magazine and the Associated Press. He is shown at Wilkinson High School around 1954, near his darkroom, holding the Graflex 22 camera that he used to take many of his photographs. He has authored several books outlining the struggle for equal rights, including *Out of the Box in Dixie* and *Freedom and Justice: Four Decades of the Civil Rights Struggle as Seen by a Black Photographer in the Deep South.* (Courtesy of Cecil Williams.)

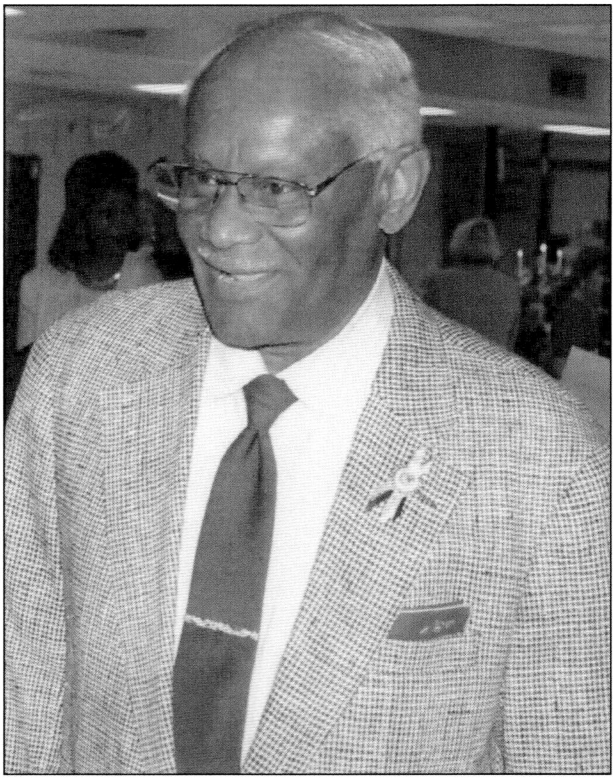

An educator for over 50 years, Robert E. Howard was a native of Georgetown and a graduate of South Carolina State College. In 1942, he became an instructor at Wilkinson High School and was later principal. In 1970, the African American Wilkinson High School and the white Orangeburg High School merged to form Orangeburg-Wilkinson High School. Howard and William J. Clark worked side by side to ensure a smooth transition to the integrated school system. Howard was also the voice of South Carolina State basketball games for over 40 years. The Robert E. Howard Middle School, formerly Wilkinson High School, was named in his honor. (Courtesy of Orangeburg County Consolidated School District No. 5.)

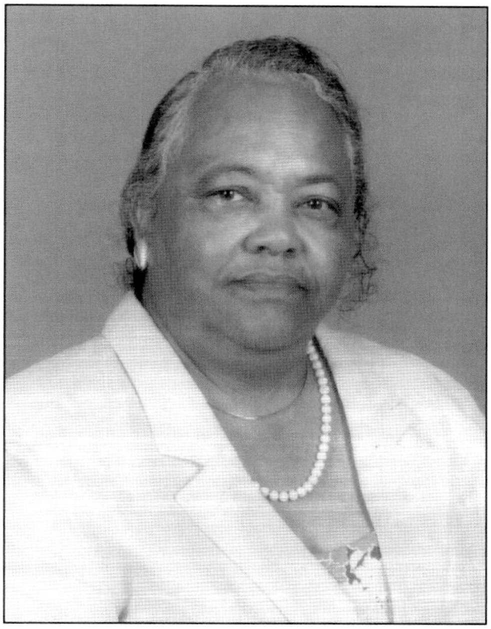

Sybil Jenkins Jamison (1924–2004) of North was a retired educator, civic leader, and councilwoman. She earned her degree in elementary education from South Carolina State College and was employed in Orangeburg County School District No. 1 for 26 years, at Norfield and Neeses Primary. Jamison was a town councilwoman for 14 years in the town of North. (Courtesy of Beverly Jamison.)

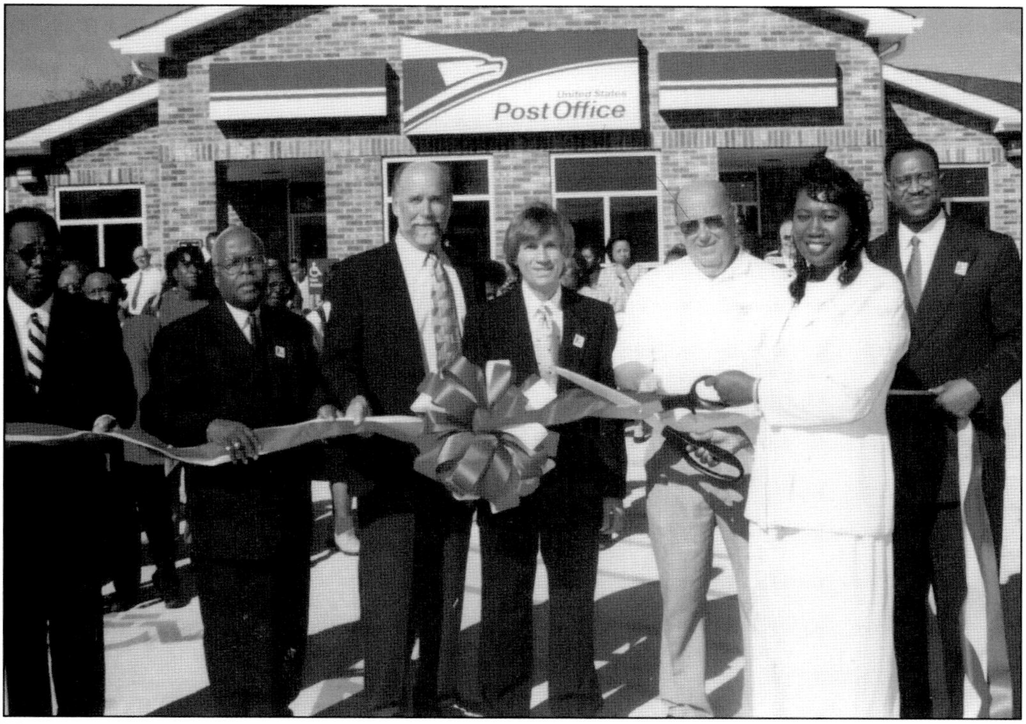

Novice Sampson Briggs, a native of Ruffin, South Carolina, is shown at the opening of the new post office in Summerton. Briggs became the first black female postmaster in Summerton in 1982 after being the officer in charge at the Eutawville post office for six months. In 1974, she graduated from Orangeburg-Calhoun Technical College with honors, and in 1980, she graduated from South Carolina State University. She was commissioned second lieutenant in 1982. While in Summerton, she owned and operated the Sunshine country restaurant and is the owner of Sampson Place Apartments in Orangeburg. (Courtesy of Novice Sampson Briggs.)

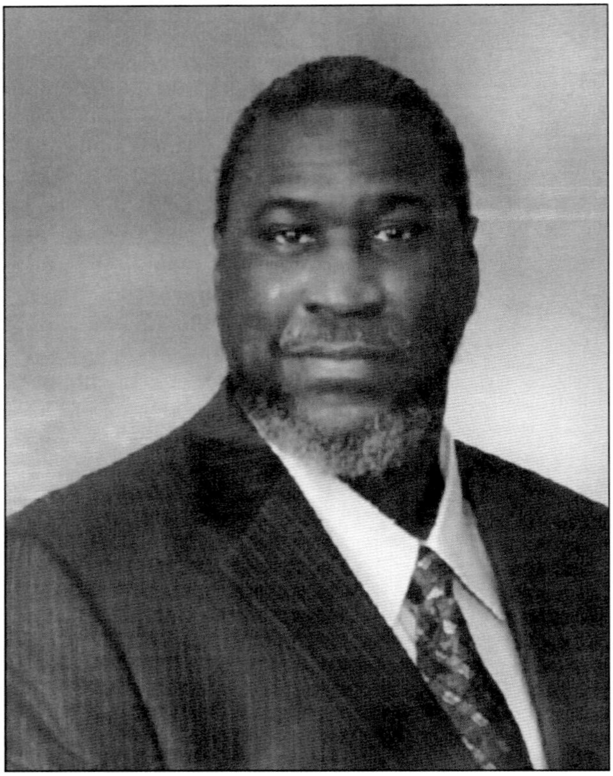

Dr. Richard Richardson was the first African American to have undergone initial medical education and advanced training in South Carolina and to be certified by the American Board of Obstetrics and Gynecology. Dr. Richardson is also the first African American surgical specialist to set up practice and actively participate in Orangeburg. He graduated from South Carolina State College in 1973 with a BS in professional chemistry, and obtained a doctor of medicine degree from the Medical University of South Carolina School of Medicine in Charleston. Since opening his practice in Orangeburg in 1981, Dr. Richardson has delivered over 10,000 babies. (Courtesy of Richard Richardson.)

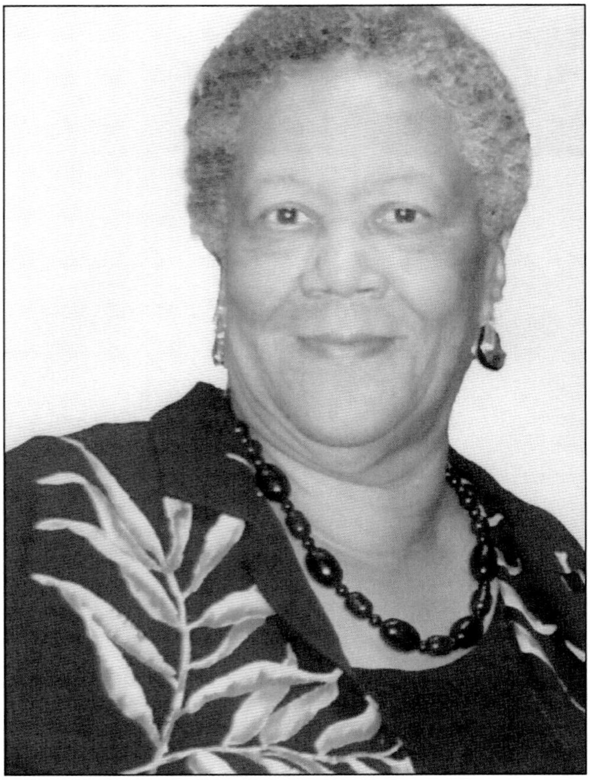

Georgia Good, the executive director of the Rural Advancement Fund, assisted low-income people in rural South Carolina and the nation for more than 50 years. She was director of the Orangeburg County Development Center in Orangeburg, and was one of the persons instrumental in developing and organizing the Family Health Centers in Orangeburg and other counties, which serve more than 20,000 patients annually. (Courtesy of Georgia Good.)

Reginald R. Thomasson (1913–1990), an educator and a musician, received BS and BA degrees from South Carolina State College, and an MA from Los Angeles State College. He was the composer of "The Evening Song" (1939), adapted as a school song at South Carolina State, and was an associate professor of music and director of bands at the school from 1936 to 1976. In 1950, Thomasson founded the South Carolina High School Bandmasters Association. He served as an elder and was minister of music of St. Luke Presbyterian Church until 1986. Thomasson, shown here around 1945, became the first college band director to be inducted into the South Carolina Band Director's Hall of Fame in 2003. (Courtesy of Carmen Sulton Thomasson.)

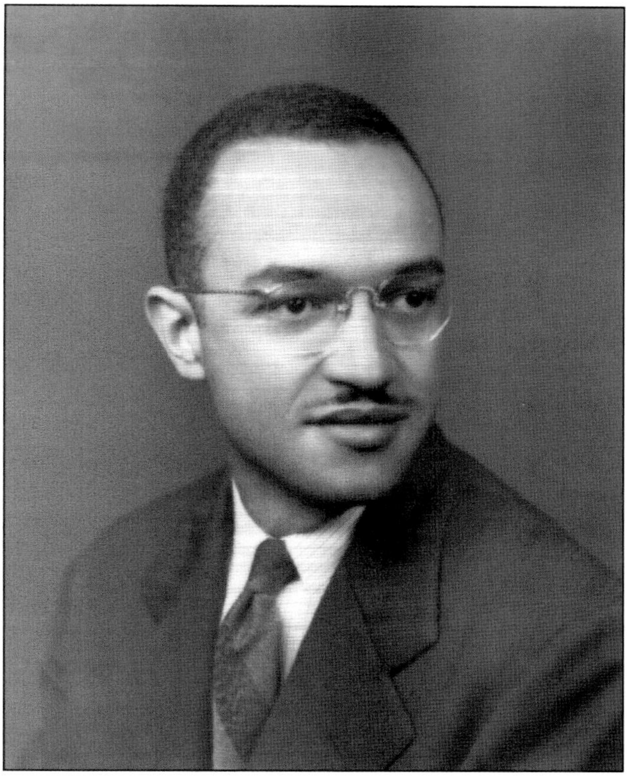

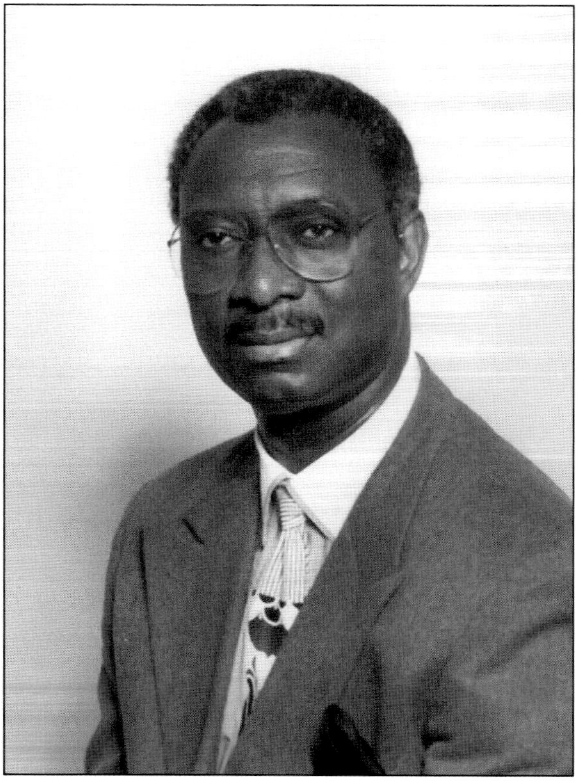

Calvin Wright is a native of Orangeburg and a graduate of South Carolina State University. He is a former Army sergeant and a Vietnam veteran. A community activist, Wright was actively involved in the civil rights movement during the 1960s. He was arrested numerous times in the pursuit of justice, and was recognized by the Voter Education Project and the American Friends Service committee for his work on voting matters, including education, registration, and suppression. For over 30 years, he has served as the executive director of OCAB, a private, nonprofit corporation whose mission is to eliminate the causes and conditions of poverty. (Courtesy of Calvin Wright.)

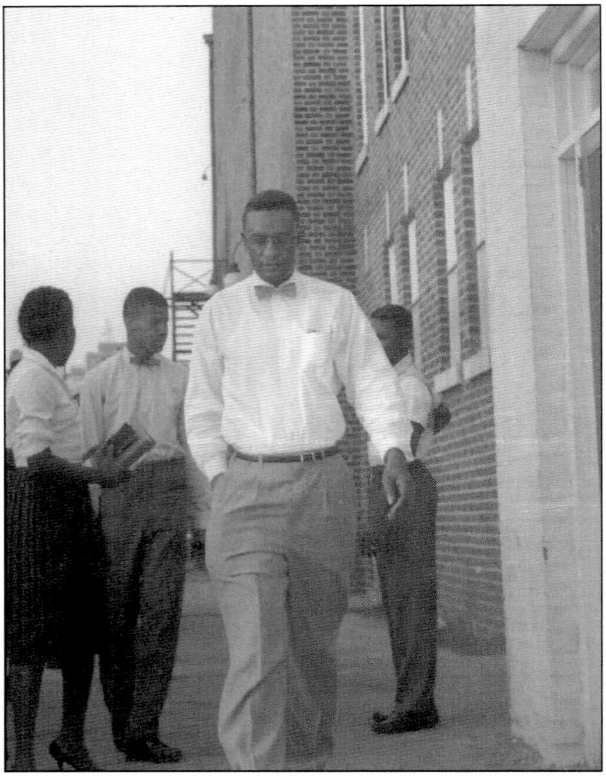

W. Newton Pough was an attorney and businessman in the city of Orangeburg. He practiced law for over 50 years in Orangeburg County. He is shown here in 1960, leaving the Orangeburg City Jail after arranging to pay fines for four students arrested by city police following demonstrations protesting segregation. (Courtesy of Cecil Williams.)

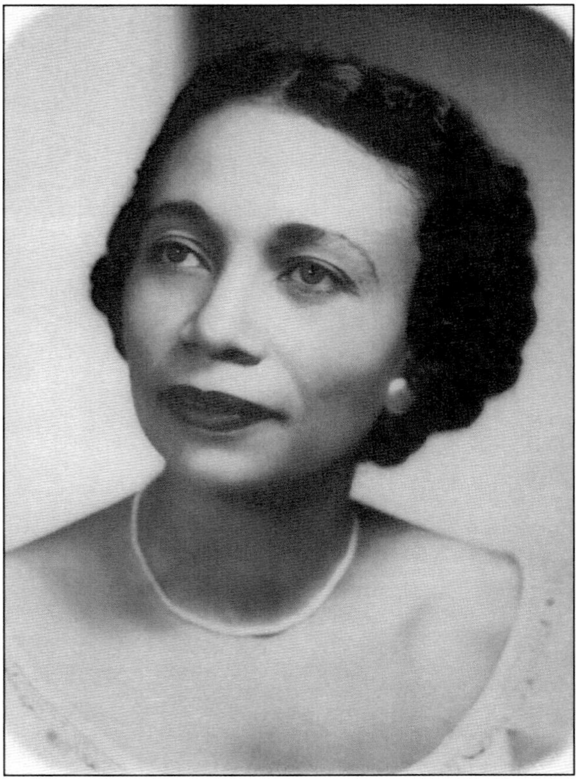

Dr. Clemmie Webber (1913–2012) was an educator, businesswoman, community leader, and author. Dr. Webber, of Orangeburg, was a member of many organizations and the recipient of the Order of the Palmetto, the highest honor a governor of South Carolina can bestow on a citizen. She was a retired professor of science education at SC State University. She and her husband, Paul Webber, owned and operated two soda shops. They employed college students, which allowed the students to ease college expenses. In 1983, she was selected as National Mother of the Year from a field of candidates from each of the 50 states. Dr. Webber always showed a philosophy of universal love and open communication. In her later years, she authored two books, *The Treadwell Street Saga* and *The College Soda Shop.* (Courtesy of the Webber family.)

Annie Jamison, of Orangeburg, was an educator and community leader. She received a bachelor's degree and a master's degree from South Carolina State College, and was elected Miss South Carolina State College in 1955–1956. She was the founding member of the New Brookland Improvement League, a nonprofit organization that provides programs to help needy individuals in and around the New Brookland community. She and her husband, Dr. Marion Jamison, helped establish endowments at Claflin University, South Carolina State, and Xavier University of Louisiana. The family-owned business, Jamison's Pharmacy, on Goff Avenue, has been a staple in the community since 1961. (Courtesy of Mary Jordan.)

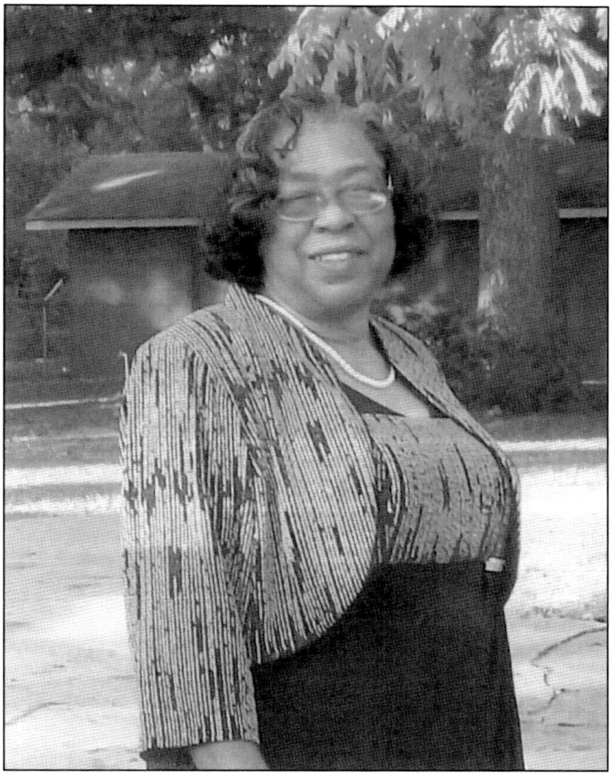

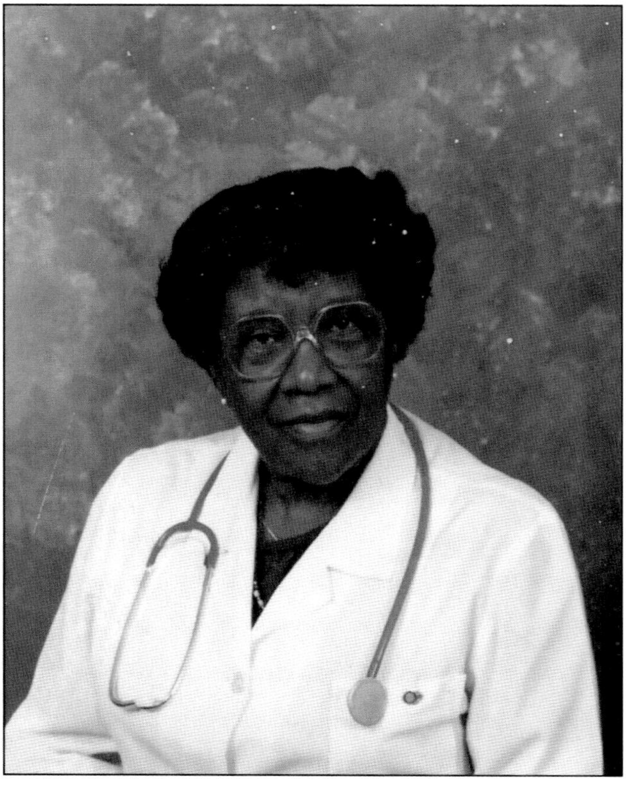

Lillie R. Owens was an educator, community leader, and healthcare worker. She was known to work three jobs on many occasions to provide for her family. She taught school for 11 years in various counties, including Orangeburg. She was employed with Dr. S.C. Disher for over 40 years. She was also known for housing females so they could attend the local colleges. She always stressed the importance of an education. (Courtesy of Willie B. Owens.)

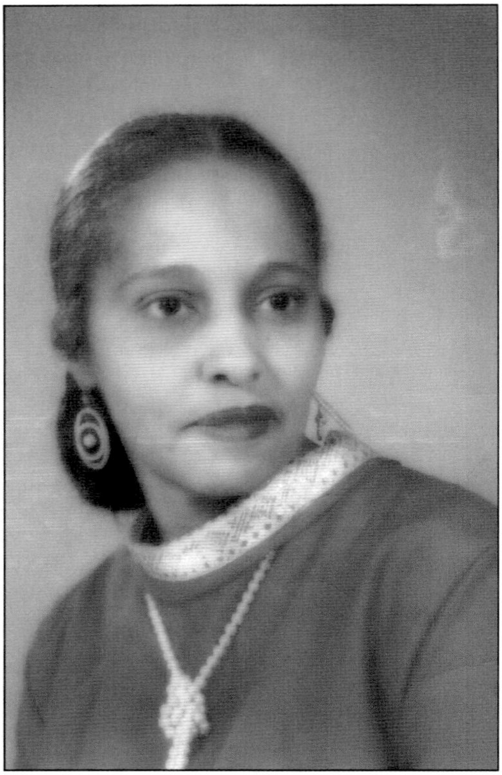

Geraldyne Zimmerman, shown here around 1958, was an educator and community leader. She was affectionately known as "Mrs. Z" and lived to be 100 years old. For over 60 years, she worked with the Girl Scouts as a troop leader and in many other capacities. She was a graduate of Fisk University and received her MA degree from South Carolina State in 1948. Zimmerman was also an outstanding instructor at South Carolina State. For the state's department of education, she wrote and produced three acclaimed educational videos on contemporary mathematics for elementary school. In 1963, she organized the Helen Sheffield Girls Club, a community service club for high school girls. In 1984, Mrs. Z took on the project of refurbishing and cleaning the historic Orangeburg Cemetery on Bull Street. For her efforts with the citizens of Orangeburg and the city council, a community center for the city's youth was named in her honor. She was also the subject of a book, *Ahead of Her Time in Yesteryear*, by Dr. Kibibi Voloria Mack-Shelton. Mrs. Z died in 2011. (Courtesy of D. Malone Zimmerman.)

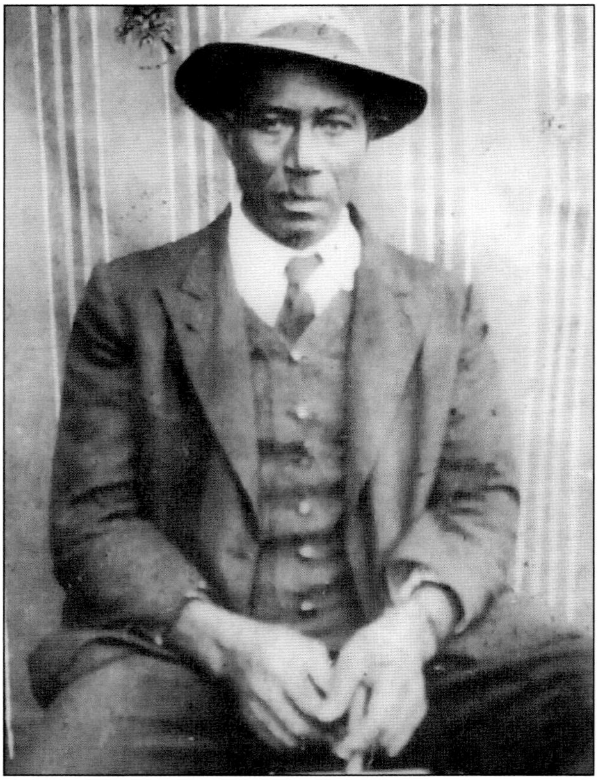

Douglas Spells (1891–1958) was born in Springtown, South Carolina, and settled in Bowman. He was a successful farmer, Methodist lay leader, and community leader in the St. Stephen community near Bowman. He first worked at the local lumber mill before purchasing a 90-acre tract and becoming a farmer. Spells married Merchie Kelley in 1913 and they had 10 children: Willie, Vernon, Bernice, Marion, Benjamin Frederick, Thelma, Roberta, Hollis Sylvester, Curtis Nathaniel, and Leroy Spells. (Courtesy of John D. Spells.)

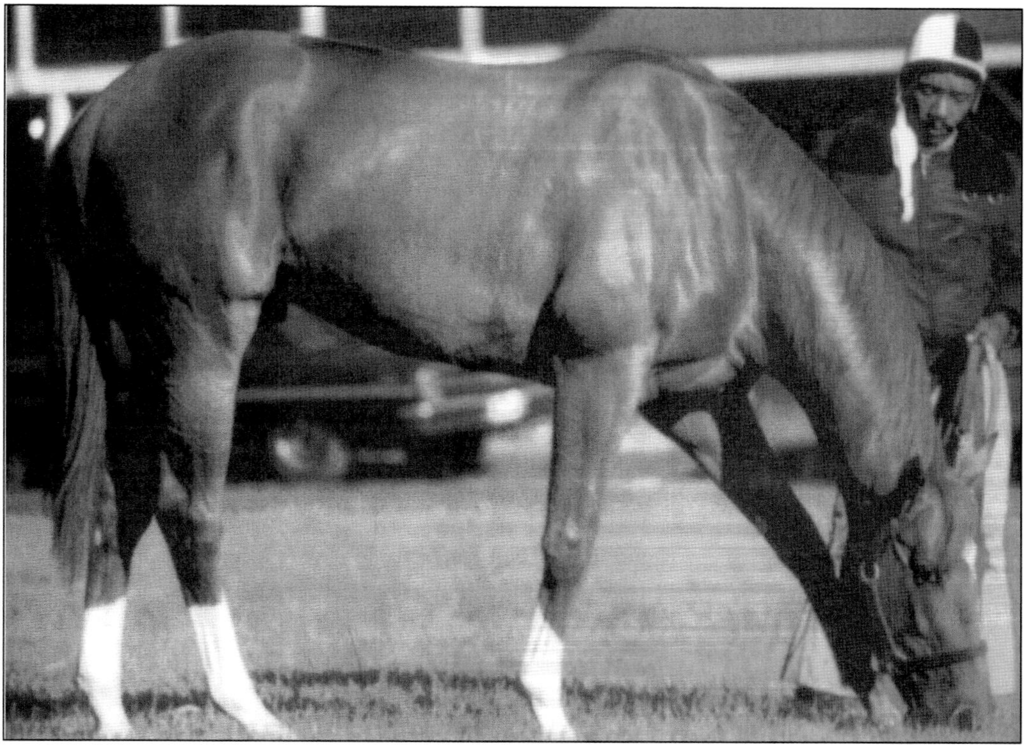

Charlie Davis is a native of Eutawville. He is shown here with the 1973 Triple Crown winner, Secretariat. Davis was an exercise rider for the famous horse in the early 1970s. Eddie Sweat, a native of Vance, was the horse's groom. They were hired by Lucien Laurin, who owned the Branchdale Race Track, now known as the Holly Hill Training Center. Davis and Sweat were depicted in the acclaimed 2010 Walt Disney movie *Secretariat*. (Courtesy of Gwendolyn Wright-Barksdale.)

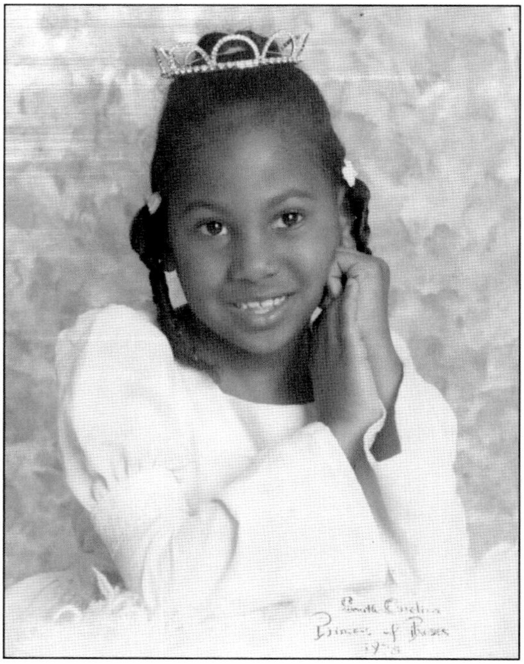

Tina Carmela Williams, daughter of Francena and George Williams of Orangeburg, was crowned the first African American Princess of Roses in the South Carolina Festival of Roses in 1973 in Orangeburg. In 1974, Rachelle Jamerson, daughter of Brenda and Broadus Jamerson III, was the second African American Princess of Roses. (Courtesy of Francena Williams.)

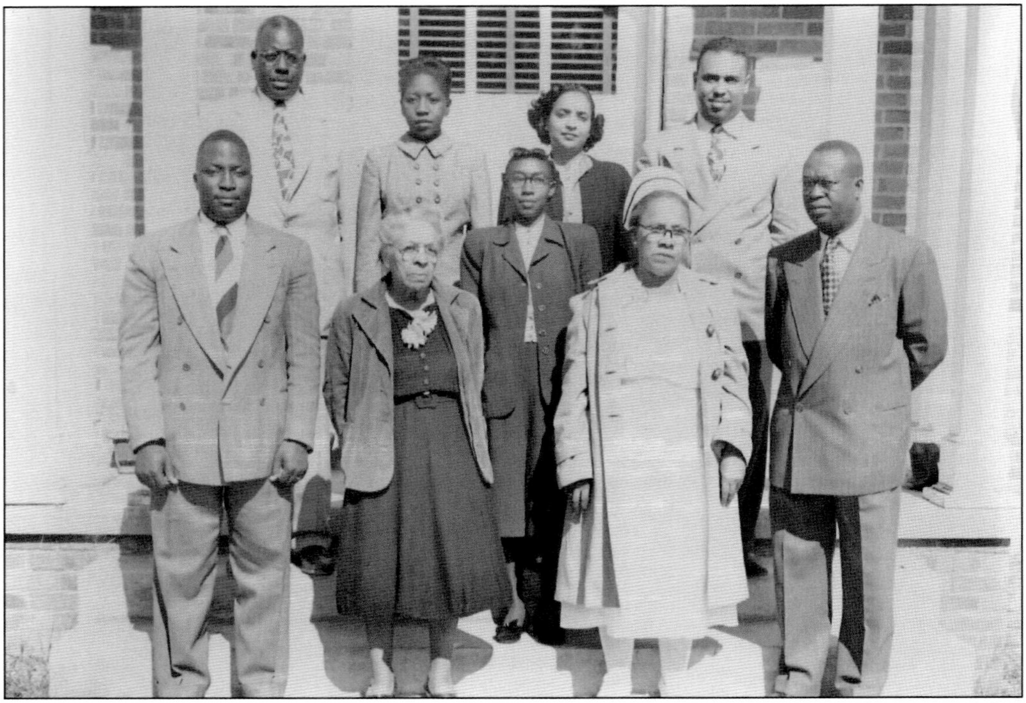

John J. Seabrook (first row, far right) was the president of Claflin University at the time of this staff photograph. H.V. Manning (first row, far left) was a faculty member and later president of the university. Since Claflin's founding in 1869, it has been served by seven presidents: Dr. Edward Cooke (1872–1884), Dr. Lewis M. Dunton (1884–1922), Dr. Joseph B. Randolph (1922–1944), Dr. John J. Seabrook (1945–1955), Dr. Hubert V. Manning (1956–1984), Dr. Oscar A. Rogers Jr. (1984–1994), and Dr. Henry N. Tisdale (1994–present). (Courtesy of Claflin University Archives.)

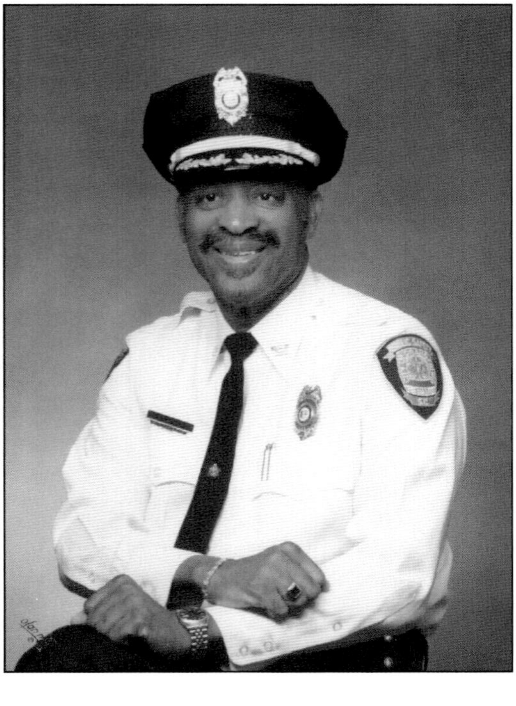

Robert Lee Keith, a retired law enforcement officer, began his career in the Orangeburg Police Department in 1960. He held positions as patrolman, corporal, sergeant, lieutenant, captain, and major; then, in 1990, he became the first African American chief of police in the city of Orangeburg. After retiring from the city in 1992, he was employed at the Orangeburg County Sheriff's Department. Chief Keith is a lifetime member of the Palmetto State Law Enforcement Officers Association (PSLEOA). (Courtesy of Robert Lee Keith.)

An unidentified woman who was known as a lay midwife is shown here. For decades, midwives provided the cornerstone of prenatal care and strong support for a large portion of rural South Carolina. (Courtesy of Shirley James.)

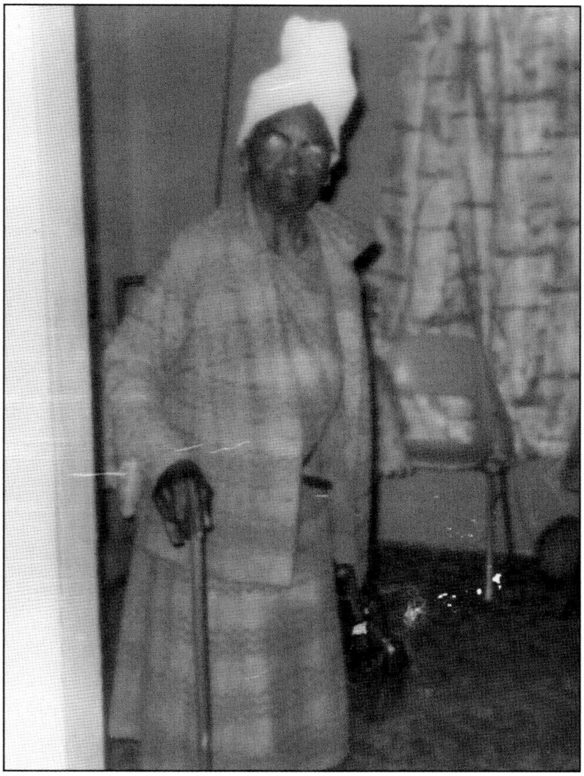

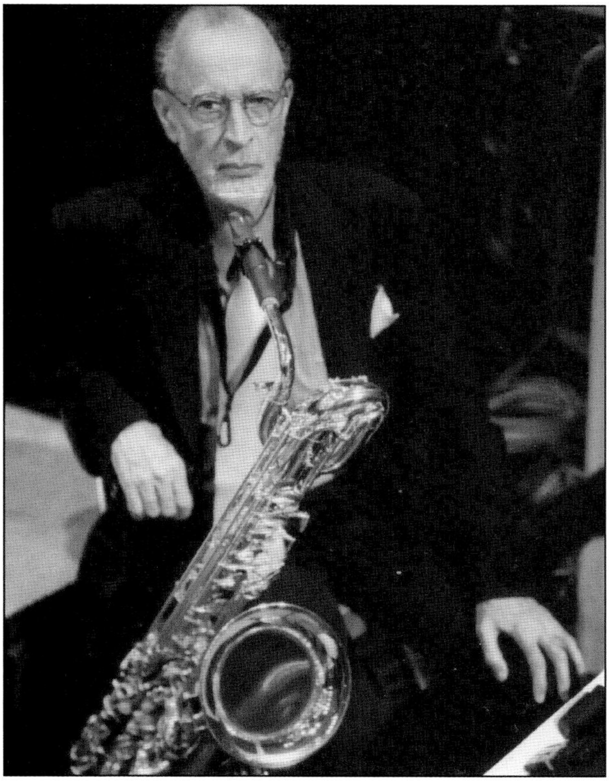

Orangeburg native John "Johnny" Williams Jr. is seen here around 1999 posing with his saxophone. A 1958 graduate of South Carolina State College, Williams served in the US Army and is an accomplished musician. While in the Army, he studied at the US Navy School of Music in Washington, DC. He encountered musicians from all over the world and played for such Motown acts as Smokey Robinson, Gladys Knight and the Pips, the Fifth Dimension, and Stevie Wonder. In 1968, Williams joined the Ray Charles Band, a group well known for its rhythm & blues and jazz renditions. In 1970, he earned a seat on the famous Count Basie Orchestra. (Courtesy of John "Johnny" Williams Jr.; photograph by Y. Yoneda.)

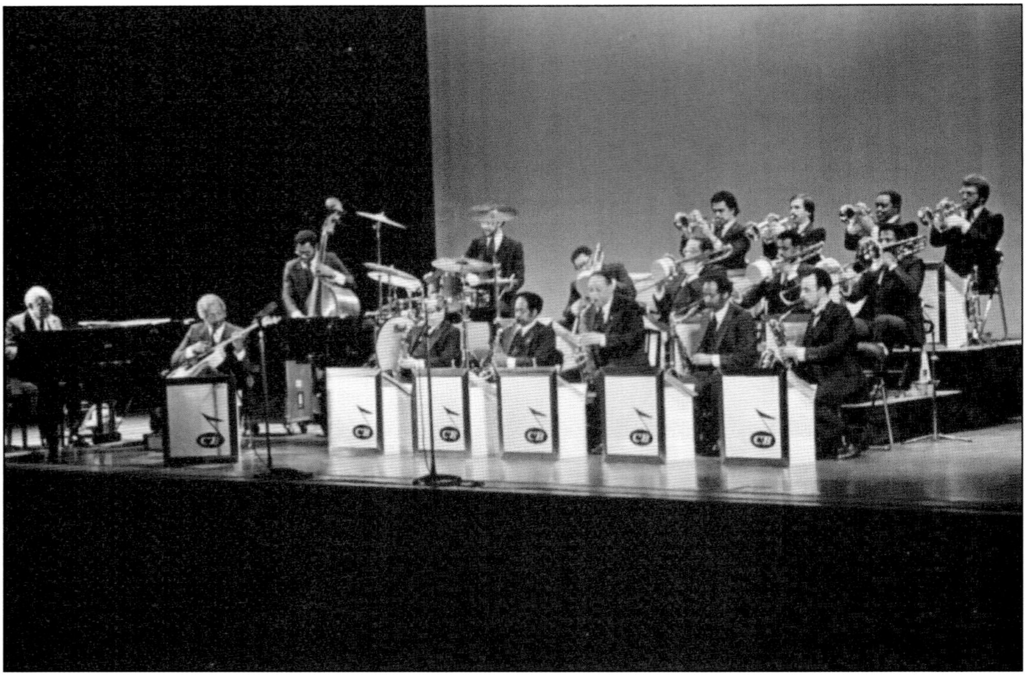

The Count Basie Orchestra is seen here performing in Japan. Johnny Williams is in the front row at far right. Williams recalls being notified of his selection for the band by Eddie "Lockjaw" Davis, a tenor saxophone great who was the manager at the time. The first baritone saxophone that Williams owned, he recalls, was bought in Paris, France. (Courtesy of John "Johnny" Williams Jr.; photograph by Y. Yoneda.)

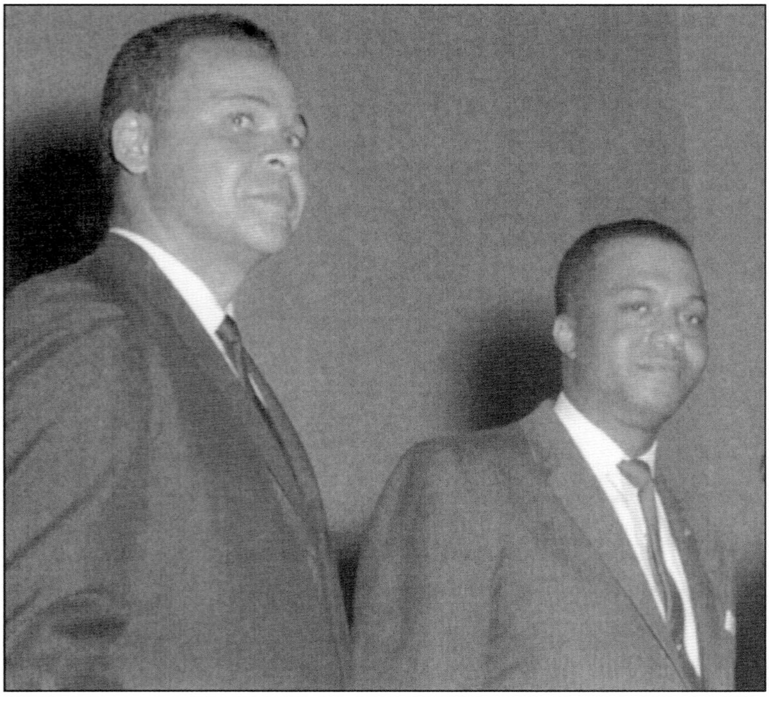

James Sulton (left) and Harlowe Caldwell, shown here in the late 1950s, were key leaders in the Orangeburg branch of the NAACP. During that time, tensions ran so high that the Orangeburg NAACP had only three active members: Rev. Matthew D. McCollom, president; John E. Brunson, secretary; and James E. Sulton, treasurer. (Courtesy of Cecil Williams.)

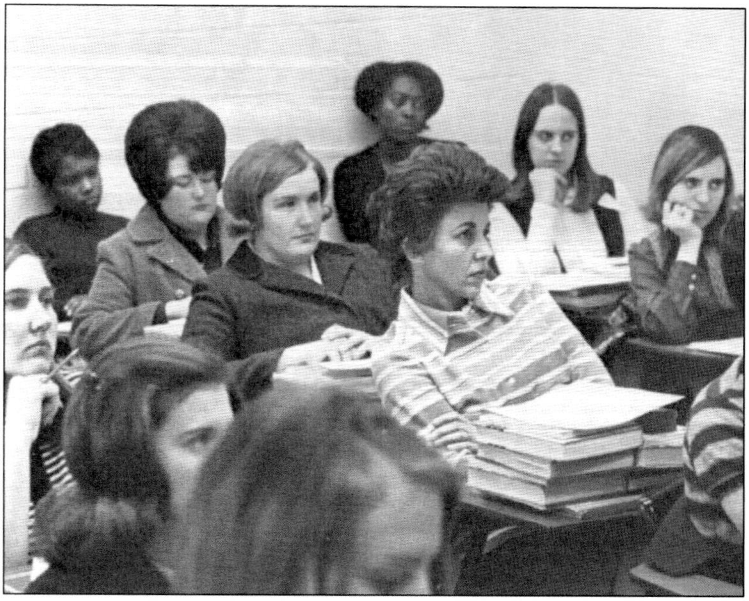

Margaret Thompson (center, in back) is shown in 1971 sitting in the rear of a class as a secretarial science student at Orangeburg Calhoun Technical College. In 1990, she was the first black probate judge elected in Orangeburg. (Courtesy of Orangeburg-Calhoun Technical College Library.)

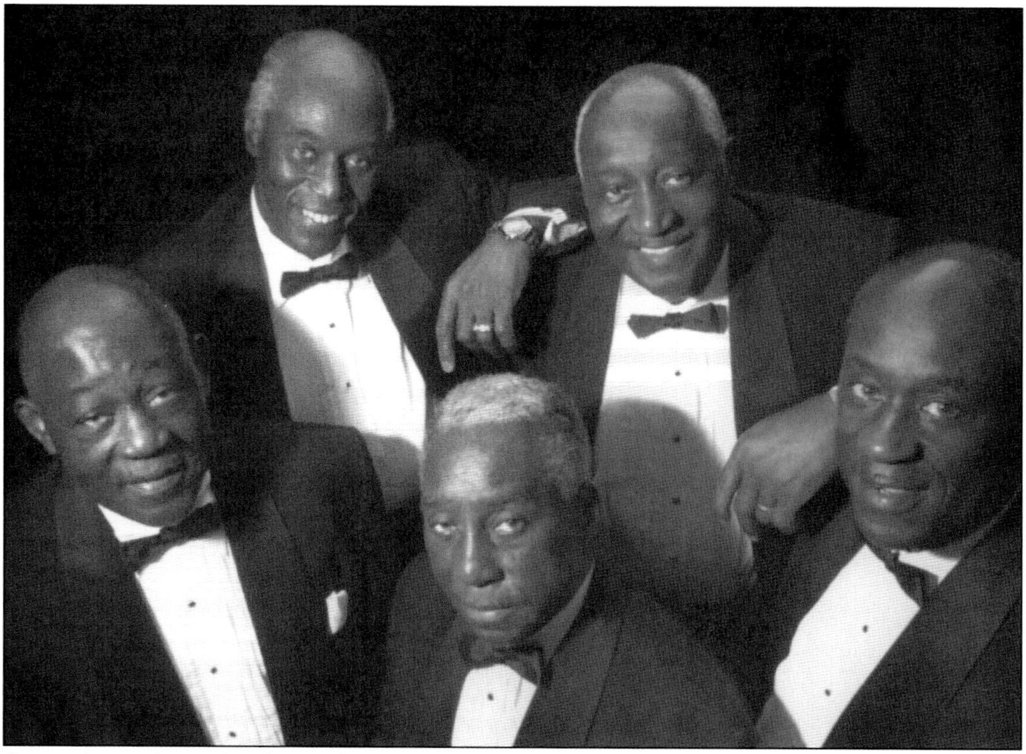

Orangeburg's finest family vocal musical group is the Jarvis Brothers Quintet. The brothers are, from left to right, Reginald, Donald, Ulysses, Anthony, and Rogers. They were born in Orangeburg and started singing on the front porch of their home. Their mother played the piano. All of the brothers were active in music while they were in college, and they all attended South Carolina State College except for Reginald, who attended Claflin College. All are retired from the education field except for Rogers, who is a pharmacist. After the death of Reginald, Donald's son Cornell stepped in. (Courtesy of the Jarvis Brothers.)

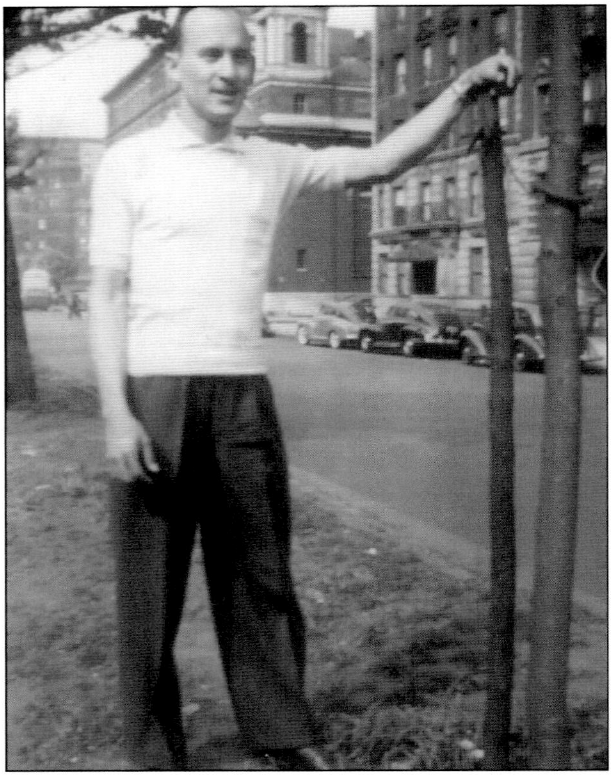

Eugene Pinson (1925–) is a retired educator and musician. Pinson served in the US Army during World War II, from 1944 to 1946. He is a graduate of the Colored Normal, Industrial, Agricultural, and Mechanical College, now known as South Carolina State University. He was hired as an assistant professor in 1949 at Claflin University. Pinson taught for more than 50 years, at institutions including Claflin, Morris College, Voorhees College, and South Carolina State. He is an accomplished pianist and noted choral director, but is best known as a tenor soloist. (Courtesy of Eugene Pinson.)

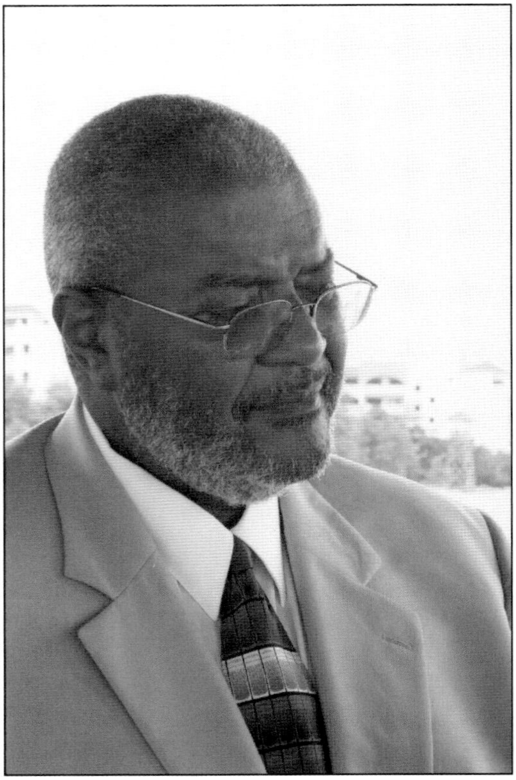

Dr. Charles Kilgore is the first African American doctor specializing in pediatrics to practice in Orangeburg. He is a graduate of North Carolina Agricultural and Technical State University (North Carolina A&T), in Greensboro, and the Medical University of South Carolina in Charleston. He completed his internship and residency at Richland Memorial Hospital at Richland School of Medicine in Columbia. He has been practicing in Orangeburg since 1984. (Courtesy of Charles Kilgore.)

Leonard Johnson and his wife, Toka, pose for a photograph after their wedding in 1959. Johnson, in the US Air Force at the time, served in the Korean and Vietnam Wars. (Courtesy of Catherine Phillips.)

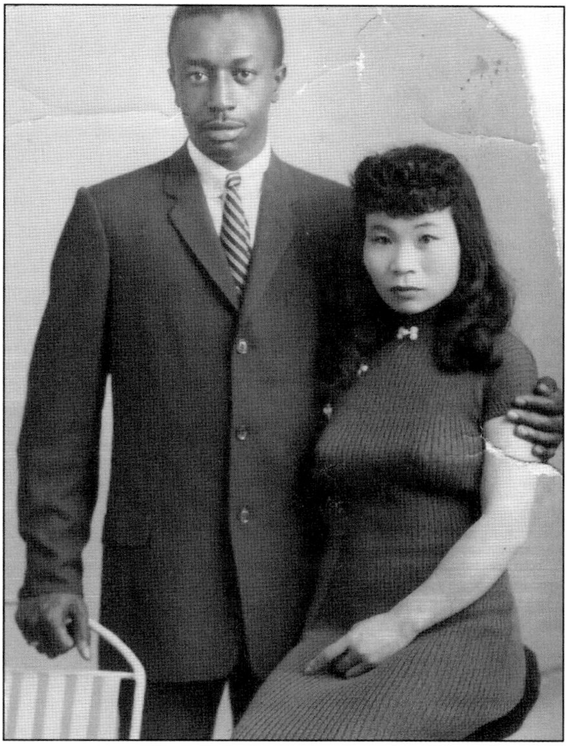

This is a scene from the 1970 tricentennial production of *Porgy and Bess* in Charleston, South Carolina. Shown are, from left to right, Eugene Pinson (as Sportin' Life), Annette Anderson (Bess), and Rubin Wright (Porgy). Pinson later served as musical director in the production at the Theater of Stars in Atlanta. (Courtesy of Eugene Pinson.)

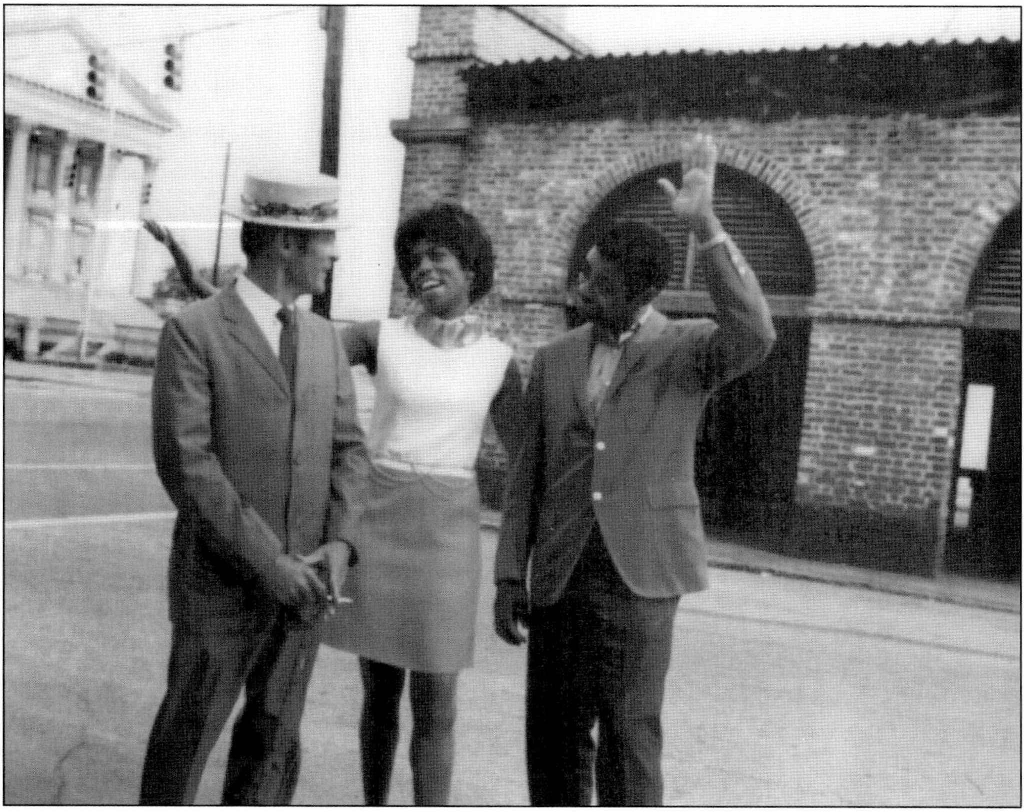

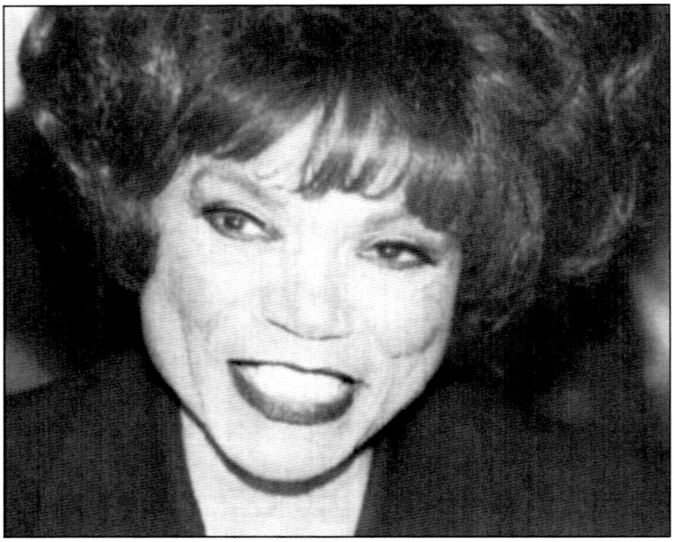

Eartha Kitt was born on a cotton farm in North in 1927. She became a famous singer and movie actress, earning a star on Hollywood Boulevard. Her 1953 recording of "Santa Baby," and her recurring role as Catwoman on television's *Batman*, are familiar examples of her work. In 1997, she returned to South Carolina to perform a benefit concert at Benedict College in Columbia, which established a scholarship fund for dance students. (Courtesy of the *Times and Democrat*.)

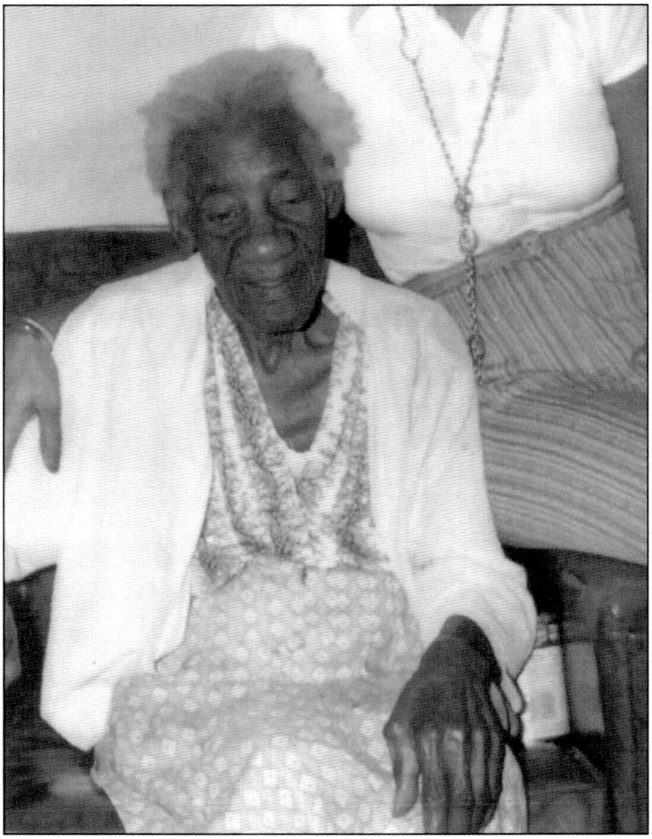

Hester Jones Walker was a native of Springfield, South Carolina, who lived to be 110. She died in 1978. She was still picking cotton at 100 years of age. She continued to wash her own clothes and care for herself until she passed. Her mother and father were born into slavery. (Courtesy of Emma Kelly.)

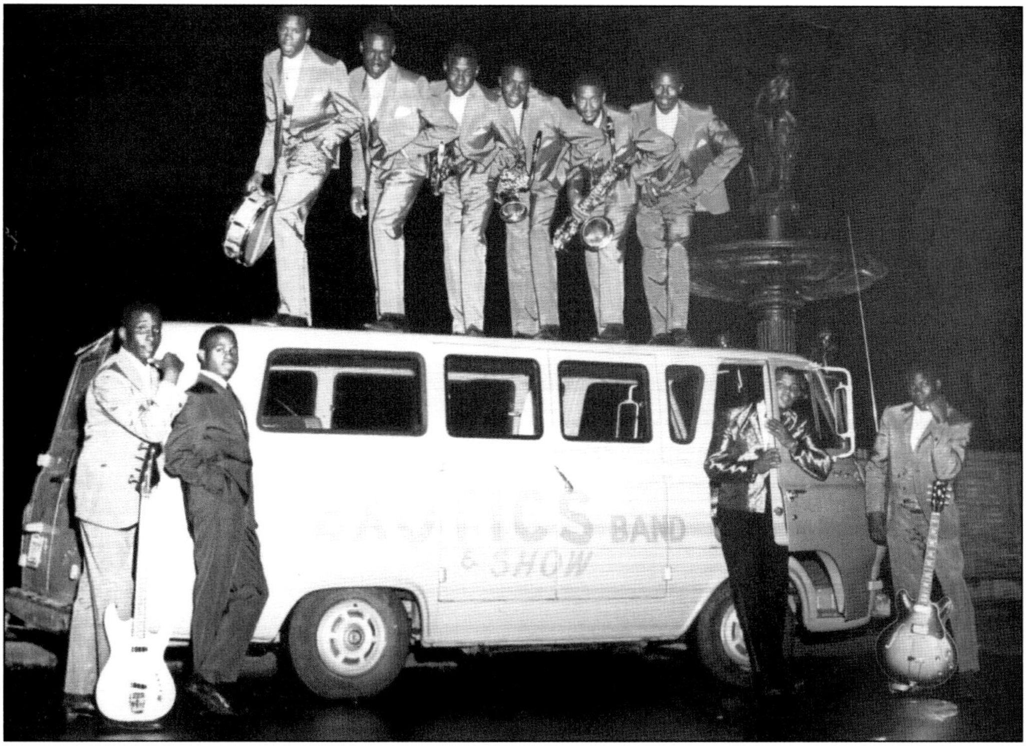

The Exotics Band, shown here in 1966, was popular in the 1960s. The founding members were Walter Bowers, Dwight McMillan, Roger Jarvis, and Harry Palmer. The band was organized in 1960 as Bogama and the Stereos, and later changed its name to The Exotics. They were from Orangeburg and performed all over the United States. On October 3, 1969, tragedy struck on their way to a performance at Western Carolina. Two band members, John Riley and Lemuel Alston, were killed and the others were injured when the band's bus went over an embankment about 10 miles south of Cullowhee, North Carolina. Members shown here are, from left to right, (on ground) Coleman Sistrunk, Joseph Lindsay, John Riley, and Lemuel Alston; (on bus) Harry L. Palmer, Roger Jarvis, Francis Thompson, Leroy Chisolm, Dwight McMillan, and Leroy McClain. (Courtesy of Harry L. Palmer.)

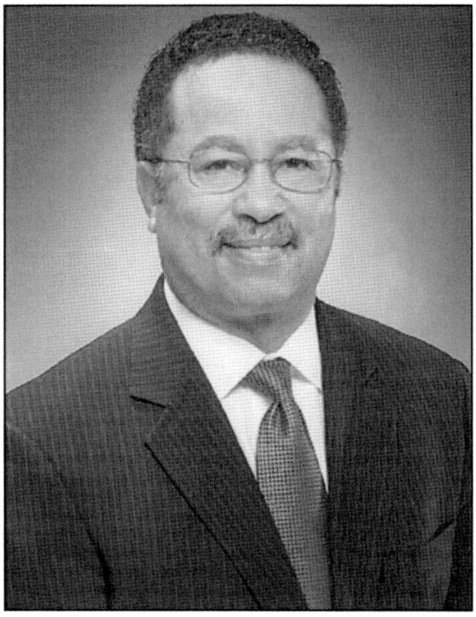

Luther J. Battiste III, a native of Orangeburg, was one of the first two African Americans elected to the Columbia city council since Reconstruction. He became the first president of the Richland County Bar Association and the first president of the South Carolina Trial Lawyers Association. Battiste is a practicing attorney in Orangeburg and Columbia. He is a partner in the Johnson, Toal & Battiste law firm. (Courtesy of Luther J. Battiste III.)

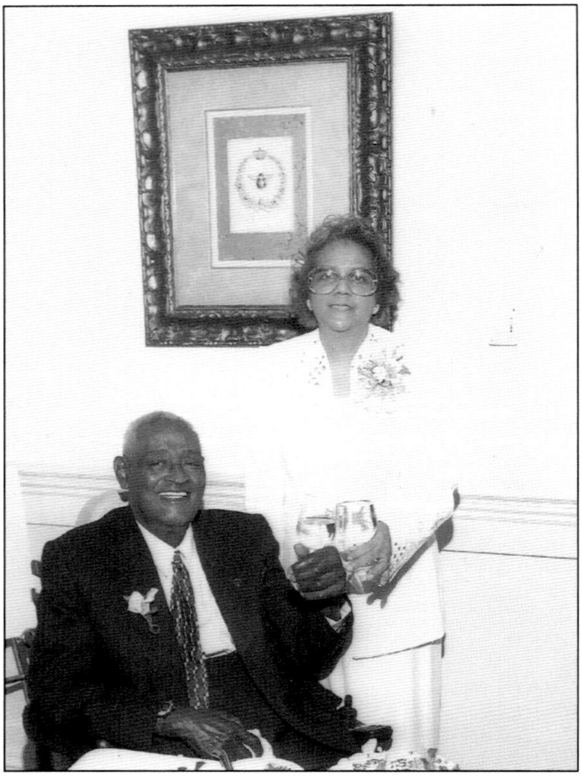

Robert Shaw Evans Sr., pictured with his wife, Beatrice, was well known in the Orangeburg community. On the campus of South Carolina State College, he served as assistant food service director in 1961 and director of food services (Boss Man) in 1964. He retired after 40 years of unselfish service to South Carolina State University, having provided administrative oversight to five food facilities and numerous campus functions. He received several awards, including a proclamation from the City of Orangeburg naming February 25, 1989, as Boss Man Day. He was inducted into South Carolina State University's Athletic Hall of Fame. Robert Evans was equally loyal as deacon of Mount Pisgah Baptist Church. He was a member of many organizations, including VFW Post 8166, the NAACP, and the Xi Psi chapter of Omega Psi Phi fraternity. (Courtesy of Beatrice Evans.)

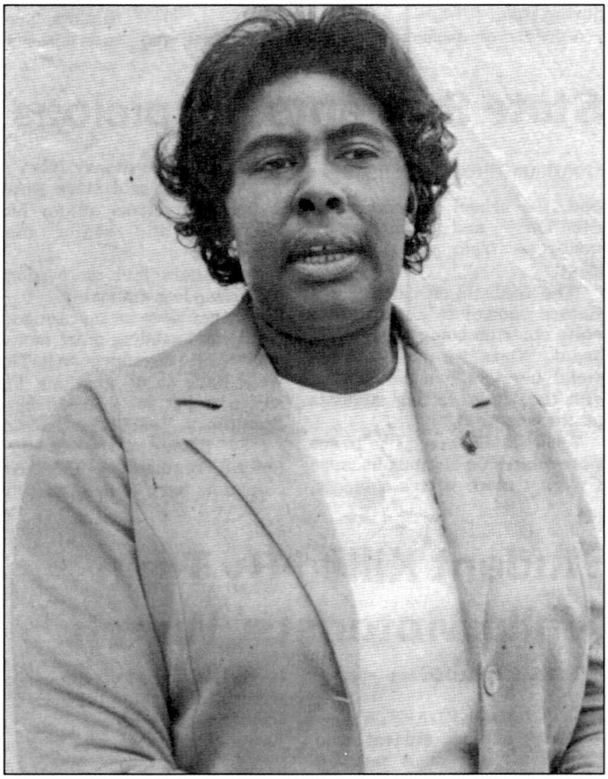

Liz Zimmerman Keitt became the first African American female elected to the Orangeburg city council in 1988, and the first to act as mayor pro tem. She is also the founder of Positeen, an afternoon program for children from kindergarten through the 12th grade. (Courtesy of L. Zimmerman Keitt.)

Roger Cleckley is a veteran and community leader. In 1986, Cleckley was elected the first African American auditor for Orangeburg County. He served two years of active duty, including a one-year tour of duty in Vietnam as a combat infantryman. He was honorably discharged in 1971 with the rank of sergeant. He is presently serving his seventh four-year term as auditor of Orangeburg County. This makes him the longest-serving locally elected African American official in Orangeburg County. (Courtesy of Roger Cleckley.)

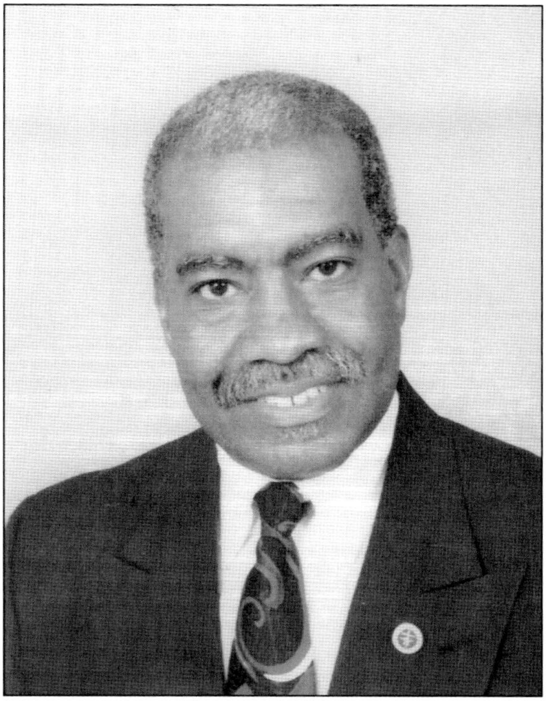

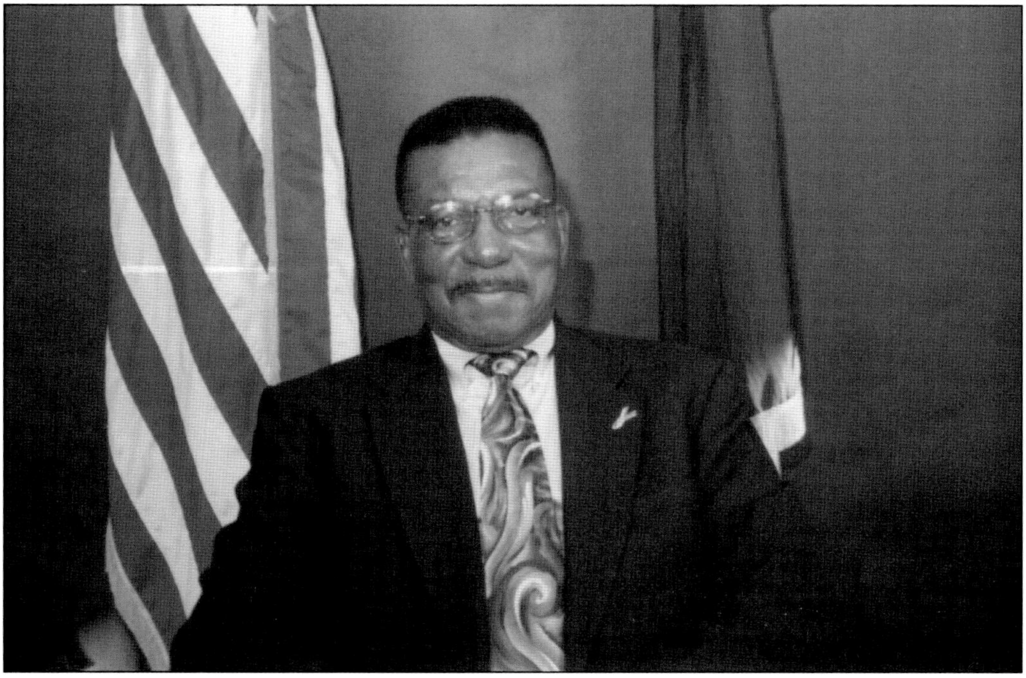

Silas Seabrooks Jr. is a community leader, former councilman, retired self-employed plumber and brick mason, veteran, and former mayor of Santee, South Carolina. He served in the US Army during the Korean conflict. In 1972, Seabrooks became the first African American mayor of Santee, a resort town in Orangeburg County. He served as mayor from 1972 to 1983. He is a member of the Elloree-Santee branch of the NAACP and of many other organizations, and serves as a deacon of Chapel Hill Baptist Church in Santee. (Courtesy of Silas Seabrooks Jr.)

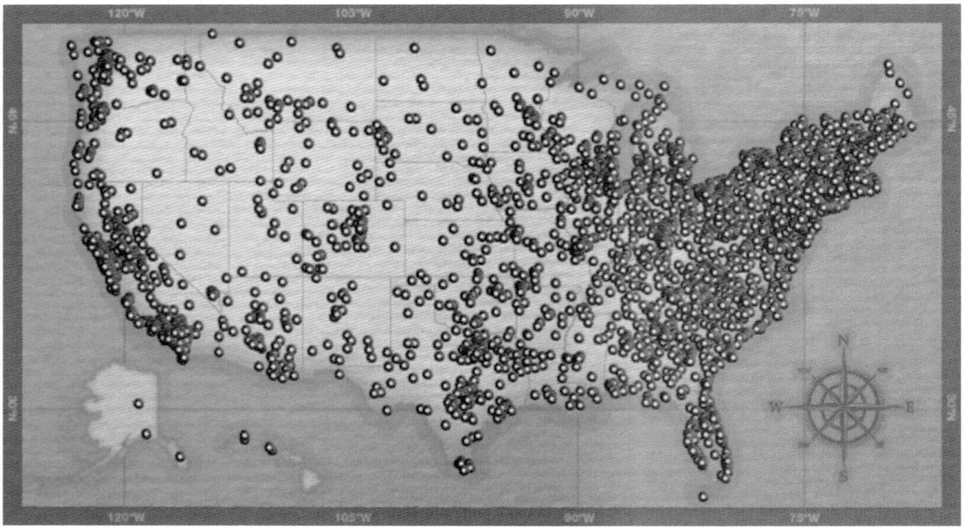